"David Fitch continues his constructive wo[...]
presence the church makes possible in a worl[...]
The disciplines he calls attention to are life giving because they are the disciplines
God has given us to be a faithful presence. Hopefully this book will be widely read
and used in churches everywhere."

Stanley Hauerwas, Gilbert T. Rowe Professor Emeritus, Duke Divinity School

"David Fitch can write this book not just because he has a heart for mission, but
because he has attended faithfully to the presence of the Spirit of the living Christ
poured out on all flesh. If you want to know more about Spirit-empowered mission,
read this book. But be careful, as it will transform—discipline, even!—your life, your
family, and your church according to the shape of the coming reign of God."

Amos Yong, professor of theology and mission, Fuller Theological Seminary,
author of *Hospitality and the Other*

"Do you want some practical, pastoral, and theological wisdom and encouragement on how to *be* the church, rather than merely *go to* church? Do you want
to be a people for God's name and faithful presence—for one another and the
world? Read this book. Learn nonnegotiable practices that Fitch and his communities have learned through their communion with a faithful God. These disciplines (including being with and for children), practiced together by the power
of the Holy Spirit, will conform us to Jesus. Joined to him, one another, and those
he's given us to love with him, we are intentionally shaped for God's missional life
among us."

Cherith Fee Nordling, associate professor of theology, Northern Seminary

"Like leaven in the dough, like a mustard seed in the soil, like light in the darkness,
the church must be faithfully present in our communities as an outpost of heaven.
David Fitch's new book will help us all to practice the kingdom lifestyle now. I encourage you to read, share, and live it!"

Krish Kandiah, founder and director, Home for Good, author of *Paradoxology*

"Are missional churches merely traditional churches with some justice projects
added on? In *Faithful Presence*, David Fitch says no. Instead, Fitch argues, following
the *missio Dei* and living incarnationally only occurs as we practice faithful presence
in the world. And such presence requires disciplines. *Faithful Presence* is a meaty
and delicious book."

Michael Frost, author of *The Shaping of Things to Come* and *The Road to Missional*

"In *Faithful Presence*, a book long overdue, David Fitch provides a corrective to the work of James Davison Hunter. He offers a winsome vision for following Jesus into the world that Christians across multiple traditions will find challenging, compelling, and inspiring."

Anthony B. Bradley, associate professor of religious studies, The King's College

"When I get up on the average day, I don't know how to transform the world. But I know how to pray, show hospitality, and proclaim truth. With scholarly care and pastoral zeal, David Fitch reminds us that it's in long-term, communal devotion to small but transformative practices that we both discover and reflect the faithful presence of God. *Faithful Presence* gives us permission to step aside from our own efforts at greatness, encouraging us to give our time and attention to disciplines that reveal and proclaim God's presence in our churches, homes, and neighborhoods."

Mandy Smith, lead pastor, University Christian Church, author of *The Vulnerable Pastor*

"In *Faithful Presence* David Fitch brings heard-it-all-before church leaders both profound insight and a new imagination for spiritual practices that lead seamlessly to an authentic, faithful presence with God in the world—a faithful presence that results in intuitive and organic mission in all aspects of our everyday lives."

Todd Hunter, bishop, Churches For the Sake of Others, author of *Giving Church Another Chance*

"The relationship between worship and mission, between the life and practices of the church and its witness to the world, is a matter of continual debate. David Fitch has done us a great service by identifying a holistic pattern of worship and witness rooted in disciplines given by Christ, to be practiced in the different contexts of our lives as disciples. *Faithful Presence* is both theologically grounded and very practical. The only problem with books like this is that you can't just read them, you have to live them."

Graham Cray, former leader, Fresh Expressions, Church of England

"Faithfulness is an intimidating idea, so the church can be tempted to find speedy shortcuts to growth, mission, and relevance. David Fitch is helping the church outgrow its obsession with fads to break open space for the reappearance of God's real-time presence in our neighborhoods. There is certainly unflattering press about the church in today's headlines, but *Faithful Presence* gives me genuine hope about what the body of Christ can be when it gathers around these seven practices. This book is appropriately critical at times, but it is fundamentally grounded in inspiring the shaping of a community for God's witness in the world. David Fitch has laid out a pathway for the church being the church again!"

Dan White Jr., cofounder, The Praxis Gathering, author of *The Church as Movement*

FAITHFUL PRESENCE

SEVEN DISCIPLINES THAT SHAPE
THE CHURCH FOR MISSION

DAVID E. FITCH

IVP Books

An imprint of InterVarsity Press
Downers Grove, Illinois

InterVarsity Press
P.O. Box 1400, Downers Grove, IL 60515-1426
ivpress.com
email@ivpress.com

InterVarsity Press® is the book-publishing division of InterVarsity Christian Fellowship/USA®, a movement of students and faculty active on campus at hundreds of universities, colleges and schools of nursing in the United States of America, and a member movement of the International Fellowship of Evangelical Students. For information about local and regional activities, visit intervarsity.org.

Scripture quotations, unless otherwise noted, are from the New Revised Standard Version of the Bible, copyright 1989 by the Division of Christian Education of the National Council of the Churches of Christ in the USA. Used by permission. All rights reserved.

While any stories in this book are true, some names and identifying information may have been changed to protect the privacy of individuals.

Cover design: Cindy Kiple
Interior design: Beth McGill
Images: Shanghai road junction: © snvv/iStockphoto
  empty yellow booth: © Kevin Russ/iStockphoto

ISBN 978-0-8308-4127-1 (print)
ISBN 978-0-8308-9941-8 (digital)

Printed in the United States of America ∞

green press *As a member of the Green Press Initiative, InterVarsity Press is committed to protecting*
INITIATIVE *the environment and to the responsible use of natural resources. To learn more, visit greenpressinitiative.org.*

Library of Congress Cataloging-in-Publication Data
A catalog record for this book is available from the Library of Congress.

P 23 22 21 20 19 18 17 16 15 14 13 12 11 10 9 8 7 6 5 4 3 2 1

Y 36 35 34 33 32 31 30 29 28 27 26 25 24 23 22 21 20 19 18 17 16

For McKnight ;)

Contents

Introduction

Searching for the Real Church

When I was seventeen, my father dropped me off at a small Midwestern Christian college. As he drove off, I waved goodbye—and then it dawned on me: for the first time in my life I was completely on my own. Among other things, I could now choose which church to go to and indeed whether to even go to church at all. Up until then, that had all been determined by my family.

The Student Affairs office encouraged all new students to find a church, so I immediately began shopping for a good one. I listened to the upperclassmen, who told me there was this church where the pastor was "hip," dressed in normal clothes and talked with you as if you were a real person. *Imagine that,* I thought, *a pastor who treats you like a real person.* Predictably, many of us settled on that church. Nonetheless, this whole experience jolted me. For years I had attended church without asking why. I came face to face with the fact that, apart from my family, I felt little connection to church. I didn't see why it was necessary for me. Now I was not only asking, Why would I go to one church over another? but, Why would I even go to church? Is the church even necessary for me to impact the world?

Many Christians I meet are asking similar questions. We've grown tired of church programming that tries harder each year to keep our attention by any means. Amid a frantic life, many of us are merely happy to have made it to church on Sunday. And then we find it doesn't connect with the rest of our lives. And so we are fatigued by church. Why bother?

Yet many Christians still go to church. Old habits die hard. We still connect with God in worship on Sunday. But after Sunday morning worship, we step out into our everyday lives and suddenly are in a different world. The Sunday sermons give us some to-dos for the week, and we try to be better Christians. But all this proves uninspiring when the rubber meets the road. When broadcast news or social media blare out the reality of the gross injustices of our world, the racial injustice, the sexual confusion, we find it impossible to relate our life on Sundays to these imposing struggles.

Does the church have anything to offer a world full of injustice? Can the church reach out to the worlds around me in a way that doesn't judge them, alienate them, or ask them in some way to come to us? Can the church engage the hurting, the poor, and the broken with something more than just handouts? We have seen the programs, the missional church, the justice teams, the church in a coffee house or a bar, and nothing seems to change. Can't we do all of this better without the church?

In this book I propose to answer these questions with the phrase, *faithful presence*.

Faithful presence names the reality that God is present in the world and that he uses a people faithful to his presence to make himself concrete and real amid the world's struggles and pain. When the church is this faithful presence, God's kingdom becomes visible, and the world is invited to join with God. Faithful presence is not only essential for our lives as Christians, it's how God has chosen to change the world. In this book I aim to describe what this faithful presence looks like.

But even more than describing this reality, I want to get intensely practical. I want to suggest that certain disciplines given to us by Christ shape us into being this kind of presence in the world. It doesn't just happen. We need practices that shape us to be a community of his faithful presence. And so the biggest part of this book will explore seven disciplines through which Christians are shaped by Christ to be his faithful presence in the world. Recovering these disciplines drives this book. It is, I contend, what it means to be the church.

Faithful Presence as the Calling of the Church

Several years ago I started going to a McDonald's in my neighborhood. There, early in the morning, I would drink coffee, grade papers, do research, have meetings, and do other things pastors and professors do. A friend eventually challenged me to see this local McDonald's as the arena of God's Spirit at work. Instead of seeing it as merely a place to do my own work, instead of even seeing the hundreds of people that pass by as candidates for my "come to Jesus" evangelism speech, I was challenged to see this place as a vibrant arena where God was truly present. I was exhorted to enter this place peacefully and be present with every person who came my way, pay attention to all that was going around me, and tend to God's presence here. For a few hours in the early morning, I started to do that regularly.

As time went on I started to meet an array of people in surprising conversations. I got to know people struggling to hold onto a job, abused by a spouse, or mistreated by police. I got to know some police themselves. I shared tables regularly with people who lived in cars and vans. I became enmeshed in a network where God was working in people's lives, and I was swept up into it. I had never been invited into the lives of so many people as I was at this McDonald's (not even in a church). We encountered God together. I saw miracles of God's presence materialize before my very eyes (some of which I'll tell about in this book). I found myself joined with people in prayer, reconciliation, healing, and proclaiming the hope of the gospel. I became a participant in God's work. I was learning how to be faithfully present to his presence. I was catching a glimpse of what faithful presence might look like in the world.

Although in many ways that McDonald's became another church for me, my own organized church community—Life on the Vine Christian Community—shaped me to be present and recognize God's work in that place. A few Viners (the nickname for people who were members of my church) started to hang out with me at McDonald's. Something that was part of my everyday life, my little McDonald's, had become an extension of Christ's presence as experienced at Life on the Vine without me really knowing it. I now believe every neighborhood, coffee shop, community center, Black Lives Matter protest march, YMCA, workplace, racial reconciliation village hall meeting, prison, city hall, homeless shelter, MOPS group, labor union hall, and hospital is a potential arena of God's presence similar to McDonald's. These places (and more) are fields of his presence waiting to be opened to the kingdom through Christians being present to his presence. Dare I say, they are starting points for changing the world, a revolution of the kingdom.

This grand revolution starts with a group of people entering into God's presence. It begins as we gather in worship and extends into every place we live. It is one and the same life. Amazing things start to happen as we gather, and then, as we become present to others, even more amazing things happen among the people around us. People are reconciled to God and to each other. Systems of evil are exposed and shut down. The kingdom becomes visible in our neighborhoods. The world takes notice and we invite them to join in to see it with us. Outbursts of his kingdom spread. And this process continues until in his reign, "all things are put in subjection" (1 Cor 15:27), and the new heaven and the new earth are completed (Rev 21:1).

All of this, every word of it, I contend begins with a group of people being restored to God's presence in Jesus Christ and then being faithfully present to him in the world. This faithful presence is at the heart of what it means to be the people of God. This is the thing we do that we call church. This is how God changes the world.

JAMES DAVISON HUNTER ON FAITHFUL PRESENCE

In 2010 James Davison Hunter of the University of Virginia wrote a well-known book about faithful presence titled, *To Change the World*.[1] In the book, Hunter proposes that Christians change their tactics for engaging culture and changing the world. He asks Christians to turn away from grabbing power in the broader culture through traditional political means. Quit trying to win the battle of ideas through political rallies, voting schemes, cultural confrontations, and campaigns of persuasion in churches and political forums. Instead, let Christians commit to a "new city commons" free from the power struggles and culture wars. He calls for Christians, shaped by an alternative covenant community of the kingdom, to humbly inhabit the places where we live and work with a new on-the-ground presence that dialogues and interacts with those around us and the institutions we are a part of. By being faithfully present, he says, Christians bring the subversive ways of Christ's kingdom into the spaces of our lives. We create new culture. We inhabit power differently. For Hunter, this is how God brings real change on his own terms. Hunter's vision and call overlaps with this book in many ways.

But Hunter, in my opinion, runs out of space in that book before he can flesh out what the actual practice of faithful presence might look like. For sure, he talks conceptually of the importance of each individual's formation in a community, its worship, and discipleship. He calls for the rejection of the Constantinian posture and for incarnational direct relational engagement in the spirit of Jeremiah 29:4-7 (themes echoed in this book).[2] He urges Christians to bring shalom to the actual circumstances we live in day to day. He calls Christians to engage in new culture making in education, the arts, and medicine—altruism that is based on who we are as Christians yet aims for the common good of the world. Yet Hunter, in my opinion, jumps the gun on assuming that such a community can exist without a new kind of formation.[3] If he is calling for the church to change and be a faithful presence in our culture, Hunter skips the question, How might our churches themselves be changed so as to be capable of faithful presence?

As a result, I fear that churches who follow Hunter's call for faithful presence will see their mission as training individuals to do this thing called faithful presence in their spheres of influence. The goal becomes for each individual to be sent out to be a faithful presence in their jobs, vocations, and spheres of influence. These individuals however, in the process, become isolated in the world. They are prone to being absorbed by the systems of the broader culture and then lose their distinctiveness. The power structures of this world are not challenged. In the process the reality of church community as a social reality witnessing to God's kingdom in the world gets put aside. As a result the world will not be changed, but once again Christians will be. The very thing that Hunter seems to be working against will happen all over again.

Faithful presence, I contend, must therefore be a communal reality before it can infect the world. It must take shape as a whole way of life in *a people*. From this social space we infect the world for change. Here we give witness to the kingdom breaking in and invite the world to join in. For this to happen, however, we need a set of disciplines that shape Christians into such communities in the world.

To this end, this book offers a set of disciplines (from Jesus himself) to shape communities of faithful presence. I contend these disciplines make faithful presence a live social possibility for churches inhabiting their neighborhoods, workplaces, play, art, and families with the kingdom of God. Though I differ with some of Hunter's analysis of the church, I hope that what follows advances his call to faithful presence.

An Invitation

Part one of this book describes God's presence and what *faithful presence* means as a way of inhabiting the world. It then describes how the disciplines function within God's triune work to make his presence real, concrete, and visible in all the spaces of our lives. It explains the disciplines as entry points into the new reality God has begun in the world through Jesus Christ: the kingdom of God.

Part two of the book, the main part of the book, then turns to the seven disciplines themselves, in which Christ promises to be faithfully present to us and we in turn become his faithful presence. I invite you to discover a world where spaces are opened up with our cooperation through these disciplines. Amazingly Christ's presence is made real. We become wonderfully grafted into what he is doing in the world. In the process we find ourselves being shaped as a community in his presence for the world. We become his faithful presence.

Throughout the book, I tell many stories of faithful presence. In every case I have changed the names and circumstances of people in these stories to protect their identity. So come and explore a world that for many in the West has been lost. It is a journey of searching through the rubble of Christendom and finding the way of life in the kingdom made possible by the triune God in the sending of the Son. In the process I hope that these disciplines, which have been with us for approximately two thousand years, get rediscovered. In their practice lies a world to be discovered in the Bible all over again. It is the world as it is under Jesus as Lord bringing in his kingdom, slowly, patiently, with love, through his faithful presence.

PART ONE

GOD'S FAITHFUL PRESENCE

1

God's Faithful Presence

He . . . has made him the head over all things for the church,
which is his body, the fullness of him who fills all in all.

EPHESIANS 1:22-23

For a while now in North America we've been missing something. Most of us haven't even noticed. We've been rushing back and forth to work, to meetings, to malls, to kids' sports programs. We've been striving to do our jobs, have a respectable career, and pay our bills. All the while we've missed that God is present all around us and is at work; all we have to do is take notice.

For most Christians in the West, God is an individual belief, a personal relationship, a private experience, something we fit in between all the other things in our lives. The notion that we can be present to God, and he to us, is not on the horizon of our awareness. We do not imagine that God is present outside of me or between me and the other person I'm with, that he will confront me in the middle of my world if I will open myself to him.

A few years back I was sitting in a gathering of my local church on Sunday morning. There were about two hundred of us sitting in the round, as was our custom. Even though there was a large table in the middle of the circle, we still sat across from one another in full view of what everyone was doing. So we can be easily distracted. This particular morning I became distracted by how distracted everybody else seemed to be. We were preparing to partake of the Lord's Table together. We were supposed to be silent, but people were moving and shuffling. As the pastor came to the table to present the bread and the wine, a few people got up and went to the bathroom. Others were tending to their children's needs. A few looked at the clock, shaking their legs impatiently.

I noticed that George, who I had known for a couple years, could not sit still. He had been a heroin addict and was fighting the hold that the addiction still had on his life. A few times during the gathering he got up, went to the foyer and then to the nursery, where he picked up his infant. Then he went and got a drink of water. It was obvious he was struggling to connect and be present with what was happening in the gathering. But he was not alone. Many were struggling to sit and be present. No doubt George was battling physiological issues. Many had to tend to their children. (We welcome all children to be present in the gathering around the table.) Nonetheless, I was struck by how unimpressed everyone seemed to be by the table. There was little sense in the room that Jesus was present among us.

I wondered to myself how the striving in the room would change if indeed we were all gripped by an irruption of God's presence (in Christ) around the table. How would we all be transformed if we could actually recognize Christ in our midst? Would George's internal struggles be changed? What if people approached the table like the Israelites approached the ark of the covenant in the Old Testament, fearing imminent sickness or even death if they approached the table unworthily (see 1 Cor 11:29-30)? How would that kind of awareness of God's presence affect George and the rest of us as we gathered around the table? I don't wish anyone harm, of course. But I was struck with this question as I sat there that morning: How have we become so distracted from such a palpable reality as the presence of Christ at the table?

"God's presence is the central fact of Christianity," said American pastor A. W. Tozer. The heart of the Christian message is that "God is waiting for us to push into conscious awareness of his presence."[1] A perusal of Scripture testifies over and over again that Tozer is right: God comes to be present with his people.

The Story of God's Presence

At the very beginning God created the heavens and the earth as the place of his presence. "Heaven is my throne," says the Lord, "and the earth is my footstool" (Is 66:1 NIV). "The garden of Eden . . . is a place where God dwells and man should worship him," says Old Testament scholar John Walton.[2] Humanity was created to be in God's presence, and Eden was God's sanctuary.[3] But Adam and Eve usurped God's authority and broke fellowship with him, and when they heard the sound of the Lord God walking in the garden the next day, they "hid themselves from the presence of the Lord God" (Gen 3:8 NASB). God's presence with humanity had been disrupted. And violence broke out (Gen 6:5).

After the Noahic flood, God set out to restore his presence with his creation. God called Abraham and birthed a people to bless the nations. God would be present in this nation. Through a series of events, this nation ended up in Egypt, where they were enslaved. After many years of suffering in Egypt, God manifested his presence to Moses at the burning bush and sent Moses to deliver his people. In that sending, God promises to be "with" Moses (Ex 3:10-12). The pattern of God's presence being *with* those he sends runs constant throughout the entire story of God in the Bible.

Moses, as we know, then leads God's people out of Egypt. They come to the same mountain where God had earlier spoke to him, and God calls Moses up the mountain to be "with" him. While Moses is with God, the people of Israel fashion a golden calf and worship it. So God, in great anger, sends Moses onward and withdraws his presence from Israel "because you are an obstinate people, and I might destroy you on the way" (Ex 33:3-4 NASB). But Moses intercedes, "If Your presence does not go *with us*, do not lead us up from here. . . . Is it not by Your going with us, so that we, I and Your people, may be distinguished from all *other* people who are upon the face of the earth?" (Ex 33:15-16 NASB) God's people are not his people apart from his presence.

God relents and consents to go with his people. Shortly thereafter a traveling tabernacle is built to house God's presence among the people. The next several accounts of Moses encountering God's presence around the tabernacle tell of the care needed for anyone in physical proximity to God's presence. God's presence is so viscerally real that they all must know how to approach God. His presence is at the core of his work among his people.

Time and again the Psalms repeat the theme of God's presence with his people. My favorite is Psalm 46.

> God is our refuge and strength,
> A very present help in trouble. . . .
>
> There is a river whose streams make glad the city of God,
> The holy dwelling places of the Most High.
> God is in the midst of her, she will not be moved;
> God will help her when morning dawns.
> The nations made an uproar, the kingdoms tottered;
> He raised his voice, the earth melted.
> The LORD of hosts is with us. . . .
>
> He makes wars to cease to the end of the earth;
> He breaks the bow and cuts the spear in two;
> He burns the chariots with fire.
> "Cease *striving* and know that I am God;
> I will be exalted among the nations, I will be exalted in the earth.
> The Lord of hosts is with us;
> The God of Jacob is our stronghold. (Ps 46:1, 4-7, 9-11 NASB)

Notice the words *with, in the midst, present,* and *dwelling* in this text. Throughout the Bible they are some of the important code words for God's real presence. As Psalm 46 makes clear, his presence dispels violence; it brings peace and stops all striving. He rules as Lord. He rules in and through his presence, which brings the richness of love, reconciliation, and justice. He will never coerce his people. Israel disregards his presence often, and God challenges them to be still and be present with him (Ps 46:10).

Years later, in the Promised Land, the temple stood in the middle of Jerusalem as the nation's meeting place with God's presence. This is where the people came to be reconciled with God, be present with God, and pray in the presence of God. When God's people rebelled and disregarded God for false idols, God left the temple (Ezek 10). The temple was eventually destroyed, and the people were dispersed in exile. Nonetheless, God promises to renew his presence among his people (Ezek 37:27). God would come again to renew the broken relationship, forgive the people of their sins, break the hold of violence, and be among them. God will heal Israel and the world through his faithful presence.

This promise was fulfilled in the form of Jesus Christ, the incarnate God, "God with us" in flesh. In Matthew's Gospel, Jesus is born of Mary in fulfillment of the prophecy, "THE VIRGIN SHALL BE WITH CHILD AND SHALL BEAR A SON, AND THEY SHALL CALL HIS NAME IMMANUEL," which means "God with us" (Mt 1:23 NASB). God has come in flesh to be the very presence of God among us. The Gospel of John describes this same dynamic, invoking the language of the tabernacle in the wilderness. He declares that "the Word was made flesh, and dwelt [tabernacled] among us" (Jn 1:14 KJV). The amazing reality of the living God having come to dwell with us cannot be missed in the presence and mission of Jesus.

In the farewell discourses of John's Gospel, Jesus tells the disciples that though he goes, he will not "leave [them] as orphans" (Jn 14:18 NASB), but instead the Holy Spirit will come. The Father and the Son by the Spirit will make their "abode" with them (Jn 14:23). "Abide in Me, and I in you" (Jn 15:4 NASB). God's presence has been renewed to us in Christ by the Spirit as Jesus goes and the Spirit comes in his place (Jn 16:5-7). In Jesus' parting words in Matthew's Gospel he promises, "and, lo, I am with you always, even unto the end of the world" (Mt 28:20 KJV).

God fulfills this promise through the outpouring of the Spirit's presence on men and women, sons and daughters, prophets and prophetesses (as proclaimed in Peter's sermon on Pentecost, reflecting the fulfillment of Joel 2:28-32) at Pentecost (Acts 2). God has come again to be among his people. Through Christ, God has restored his presence among us, which began with his people at Pentecost. According to the apostle Paul, we the church, God's own people, are his "temple" in the midst of the world (2 Cor 6:16). We are no longer strangers to God but fellow citizens of "the household of God," being knit together into "a holy temple in the Lord; . . . for a dwelling place of God in the Spirit"

(Eph 2:19, 21-22 RSV). God's presence in Jesus does not end with Jesus' death, resurrection, and ascension. In Jesus, God extends his own presence by giving of the Holy Spirit to his people, and subsequently sends them into the world (Jn 20:21-22).

In the final chapter of the book of Revelation we are told where this is all going: the coming of the new heaven and the new earth. Revelation depicts the image of the new city of Jerusalem as the place of God's indwelling, where no temple is needed. Indeed, the new heaven and earth are described in terms of the dimensions of the temple, the dwelling place of God among Israel.[4] And so the voice in Revelation 21:3 says, "Behold, the tabernacle of God is among men, and He will dwell among them, and they shall be His people, and God Himself will be among them" (NASB). This is the goal of God's redemptive work: that we will be restored, along with all of creation, to be with God and he with us. His presence will flood the new heaven and earth, and everything will be made new.

The Scriptures, from beginning to end, tell the marvelous story of God returning his presence to all creation. It always was God's intent to be *with* his creation in the fullness of his presence.

THE LOSS OF PRESENCE IN OUR WORLD

But this sense of God's presence has been lost in our modern world, even among Christians. Daily, we obsess about holding our lives together. We walk in isolation and protection from other people. We pass homeless people on the street and give a dollar, but we do not know them. Indeed, we dare not know them. At work we look at clients as profit-loss statements. Even our most intimate relationships can turn into negotiated contracts. As a result there's a distrustful distance between people in all types of relationships. We are empty and long for some kind—any kind—of presence.

Ultimately this is a longing for God. But God has not left us. We, in all our striving and independence, have not allowed any space for him to be present between us and the people we do life with. We roam frantically in a maze of disconnected souls.

Even when we go to church, we find no respite from this frenzy. Though there's a flurry of activity and programming in our church buildings, it seems as if we're avoiding something. We see our pastors projected on video screens, separated by technology from the people they are preaching to. We do not really know the pastor, or anyone else in this gathering for that matter. And when the well-produced worship experience is over and we leave the church building, something gnaws at our souls. Emptiness creeps back in, alerting us that there was something missing in that building.

Rarely do we gather to be present in our neighborhoods. More often than not, church leaders teach us how to defend ourselves against the forces of darkness "out there." We don't learn how to recognize God's faithful presence in the neighborhood. We are lost in our inability to be present before God, among ourselves, and in our neighborhoods. We want another way of life.

This stunning loss of presence in our society is glaring. But God is still there, and we still long for presence with God and with other people. We long to be truly known and to truly know someone. We long to be with someone on a journey that means something. We groan in the depths of the night—groaning for God's presence.

IT'S TIME FOR US TO PAUSE

When things get crazy at my house, we try to stop everything and clear some space. I find myself saying things to my ten-year-old son like, "Max, I will not play the goof-off game with you anymore until we at least have some face time. One serious conversation!" "But Dad! Come on Dad, you never goof off with me anymore." And right there, rather than giving in, I must own up to my own unhealthy habits of always wanting to be distracted, have fun, and avoid the hard work of parenting. I must take this God-given opportunity right now to pay attention and nurture some space when he is ten, or it may be too late in just a few short years.

Nothing, absolutely nothing, is as life transforming for either me or my son than actually being present with each other and to God. When we sit face to face, listening and tending to what's going on in the other person, and when we do the same together with God, amazing transformation and goodness begins.

Many of us Christians in North America have reached a similar moment. God's presence has been structured out of our crazed existence. We must stop everything and make space to be present to God. We have heard about the marvels of God's presence to his people in Scripture. And yet so much of the world we live in today remains dark to the presence of God. The light of his presence seems not to have been turned on. How does God restore his presence over the whole earth? And what do we have to do with it?

How God Changes the World

The Bible's answer to this question is the church. God's plan is to become present to the world in and through a people, and then invite the world to join with him. How does this happen? In the simplest of terms, a group of people gather and become present to God. In our life together, we recognize God in the presence of Jesus Christ through disciplines in which he has promised, "I am in your midst." By knowing God's presence in Christ in this way, we are then able to recognize his presence in the world. We participate in his work in the world, and his presence becomes visible. The world then sees God's presence among us and through us and joins in with God. And the world is changed. This, I contend, is faithful presence. This is the church. And this is how God has chosen to change the world.

But doesn't this limit God's presence too strongly to the church? Isn't God already present over the whole earth? Why do we need the church to be his faithful presence in the world?

Certainly God is present (and at work) in the whole world. As the psalmist declares, "Sing praises to God! . . . For God is the king of all the earth. . . . [He] reigns over the nations" (Ps 47:6-8 RSV). Time and again, Old Testament texts declare God's sovereign rule over the whole world. Nonetheless, he becomes uniquely present and visible in (and through) a people: first among his chosen people Israel (concretely symbolized in the temple) and then through Christ in the church, his body. Here among a group of people, his subjects, he is present and brings in his kingdom. And then, through this people, he reveals his presence elsewhere in the world. He invites the whole world to join in.

THE EXAMPLE OF LAWNDALE

When my friend Wayne Gordon moved into the Lawndale neighborhood in 1975, it was one of the poorest and most crime-ridden neighborhoods in Chicago.[5] Few could imagine anything good coming from this place. Nonetheless, God was already working there. He was present. Wayne took a job as a football coach and history teacher in the local high school. He opened a weight-lifting room in the first-floor storefront room below his apartment. There he gathered a group of ten to twelve young football players who met to study the Bible and be with each other in the struggles of Lawndale. More people came. Wayne spent hours listening to them, the stories being told and the needs pressing in on them. Wayne became present to them and to God among them.

Listening to the needs of the neighborhood, this group opened a free-style exchange laundromat where every user would contribute in some way to its functioning. Over the next few years, hundreds of people intersected in that small room of washers and dryers. This became an entry point for God to become especially present. As people became present to others and then discerned Christ's presence in their midst, one miracle at a time happened. They prayed and denounced the powers of evil. Reconciliation happened. Finances were shared. Life was reordered. Slowly, over many years, God made his presence concrete in Lawndale.

And yet, as Wayne once said to me, "If you had been here after fifteen years you would have said nothing is happening here." God's presence is not always obvious. He requires witnesses. God comes humbly in Christ. He so loves us, he never imposes himself on us. Instead he comes *to* us, to be *with* us, and in that presence he reveals himself. In his presence there is forgiveness, reconciliation, healing, transformation, patience and, best of all, love. In his presence he renews all things. *Presence* is how God works. But he requires a people tending to his presence to make his presence visible for all to see. In that tiny group of people in Lawndale, Christ became present for all to see.

Thirty-five years later, the transforming work of God in Lawndale has now become so visible that people from around the world come to see what God has done: a church gathering of almost one thousand, hundreds of renovated apartments, a hospital with 450,000 patient visits a year to people based on what they can afford, a "hope house" that provides a recovery place for those escaping various hideous addictions.

As Wayne frequently reminds people, "Not one thing or idea has been done here that did not come from within this Lawndale community itself." God was at work here long before Wayne arrived. But a visible community starting with twelve young people made space for Christ's presence to become visible in a specific place. By tending to God's special presence in Christ in a people, what God was already doing became visible to all who would see. And now Lawndale is influencing Chicago and beyond.

God is present over the whole world, yet he becomes visibly present through a people who make his presence known.

THE RELATIONSHIP BETWEEN KINGDOM AND PRESENCE

There is one last piece to this puzzle about how God becomes present in the world: God's kingdom and how he rules through his presence. People often think of the kingdom of God as the primary metaphor for how God works in the world. But the kingdom of God runs parallel to the presence of God in the history in Israel. They play off one another. The kingdom metaphor helps us see the dynamic of how God works through his presence.

God's presence actually precedes chronologically the kingdom in the history of Israel. The tabernacle, which was replaced by the temple, precedes the monarchy of Israel. Giving Israel a king was a concession by God to Israel.[6] The prophet Samuel actually complains that Israel was not content with God's presence. Israel wanted a king like the rest of the nations. They were not content with God's way of working *among* a people through prophets, priests, and judges. Samuel resisted giving Israel a king, but God told him to do it anyway, saying, "they have not rejected you [Samuel], but they have rejected me from being king over them" (1 Sam 8:7). But this kingship could never replace the presence of God, and Israel would later regret having a king (1 Sam 8:9). Years later, after the debacle of the monarchies, Israel returned from exile. At this time the temple (the sign of God's presence) was restored to Israel, but not the monarchy. Israel had forgotten God's presence in lieu of a king. God was calling them back to his presence.

But God did not totally throw away the kingdom idea. It ran deep in Israel's history. Jesus keeps the language of kingdom but redefines it.[7] He says before Pilate, "My kingdom is not of this world" (Jn 18:36 ESV), meaning his kingdom does not operate on the basis of the worldly power and coercion formerly associated with Israel's (and Gentile) monarchies. Instead Jesus comes to fulfill the idea of God's rule as his presence among us. He is turning the notion of kingdom upside down. He says to the disciples as they gather round the table, "As my Father has conferred on me, so I confer on you a kingdom" (Luke 22:29, my translation). He is inaugurating in his disciples a new way of being together in his presence around this table that foreshadows the completed reign of God. It is in and through his presence with them and one another that this kingdom will come to be.

Throughout the Bible the kingdom of God is located wherever a people come together and submit to his rule over their lives. God calls a group of his subjects together, and in this space he rules. God reigns over the whole world, but it is here in these places that his reign takes visible shape among this peculiar group of people called Israel, who are his subjects for the rest of the world to see.[8] And it is here, most importantly, that he comes to be present and manifests his ways among a people.

And so the apostle Paul uses the body of Christ metaphor more than any other to describe the church as Christ's presence in a body. Yet here also, in this people, Christ reigns as head of a physical body by the Spirit. He is still Lord over the world, but he rules in this space. And so he calls the church "God's temple" (1 Cor 3:16), the meeting place of God's presence in the world (Eph 1:23; 1 Cor 3:9, 16-17).[9] In a wonderful summary Paul puts it like this: "And he has put all things under his feet and has made him the head over all things for the church, which is his body, the fullness of him who fills all in all" (Eph 1:22-23).

His kingdom and his presence go together. In the church God will uniquely dwell and make his presence known in Christ. With his presence always comes the justice, reconciliation, renewal, and healing of his new reign. This is faithful presence. It is the way God works. This is how God will change the world. This is the mission of God.

WHERE IS THIS CHURCH?

At this point you may be thinking, *where is this church?* This does not sound like any church I know.

Strangely, I believe this church exists among us. It has existed ever since Christ first sent his Spirit with the disciples (Jn 20:21-23). We see glimmers of it when people are transformed within a church community or whole communities are affected by a church community's love, care, and generosity in a neighborhood. But this church also regularly, down through history, has been dislodged from its call to faithful presence. This church has been dislodged, for instance, when it has aligned itself with worldly power. Too often we rely on government or money to do the work of God's presence. We lose our calling. Likewise, whenever the church focuses on self-preservation, keeping people happy, coming back every Sunday, and filling the offering plates, the church turns in on itself and loses its way again. Down through the annals of church history, under the pressure of keeping the church going, time and again we Christians have lost the call to be God's faithful presence in the world.

But today, as North American Christendom wanes, with fewer and fewer Christians to be kept happy, with churches shrinking and the injustices of the world pressing on us, it has never been more urgent for the church to be faithfully present in the world around us. Surely it is time to return to discerning the presence of Christ among us and in the world. It is time for a new faithfulness to his presence.

How do we do this? To this question I now turn.

2

To Change the World

*Don't you know that you yourselves are God's temple
and that God's Spirit dwells in your midst?*

1 CORINTHIANS 3:16 NIV

One time a man from our church, I'll call him Joe, lost his job because he had become violent with his boss. At the same time, he had not paid his rent for two months and was being evicted from his apartment. He claimed the landlord had been unjust by allowing the landlord's mail to go into Joe's mailbox (a mailbox Joe technically hadn't paid rent for in two months). Meanwhile, Joe, an ex-con, was becoming violent with his wife. Some old, painful cycles in his life were kicking in. In short, God's presence was absent from Joe's life and all his various relationships: work, marriage, landlord, and so on. It was all heading for a crisis.

So a group of friends met with both Joe and the landlord. We saw an openness in the landlord but still no resolution happened. Then the Christians among us invited Joe, some of his friends, and the landlord to gather around a table and be present to each other and to God. Following Matthew 18:15-20, we asked to hear their grievances toward each other. The landlord was surprisingly open to the idea and agreed to join us. We opened the gathering by praying "Thy kingdom come" and invited Christ's presence into our midst. We read Matthew 18:15-20 and promised to submit this whole episode to Jesus as Lord as well as to one another, being very careful to listen and confess sin. The landlord admittedly was puzzled at some of this language but went along anyway. In doing so, we became present to each other and to the presence of Christ among us.

We listened to Joe's accusations against the landlord. We listened to the landlord and his grievances against Joe. We asked questions. We submitted to each other and to Christ in our midst. There was a hush over the room as we watched entrenched power positions break down. Joe was so convicted he went outside and hid in a tree for two hours. Eventually, he confessed his wrongs against his landlord, feeling remorse for his sins. While Joe was in that tree, stunningly the landlord forgave two months rent and added on another month free. When Joe came back he started to deal with the anger deep in his life. Abuse and pain was uncovered and forgiven. In the coming weeks, true reconciliation began between Joe and his family members. Some healing and growth started that night between Joe and his wife. Many in the neighborhood heard what had happened. The kingdom broke in and became visible in real socioeconomic relationships. It reminded me of a New Testament miracle story.

What happened with Joe, the landlord, and our church that night did not happen spontaneously. We were practicing a very specific discipline that day. It was the discipline of reconciliation taught by Jesus Christ himself (see Mt 18:15-20). God was surely present in the neighborhood before we gathered that night. But in gathering together in this practice of reconciliation, Jesus promised to be present there: "I will be in the midst of [with] you" (Mt 18:20, my translation). In the space of that discipline, our lives were formed by the thick meanings of Christ's work on the cross, his forgiveness, his reconciliation, his renewing of all things. By mutually submitting to one another under his lordship through this discipline, a space was opened up for his presence, and the kingdom broke in.

The church, I contend, is built on disciplines like this. The church is more than a space where some individuals gather to affirm they believe in something. It is the place where God's people discern his presence and submit to Christ's concrete rule. He has given us disciplines for doing this. Here a new world is born that is nothing less than his kingdom breaking in. Here an incredible faithful presence takes shape.

THE GREAT COMMISSION

If I were to describe metaphorically what happened around the table that night, I would say that a few Christians joined hands with God, who is already at work in the world. We discerned God at work in the neighborhood and then cooperated with each other to open space for his rule among us. There, around that table, with Joe, the landlord, and some friends, Christ became present (literally) and renewed our lives according to his purposes.

The landlord's openness to our meeting was evidence that God was already present in the neighborhood. God was even active in those disputes between Joe and the landlord. God was there in all the other disruptions going on in Joe's life. But in coming together around that table via the discipline of reconciliation, a space was cleared for Christ's presence to be recognized, his conviction to be discerned, his power to break in. As a result, we all became witnesses to his kingdom, and the neighborhood looked on.

This, I contend, is the way God works. This is the way God will change the world through Christ. His work will begin small, in little places like this. And from there it will expand to change the world on a larger scale.

God's work is necessarily twofold. God first is present and active in the whole world. But God also chooses to become present in and through a people locally. He, in essence, completes his work in the world in the concrete lives and circumstances of a people through the real presence of Christ.

Jesus' Great Commission (Mt 28:16-20) confirms this twofold movement (see appendix 3). Jesus, before the ascension, sends his disciples into the world and says, "All authority in heaven and on earth has been given to me" (v. 18 NIV). His rule and power is now over the whole world ("heaven and earth").[1] The word used by Matthew here for "authority" draws on the ways Old Testament Israel talked of God's lordship over all creation.[2] Through Christ the whole world has now become the arena of God's mission, and this moves beyond Israel or the church. This is the *missio Dei* (emphasizing that the mission of God is beyond the church), part of the Great Commission.

But Christ also goes *with* his disciples into the world as they live, teach, disciple, and baptize under his authority. The ending sentence of the Great Commission says, "and lo I am *with* you always, even unto the end of the age" (v. 20, my translation). Here Jesus uses the word that signifies the incarnation: *with*. This same word named Jesus at his birth in Matthew 1:23: Emmanuel, "God with us." This word summarizes how God will extend the presence of Christ with a people (the disciples) as they are sent out on God's mission. God doesn't only rule generally over the whole world through Christ, but this work of God becomes concrete as the Spirit extends Christ's presence visibly through the church into the world. This is the *incarnation* part of the Great Commission.

The Great Commission is fulfilled when the two (*missio Dei* and incarnation) come together in one concrete place. In this space the Father (reigning), the Son (being sent), and the Spirit (making the Son's presence real) work together. A people become present to God's presence in the world (*missio Dei*) and make space for Christ's presence to become real among them (incarnation). His kingdom breaks in. Witness happens. This is what happened that night with Joe, the landlord, and friends. The discipline of reconciliation opened up space among a people for Jesus' presence to be tended to, and in so doing brought to fruition what God was doing in the landlord and Joe. We all watched in wonder. We were witnesses. This is, I contend, the way the disciplines work.

In Matthew 28:19-20, Jesus sends his disciples to "make disciples" of all nations. Teach them "to keep" all he has commanded them to do. Jesus was not asking his disciples to enforce a new legalism. He was asking them to teach the disciplines, just as he had taught them. To "make disciples" implies the use of disciplines. This is the means by which Jesus will be *with* us and manifest his authority over heaven and earth. He says to baptize them into the life of the triune God, who is at work in the world (v. 19). In other words, teach people how to live under Jesus' reigning authority (enacted by the Father) in his presence by the Holy Spirit. In this way Jesus summarizes what it means to live faithful to his presence.

That night, around that table, a space was opened up among Joe, the landlord, friends, and neighbors for God's work in the world to become visible. Like a special visitation, Christ came to be with us by the Spirit. Those of us who were Christians tended to Jesus' presence in our midst. Others sat with their eyes wide open, wondering what they were witnessing. We all became witnesses to what God is doing to redeem the world (Acts 1:8). We saw the Great Commission of Christ fulfilled among us in that moment of faithful presence.

INTRODUCING THE SEVEN DISCIPLINES

What are the disciplines I've been speaking of? I believe there are seven disciplines given to us by Christ through his apostles. These shape us into his presence. They are the Lord's Table, reconciliation, proclaiming the gospel, being with "the least of these," being with children, the fivefold ministry, and kingdom prayer. In these disciplines Jesus has given us all we need to shape our lives into his presence for the transformation of the world. I choose these seven for a couple of reasons, not the least of which is that they are all given to us by Christ in the Scriptures. In addition, they have a long history of being practiced by the church. They have been proven over time to form the foundation of life in Christ's community. Finally, I also have experienced each of these disciplines as shaping God's kingdom in my church and neighborhoods.

I could have chosen more disciplines beyond these seven. The lists of the church's practices (marks or sacraments) has varied over the centuries.[3] But among all these lists, these seven disciplines in particular have long, compelling histories in the early church (prior to the Roman Church) as practices where the living Christ is encountered. Historically, they have led people into his presence. Even the disciplines of proclaiming the gospel and kingdom prayer have been located by the church (in the mass) around the Lord's presence at the table. These seven are disciplines of his presence.

If you are a Roman Catholic, you may notice I do not include baptism and marriage in my list of disciplines even though they are part of the seven Roman Catholic sacramental practices. This is simply because they are not repeatable. They are initiatory practices. At their best they are not repeated in our lives even though we frequently reconsecrate or celebrate our vows from time to time.[4] I have chosen to focus exclusively on the disciplines of Christ given to the church that we live daily as central to our everyday life.

In this regard these disciplines encompass all of life, including eating, fellowship, hope, conflict, sickness, death, leadership, raising a family, and life with God in mission. They are not things we merely do on Sunday but are the means by which we become present to God's presence everywhere we live.

A SOCIAL SPACE IS OPENED UP

These disciplines are always about more than just *me*.[5] Like that night with Joe, they open space for God's presence in Christ to become real among *us*. They form a community in and around his fullness. They are intensely social.

We might therefore call these disciplines social sacraments, following the Anabaptist theologian John Howard Yoder,[6] because God becomes specially present as Christ "in and with, through and under what men and women do" together in these practices.[7] Here, in these disciplines, we discover that Christ promises to be with us in a special way. Whenever you do this, "I am in your midst," he says. Because we know he is present here, we can discern his presence in the rest of our lives.

It makes sense then that these disciplines are about more than my personal relationship to Jesus. They are entry points into his kingdom. They open up space for God to rearrange the world, starting in our social relationships. These disciplines invite us into what God is actually doing in the whole world.

We know, for instance, that "in Christ" God is "reconciling the [whole] world to himself." God is working for reconciliation of all things in the world. Yet he will not overwhelm people. He works through entry points. He entrusts to us "the message of reconciliation" (2 Cor 5:19). We are "ambassadors," representatives, bridge builders, entry points into this new world. Through the discipline of reconciliation (Mt 18:15-20), we participate in the work of God, opening space for God to bring his work into concrete reality in a specific place and time.

By leading people into these disciplines, the disciplines (in a sense) lead us. As we enter into the disciplines, they shape us into his rule. Spaces of his presence are opened up. Out of our mutual submission to the King in this place, a community is formed in our midst. His authority and reign become visible among us. From these places a new world is born, and we invite the whole world to see and join us as we go where he is indeed taking the whole world.

That night with Joe, people's lives were reordered. The power and authority of God's rule broke in. "What is bound on earth is bound in heaven, and what is loosed on earth is loosed in heaven" (Mt 18:18, my translation). Marriages were renewed, broken relationships healed, economics rearranged. More than each person's relationship, individual relationships with God were set right. It was the beginning of a new social order. It did not happen in one night. But for those who had eyes to see, a new kingdom was being born in our midst. In this way these disciplines help us participate in the space where God is taking the whole world.

Kingdom, Presence, and Mutual Submission

Presence is the way Christ rules. His kingdom and his presence are inseparable. Christ's authority and his kingdom are central themes of each discipline as he teaches them in Scripture. These disciplines shape us into his kingdom, which implies into his presence.

At the core of the disciplines then is mutual submission. The disciplines gather people together into a circle of submission to his reign. Submission to the King defines each subject, and the kingdom is composed of the King's subjects. Each discipline then creates a space for surrendering our control. Each works against the impulse to take control and impose my will on a situation. In this process a marvelous space is opened up for Jesus to become Lord. We can then tend to Christ's presence among us.

These disciplines inevitably challenge our most ingrained ways of leadership in the American church. They challenge the disdain our culture has toward the word *submission*. Unfortunately, this word has been used often by the powerful to abuse those under them. Whether it be abusive spouses, abusive leaders, or abusive executives, submission always seems to imply one person over another in an abuse of power.[8] In the kingdom of God however, there is no more seizing power by someone over others. As Jesus said, this is the way of the world (Gentiles) who "lord it over [you]," but "it is not so among you." Instead, "whoever wishes to be first must be last of all and servant of all" (Mk 10:42-45, my paraphrase).

And so submission is always mutual, never unilateral. Indeed, the perceived leader, as Jesus models time and again, must first submit to everyone (v. 44). "Whoever wants to be first must be last of all" (Mk 9:35). Mutual submission is a founding principle of the kingdom. As we will see, this principle runs through all of the disciplines.

In the disciplines mutual submission lies at the root of the way God forms his church into communities of faithful presence. No one comes seeking to win. Instead, we come trusting the one Lord who reigns to work in and among us for his preferred future. There can be no antagonism at the core. There can be no violence here. There is instead presence, the fullness of Christ, the abundance that comes from the love and forgiveness of his person and work.

THE IN HERE–OUT THERE PROBLEM

The disciplines make it impossible to locate the church inside four walls of a building. They defy any in here–out there split.

A couple years ago I was on a weekend retreat with our new church, relaxing together in a Indiana beach house when an unusual conversation broke out. About twenty people were gathered on the back porch discussing where we were as a church. We had moved to our neighborhood about two years earlier and had engaged with many hurting people in our neighborhood. We had made inroads into community activities and were involved in bringing healing to some of our town's basic needs. But we were frustrated. Jonathan said, "What are we doing here? We've been here two years and nothing is happening! We haven't seen any more people come to our Sunday gathering. We haven't seen any conversions." Jonathan wasn't seeing a connection between what we did on our Sunday gatherings and the rest of the week. Meanwhile Megan piped in, "I don't know what I'm doing with Mary in the neighborhood. She's so hurting. She's homeless. And I thought I was helping her, but now you're all telling me I'm enabling her. I thought this is what we were doing here as a church. Now I'm so confused as to whether I'm supposed to be doing anything." Megan, it seems, saw any helping of hurting people as church. She was not clear on how what we did as church extended into her relationship with Mary in the neighborhood. Both cases illustrate a disconnect between our organized church life with God in worship, discipleship, and community, and our life with God in our neighborhoods.

But there is no separation between the church and the world as far as God is concerned. Returning to the twofold movement of the Son, God is at work in the whole world, including, but beyond, the church (*missio Dei*). Yet he is uniquely present in Christ (incarnation) wherever the church is faithfully present to his work in the world. The church is the extension of Christ's presence in the world, making his reign over the whole world visible.

Each of the seven disciplines therefore transgresses the traditional borders of church. What we do *in here* seamlessly bleeds into every area of our lives *out there*. We are continually discerning his presence. Neither Jonathan nor Megan were seeing that the same discernment of his presence at worship defined our discernment of his presence at work in Mary and the neighborhood. We are all surely called to help all people. Yet the church's specific task is to bring Christ's presence to, and discern his presence at work among people in our neighborhoods.

The difference between the church and the world therefore is not spatial, that is, between where God is and where he is not. There is no *in here* and *out there* when it comes to the church (see appendix 3). Instead, the church in essence experiences God's presence visibly now, ahead of the time when God shall visibly reign among the whole world. The difference between the church and the world then is just a matter of timing. The church experiences the kingdom ahead of time. The rest of the world is heading there; they just don't know it yet ("for he shall reign until all things have been made subject" [1 Cor 15:25, my translation]).

THE DISCIPLINES ON THE MOVE: THE THREE CIRCLES

With this in mind, I propose that the disciplines are best understood as *on the move.* They occupy three spaces continually—what I call the *close circle,* the *dotted circle,* and the *half circle* (see fig. 2.1)

Figure 2.1. The close, dotted, and half circles

The discipline first creates a close circle of committed subjects to Christ; all are in mutual submission to Christ and to one another. I call this the close circle as opposed to closed circle, because this circle does not exclude people from the circle. Rather, because all are committed Christians carefully discerning their submission to Christ and to one another under his reign, there is a social closeness that is supernatural. And Jesus, as the host, is at the center of this space. Here the intensity of the presence of Christ is known like nowhere else.

This incarnational presence of Christ, however, does not remain in the close circle. It is extended by these same people to a second space in the neighborhood. This space is represented as a dotted circle because, even though this space is still defined by a circle of committed followers of Jesus, there is space for neighbors and strangers to enter in and watch what God is doing in this circle. Here, the Christian disciple is the host. This disciple gathers people together (often in a home) into Christ's presence in the neighborhood via the disciplines.

Christ's presence however does not remain here either. Indeed Christ's presence *goes with us* into the many places we inhabit with the hurting and broken of the world. This space is a half circle because here the Christian goes among the world as a guest. Here the Christian also extends the special presence of Christ into the world, just as with the dotted circle. But here we discern Christ's presence as a guest among the hurting and the wandering. In this half circle the question is never whether Christ is here or not. Rather it is whether his presence will be welcomed.

All three circles are part and parcel of each discipline *on the move*. This is a pattern throughout the New Testament. The church gathers in its place of worship to encounter Christ's presence. But this same church is sent out to extend his presence into our homes, our neighborhoods, and among the marginalized and hurting in the world. The church's location therefore cannot be seen in terms of *in here* or *out there*. It is an entire way of life.

A fuller treatment of these three circles is coming in chapter three on the Lord's Table.

From Maintenance to Exhaustion to a Way of Life

That evening on the back porch in Michigan City, I remember asking the group to count the number of relationships we had with people in the neighborhoods. It could be the neighbor next door, the zoning committee chairman of the village, people we worked with in police/community relations to discuss the race issues in our community, a hurting widow we met at the coffee shop. We counted about seventy-five people we were involved with in long-term, real-life relationships in various kinds of situations. I then asked if our church was 50 people (the total who gathered on Sunday) or 125 (the total number of relationships where we were discerning the presence of Christ at work among us). I argued it was the latter.

There is a danger in thinking about the church as the number that meets only at the Sunday gathering. When we separate what happens in the close-circle gathering from the rest of life, we inevitably focus on doing the disciplines correctly, smoothly, professionally, and conveniently. We focus on maintaining and growing the close circle. In the process we get cut off from engaging the surrounding neighborhoods of God's presence. We can even become insulated and defensive. Our language becomes tribal. We get cut off from mission. I call this maintenance mode (see fig. 2.2).

Figure 2.2. The maintenance mode

In a similar vein, when we focus entirely on the half circles of our lives and disregard the close circle of his presence, we close ourselves off from the very foundation of God manifesting himself in the world. It's not that God is not present in the world but that, devoid of knowing his real presence in the close circle, we lose the wherewithal to discern his presence in the world. We end up relying on our own efforts to solve the problems of the world. We are eventually depleted and disappointed. I call this exhaustion mode (see fig. 2.3).

Figure 2.3. The exhaustion mode

It is important then to nurture presence in all three circles (for more on the dotted circle see appendix 2). In that Michigan City meeting, I saw signs of the maintenance mode in the voice of Jonathan and signs of the exhaustion mode in the voice of Megan.

Down through the centuries the church has fallen into maintenance mode. It seemingly happens when the church becomes too comfortable in society or when it aligns itself with power. Less concerned with those outside of Christ, the church retreats into itself. More reliant on secular power, it turns to running things efficiently. And when the church likes its power too much and the culture is no longer primarily Christian, the church desperately tries to preserve that power. It defends the close circle at all costs. All this results in maintenance mode.

On the other hand, exhaustion mode happens when Christians leave the close circle behind to work for justice and mission in the world. They may even reject the gathering of Christians in worship altogether (as a reaction to maintenance-oriented churches) and place their focus on being with the hurting, the poor, and the victims of injustice. All of this may appear admirable at first. But when the half circle is cut off from the close circle, it's difficult for the people to stay within the discerning posture of Christ's presence among the hurting. We are prone to taking matters into our own hands. We become exhausted as Christians. And although we may accomplish many good works of mercy (which is good of itself), in the end we will not bring in Christ's kingdom.

Each one of the seven disciplines should relentlessly move a people out of the maintenance or exhaustion mode. They drive us to be faithfully present in all three circles of life. We now turn to these disciplines, beginning with the most foundational discipline of them all, the Lord's Table.

PART TWO

THE SEVEN
DISCIPLINES

3

The Discipline of the Lord's Table

When the time comes to eat . . .

1 Corinthians 11:21

*U*SA *Today* reported that a chef named R. J. Cooper was opening a new restaurant in Merrifield, Virginia. A carpenter asked him whether he wanted a cell phone charging station at the hostess desk and answered abruptly, "No—100% a no!"[1] The article went on to report that restaurant owners are struggling to create a dining atmosphere free from the distractions of social media and electronic communications. Several restaurants have banned people from talking on cell phones at the restaurant. Social media distractions, they argue, are destroying people's ability to be present with one another at a meal. They can't be present long enough to even look at a menu and order food. As a result, time spent per customer at the tables was being extended. When they did start eating, little social interaction was actually taking place. The ambiance of the restaurant was being ignored. Cooper questioned whether his restaurant was losing its very reason for being. For Cooper, banning cell phones was an act of pure survival.

R. J. Cooper's quandary illustrates how we've lost the capacity to be present in our society. We are a mass of disconnected souls related to each other only in the most distanced and controlling ways. We don't take time or create space to be present with one another. We see it in the ways we eat. After a busy day at work, mom and dad go off to another meeting, and children go to various programs or lessons. We rarely take

time to eat together in our homes. Parents and children are rarely present
to each other. Stress over work and finances occupy the attention of the
parents. As a result, spouses rarely tend to one another's souls. At church
people rush in to Sunday services and then rush out again. Church goers
rarely have that potluck meal together that characterized American society before World War II. At work, managers rarely talk with workers,
except to review their performance. As philosopher Slavoj Žižek reminds
us, real conversation that tends to each other's lives rarely happens
around the table. It is "foreign to our fast food times, which only knows
business meals ('power lunches')."[2] We are a mass of disconnected souls
with too many tasks to do and too much stress to do them.

Nonetheless, our world starves for presence. After work is over, after
we arrive home on the train, we swarm to restaurants and bars just to
share a beverage or a meal in hope of making contact. Whole train cars
on the Chicago Metra commuter train are segregated for those who want
to bring a beverage and share conversation at the end of a long day. It's
not much, but it's something. People everywhere long to be known. Our
culture bears the signs of people wanting to share life meaningfully with
one another. The world longs for Eucharist.

THE DISCIPLINE OF THE LORD'S TABLE

The Lord's Table is about presence. Surely it is about eating, but ultimately
it's a discipline that shapes a group of people to be present to God's
presence in Christ around the table, where we eat. Then, in the process
we are able to connect with the other people around the table. Our lives
are then reordered socially by his presence. This discipline was inaugurated by Jesus himself and given to his disciples on "the night he was
betrayed." Today, almost all Christians practice it. This first discipline we
explore shapes a community into God's faithful presence.

There are of course differences among churches in the way we practice
the Lord's Table, or the Eucharist, as the high-church traditions (Anglican,
Roman Catholic, etc.) name it.[3] Nevertheless, there is a common core to
what we do together. All churches, for instance, incorporate the "words of
institution" as the means to remember together (or bring into the present,

anamnēsis [1 Cor 11:24]) the meaning of the bread and wine. "This is my body that is for you." "This cup is the new covenant in my blood. Do this, as often as you drink it, in remembrance of me" (1 Cor 11:24-25).

There is almost always a communal invitation to peace and reconciliation prior to the table. The presiding leader challenges all believers to make sure there be no enmity between us as we come to the table. For as the apostle declares, because of the divisions among the Corinthians, they are in essence denying the Lord's Supper (1 Cor 11:18-20). There is almost always a prayer of thanksgiving and a blessing that inaugurates the celebration of the table. The table, after all, is called the Eucharist (which means "thanksgiving") because it begins with a great thanksgiving, an offering of a blessing to God for all he has done through history. It opens us up to receiving from him and each another as we eat this meal. Usually the Holy Spirit is invited to this table (called the *epiklēsis*), making possible the living and real presence of Christ at the meal. This is interpreted in many different ways by various churches. Then there is the actual breaking and distribution of the bread and sharing of the cup. The logic of his broken body and shed blood becomes a meal we ingest into our bodies as the very basis of life itself.

Last, often an offering of material goods is taken as part of the Lord's Table. For some churches this comes before sharing the bread and wine. For others this comes after. Still others offer their gifts both before and after. We come bearing gifts, offering them out of the abundance of what God has already given us. These gifts are offered to God for him to return his blessings and abundance to us through his work in Christ. In essence, all we have is transformed into his purposes around the table. We believe that this abundance shared around the table will flow forth from the table through the whole of our lives and then return all over again.

It is not my purpose to treat the full breadth of the practice the Lord's Table. We all must draw on our own traditions and deepen our practice of it. Thus we will recover the discipline of the table, which will shape us into his presence for the world. But for our purposes, let's try to understand how the table shapes us to know and discern God's presence among us and in the neighborhood.

DISCERNING HIS PRESENCE

When we sit around this table and tend to his presence, our eyes are opened and we know his presence is here in a special way. The first reported time this happened post-resurrection was on the road to Emmaus when Jesus joined the two disciples on their walk (Lk 24). On this day of his resurrection, Jesus taught them what all the events of the previous three days meant, according to the Scriptures. As they came near the village, they invited Jesus to join them in their home, which always meant a meal around a table. While they were at the table, Jesus "took bread, blessed and broke it, and gave it to them," and their eyes were opened to his presence with them (Lk 24:30-32). They recognized him there. His presence became real.

Just as happened on the Emmaus road, so also today Jesus' presence is "known . . . in the breaking of the bread" (Lk 24:35). Jesus' presence historically has been uniquely real and recognizable around the table. The fact that the Corinthians were sick and dying reflects their disregard for discerning Christ's real presence around this table (1 Cor 11:30).

We know that over hundreds of years the church has struggled to understand Christ's presence here. There is no sense rehashing those controversies. But what remains is that each of us, within the boundaries of our own histories, must come to grips again (especially those Protestant traditions that have diminished the presence of Christ at the table) with the reality that Christ is present at the table in a real, sacramental way. We must tend to his special presence because his presence always brings the reordering of our lives together into his kingdom. This is what makes this table so revolutionary at the core: here God shapes a people to be his kingdom in the world.

I remember one time sitting with my discipleship group in McDonald's early one morning. We were talking about our recent vacations and I mentioned that I try to make it to the Eucharist even when I am staying in desolate cottage country in rural Canada. This often means I must go to the local Roman Catholic Church. They all wondered why. It's vacation after all! I said that tending to Christ's presence at the Eucharist, even when I can't participate (as a non-Catholic), reorients me to Christ's presence and trains me to tend to Christ's presence in the rest of my week. The discipline orders my life in profound ways. I would no sooner miss it than I would any other necessary task for living (like eating and sleeping). One of my friends said, "You believe in that hocus pocus?" That of course saddened me, but, more to the point, it reminded me of just how big the gap is between many Christians and the real presence of Jesus Christ at the table and in our everyday lives. Thus I committed to leading better at the table in my own pastoral work.

It's hard for evangelical Protestants (my own church history) to conceive that there is something unique happening around the table. Many times Protestants have to go through the "Is this anything?" exercise, akin to the game played in the 2000s on the *Late Show with David Letterman*. We must get past the rote memory games that individualize the Eucharist and tend to Christ's real presence. For here we have perhaps the single best opportunity to train ourselves to tend to his presence for our lives. Here we can recognize and receive the forgiveness that flows from his broken body into our lives, the healing of reconciliation, the renewal of all things through the cup of the new covenant relationship we have with God the Father through the Spirit. If we can recognize his presence at work around the table, we will be able to recognize his work in the rest of our lives as well.[4] If we can be trained into its logic of forgiveness, reconciliation, and renewal on Sunday, we can recognize that same logic of his presence in the world. Without such a discipline, however, we will always be tempted to take God's work into our own hands instead of recognizing his work, submitting to, and participating in it. The table on Sunday morning (or whenever we gather as Christians) trains us to discern Christ's presence in all the other places we eat during the week.

A KINGDOM IS BEING BORN

Around this table a space for the kingdom is opened up. God's kingly rule over the whole world meets his incarnational presence in this particular time and space. Our selfishness is revealed. Our grasping for control loosens. People's lives are disrupted. If we tend to his presence here, we inevitably will forgive, reconcile, and open ourselves to renewal and healing. His rule takes on flesh among us. As we submit to him, Christ's presence peacefully reorders us into the ways of his kingdom.

Jesus makes it clear that this table is the kingdom. He says, as he inaugurates it, "And I assign to you, as my Father assigned to me, a kingdom" (Lk 22:29 RSV). This table foreshadows the messianic feast to be consummated in the future ("so that you may eat and drink at my table in my kingdom" [v. 30]). The table, post-resurrection, is the beginning of the fulfillment of his kingdom.[5] It is the proleptic materialization of his kingdom. Therefore, around this table, God is reordering relationships and inaugurating a different kind of authority, the authority of his reign. The disciples at the time could not comprehend it.

First and foremost then, the table leads us into submission to Jesus Christ as Lord. There is no kingdom without subjects to the King, so we must begin by subjecting ourselves to him. As we move closer to the table, into the very core of Christ's presence there, he draws us into submission. As we submit to his presence there, we are realigned into his reign. Our submission to Jesus spreads out into mutual submission to one another. And a new social order is birthed out of this, which is nothing less than his kingdom.

In Luke 22, Jesus is inaugurating the table, and the issue of mutual submission rushes to the forefront. In the middle of the meal, around the table, an egotistical dispute breaks out among the disciples. They are arguing over who is to be the greatest among them in the coming kingdom. Jesus responds by rejecting the modes of authority associated with the Gentiles, who "lord it over them" (Lk 22:25). He says it will not be so among them. "Rather let the greatest among you become as the youngest, and the leader as one who serves" (v. 26 RSV). In John 13:1-17, Jesus gets down on his hands and knees and washes the feet of his disciples to demonstrate the point. So, in the most palpable way, Jesus inaugurates the table through mutual submission. He could not be more explicit about the way we will relate to one another in this kingdom, about the way authority will be exercised. It could not be more different than what they are used to (as with the Gentiles). The whole scene prefigures the kingdom and points to the new world coming ("that you may eat and drink at my table in my kingdom" (Lk 22:30). It displays the authority that shall characterize the kingdom until it is realized completely in the messianic age (Lk 22:29-30). This kingdom will be founded on mutual submission to one another under the lordship of Christ, where anyone who rules does so through submission to the work of God happening in the midst of us.

In 1 Corinthians 11 submission manifests itself in a different way. At issue here is that the Corinthians have come to the table caring more about themselves individually than one another. The rich are eating and indulging themselves while the poor are going hungry (v. 21). Divisions are breaking out among them (v. 18). Everyone is acting out in the most narcissistic of ways. Individuals are setting themselves above others. For Paul, this means the Corinthians have not discerned Christ's real presence at the table (v. 29). They have not submitted themselves to one another. As a result, he says, "When you come together, it is not really to eat the Lord's supper" (v. 20).

Think of how earth shaking this experience of Christ at the table must have been for the early Christians. The very presence of the risen Lord is here at this table. Something so special, even dangerous, is happening when they gather around it. Our health is at stake. It's a matter of life and death (some are dying [vv. 29-30]). Yet as each person submits to him, the issues of relationships with one another and to Christ, to authority and how we relate to each other, are opened up. The socioeconomic relationships among us are realigned as we share mutually out of what we have and what we receive. Together we become financially liable for one another.

In this space we submit all of our divisions and personal agendas to Christ's presence. All of this must die. There we sit, tending to one another and to his presence. And an amazing social dynamic breaks forth that can only be described as a new political order subverting all other allegiances. Just as the first tables of the early Christians subverted Rome and Caesar and started a new way of life before the watching world, so this table subverts all other politics of American self-preservation, accumulation, and individualism.[6] A profound flourishing in the kingdom results.

It is essential then that we lead one another into submission to Christ at the table. Because God will not impose himself on us or overwhelm us, our submission to his reign opens up space for him to work. The people who carry the most power must submit first, just as Christ did when he washed the disciples' feet. By example, the leader will lead the community into a place of submission to the one Lord and to one another under his lordship. From this submission the table opens up the world to his reign and his presence among us.

THE TABLE IN THE THREE CIRCLES

Most people think of the Lord's table as a discipline practiced only on Sunday mornings by committed Christians. But a look at the life of Jesus and the pattern of the primitive church reveals multiple spaces where this discipline of the table is practiced. These spaces can be summarized in terms of three circles referred to in chapter two: the close circle, the dotted circle, and the half circle (see fig. 2.1).[7]

The Lord's Table in the close circle. The close circle represents the first space of the Lord's Table. Here is ground zero for the table. Here the table is founded. At this table we carefully discern our relationship to God in Christ before we dare approach it. Are we in full submission to Christ? Is there any enmity between me and someone else around this table? Because of this discernment, there is the closest of fellowship and unity with one another.

No one can miss this closeness around the table on the night when Jesus was betrayed. Here, at the celebration of the Passover, Jesus is seated as the host. He presides, and yet he washes his disciples' feet in a display of utter and total vulnerability. Intimate conversation is happening. The disciple "whom Jesus loved" reclines next to Jesus in closeness, in effect leaning on his shoulder (Jn 13:23). Together they know they are facing danger of some kind, though they know not what. And the one who eats the bread unworthily walks out in disdain, to his own doom (Jn 13:27-30). He cannot stand the intensity of the closeness. It is almost as if we are all forced to deal with who we are and our submission to Jesus and his mission. Judas, in effect, must leave. He cannot stand the penetrating truthfulness. Simon Peter declares his allegiance to Jesus at all costs, saying he is willing to go to prison or even death for his Lord (v. 37). Jesus tells him the truth about himself (v. 38). The presence of Christ, by the Spirit, reveals our brokenness. It forces renewed commitment. It orders our lives intensely, either further into or away from the kingdom.

This closeness marks the table after Christ's ascension as well. In 1 Corinthians 11, as we have already seen, Paul is shocked at the Corinthians' disregard for one another in Christ's presence. The Lord's presence there is so intense that they indeed get sick and die because they have disregarded him. This table (as with all close circles) therefore requires discernment. The church has historically gathered for this close table on Sunday mornings. It's the day Jesus rose from the dead. Here we can properly discern his presence as Christians. We call this the "close table" over against the closed table or fenced table in some traditions.[8] At this table the closest of fellowship is experienced with the resurrected Jesus.

For years, at Life on the Vine Christian Community, we set aside an hour and a half once a month for our church to be present to Christ at the table. Though we celebrated the Eucharist every Sunday, on the first Sunday we took extra time before the regular worship to focus intently on the table. We would spend time in the foyer discerning our relationship to Christ and each other, making things right with those we had enmity with. Then we entered the room saying "Jesus is Lord" as a sign of our discernment and received a match from the usher. We then processed to the table and everyone lit a candle, recognizing Christ's presence among us together. The table, lit with all these candles, symbolized Jesus' magnificent presence among us. We then brought our needs, hurts, desires, resentments, and the like to the table. We surrendered them to the presence of Christ for his forgiveness, reconciliation, and renewal. We did all this in open prayers around the table, tending to one another. We learned how to give thanks around the table. We learned the *epiklēsis*, making his presence real by the Holy Spirit. We partook together. This time then *set the table* for the rest of the week and month. It set the order for our regular Sunday gatherings around the table, where the rituals were shortened but meant so much more because of this first Sunday practice. This is the way our church, Life on the Vine, sought to renew the discipline of being present to Christ's presence at the table.

The Lord's Table in the dotted circle. But the table doesn't stop there. It extends into the neighborhood. As the early church father John Chrysostom said, there is "the liturgy after the liturgy."[9] Here around the tables of our neighborhoods we gather to eat regularly. We start with Christian friends, and then, over time, our neighbors, as they look on, are welcomed around our tables. The dotted circle represents this second space for the table. It is still a circle constituted by Christians forming a circle of those submitted to Christ's presence. Yet this time there are openings in the circle, where strangers are welcomed in. So the circle is porous or dotted.

In this dotted circle the Christian in the world *becomes the host.* Most typically, this table takes place in homes in neighborhoods. But it can happen wherever Christians meet regularly to share a meal in the hospitality of Christ's presence together in the neighborhood (at restaurants, parks, community centers, preschools, etc.). This meal is initiated by a Christian, hosted by a Christian, and yet is always open and hospitable to strangers who are becoming regular parts of our lives. In these places the close circle table on Sunday is extended to a more open space, a porous circle, in the neighborhood, where there are entry points for strangers to be among us and taste of the kingdom. Christ's special presence is extended into the neighborhood.[10] Here in the neighborhood, Christians are shaped to be his faithful presence.

In Mark 6:30-44 we see thousands of people gathering around Jesus. These people were curious about what they were seeing and hearing from the apostles and Jesus (vv. 30-33). Jesus saw them as a wandering herd without a shepherd. They had no cohesion, no direction. They were not yet part of the kingdom. In many ways this is a circle of Christians ("the apostles gathered around Jesus" [v. 30]), yet with people "from all the towns" gathering as well. In other words, this is a dotted circle.

Jesus sees what is happening. The disciples come to him and report the need to send the crowds away so they can get something to eat. Jesus directs them in no uncertain terms to host the "table," saying, "You give them something to eat" (v. 37). Jesus wants his disciples to host this table. Here is where the dynamic of the dotted circle kicks in.

The disciples immediately ask, "Are we to go and buy two hundred denarii worth of bread, and give it to them to eat?" (v. 37). They have misunderstood what it means to be a host in the presence of Jesus and the in-breaking kingdom. They immediately assume that they must do everything, take control, and provide out of their own resources. But this is not what it means for the Christian disciple to host the Eucharist in the dotted circle. So Jesus takes over to show them. He asks how much food they have and tells them to bring him what they have. Nothing more, nothing less. So they bring to Jesus what they find among the crowd: five loaves and two fish. They in essence bring what they have as an offering into the abundance of the kingdom in Jesus. He *takes* the loaves and fish, *blesses* and *breaks* them, and *gives* it to the disciples for distribution. These four words signal that this indeed is a Eucharistic celebration around the presence of Christ.[11] In the midst of this meal, people meet the abundance of the kingdom as "all ate and were filled," and there was an abundance of food left over (vv. 42-43).

In this stunning story we see how the table extends the presence of Christ into places where curious onlookers are invited. We see that Christians are to host these tables. At this table however, there is no presumption that all who partake are reconciled. Certainly the Christians around the table are practicing the reconciled life. But there is no discernment required of the onlookers. Unlike the disciples in this story (who failed to discern what Jesus was doing), Christians must discern the presence of Christ and his work among us. We send no one away, including people in conflict. Via the dotted circle, we invite them to be with us among Christ. The host does not somehow take control of the table but facilitates the table around the presence of Christ, who reorders the world into his kingdom. The host allows the space to be opened for Christ to meet all our needs and more.[12] This is what Christ was trying to teach his disciples at the feeding of the five thousand.

A similar story takes place with the apostle Paul while he was traveling on a ship with prisoners in a storm in the Adria Sea (Acts 27).

After fourteen days of battling storms, after several proclamations of God's promise to deliver, Paul urges all the beleaguered sailors, prisoners, and passengers to take some food. Here again we see that the people who are invited to eat are not (at least initially) all followers of Christ. We have some evidence of people ("friends" [v. 3]) who are potentially converts like, perhaps, Aristarchus (v. 2), who is mentioned by name as someone the Christians know. Likewise the centurion in verse 43 appears to be a convert to Paul's message. And so, together with Paul and Luke, we have a circle of believers in the ship. Paul, nonetheless, offers the bread "in the presence of all" (v. 35). It is therefore a porous circle. Here Paul, the disciple of Christ, gathers them to share a meal for their deliverance (v. 34). As the host, Paul *takes* the bread, *gives thanks,* and *breaks* it. The eucharistic words used here testify that Paul is making way for the eucharistic table in the middle of this shipwreck. They are, in essence, tending to the presence of Christ among them in the eating of this meal. After the meal they are greatly encouraged. In the midst of this great suffering, the ministry of Christ's presence at the meal is stunning. They are encouraged and strengthened to journey through the suffering that lies ahead.

An instance of this dotted circle happened at our home every Friday night in our northwest Chicago suburban neighborhood. Every one of us would bring food as our offering, place it on the island, in the kitchen, hold hands, gather as a circle around the island, and pray a prayer of thanksgiving (eucharist) together: "We give you thanks for all you have given us. As we experienced this past Sunday, let us tend to your presence among us at this table. May we share the forgiveness, reconciliation, and renewal of all things by your Spirit as we eat this meal, O Lord." Then we would sit and eat and talk. But sometimes the talk became egocentric and self-serving. Sometimes mayhem erupted as everybody scurried for attention or the need to be seen and heard. People, being people, tried to attract attention to themselves.

We would gently calm all this down, generously admonishing one another to be present and listen to the other person. Some would move to another room and sit and talk to someone else while in front of the

TV. They did not yet know or understand eucharist. We had to make a rule: Everyone, no matter how many in the group, must always sit around the table. Sometimes the seating around the table expanded to two rows. Smartphones were not allowed. Of course we had to take care of children, but they too were guided to sit around the table until desert. We ate together, aware of the forgiveness, reconciliation, and renewal of all things that we had shared as a result of Sunday Lord's Table. As months rolled on, we learned how to be present with each other. We discovered a different dynamic shared across a table between me and another person. It was the presence of Christ.

It took months to cultivate the kind of mutual submission and tending to Christ's presence that defined the discipline of the Lord's Table. One might assume that I, being that type-A Caucasian male, always took charge. Instead, I had to learn how to model as best I could a posture of submission and presence to each other and Christ around the table. I had to go first in this posture of submission to Christ at the table (the one perceived in power always submits first). I would take a deep breath, chill out, and speak rarely. When I spoke, it was to direct attention to someone other than myself, and (generally) I did not speak unless spoken to. As the one who had called the gathering together, I was asked to lead. But none of this could happen if I led in prototypical American ways. I led by submitting and, when necessary, tending to the issues of presence. It took months to cultivate trust, mutual submission, listening, and paying attention to the Spirit. A year later the presence around the table was so intoxicating, people's lives, attitudes, and physical health were transformed by the interactions.

The time for dessert arrived each evening around 8 (which, along with coffee, was always a highlight). The host then posed a question that could center some conversation around what was going on in our lives. We sometimes focused on our personal lives or struggles with God, sometimes what was going on among us or sometimes our lives with God in our neighborhood.[13] Stuff would come up in our lives and the table would become a live arena for listening to each other and God and tending to God's presence among us. The gifts of the Spirit were set into motion among us. As 9 arrived, the host would call the children together (the younger ones having left to play after dessert), and we all prayed, submitting these things to God and his kingdom. This was our routine. The presence of Christ became very real among us as we became present to one another. For me, the experience was indescribable.

One time a couple in the neighborhood of one of our members was going through disruptive times with their teenage daughters. They knew about our Friday night group and wanted to attend. They were welcomed. In a way that was more comfortable than any of us had felt for the first six months of our table fellowship, they immediately began to share their wounds with us. As we did every Friday night, we called the children together after our discussions and we prayed. I asked our guests if we could include them in our prayers. They hesitated, but said yes, and we did. They saw an unmistakable glimpse of the kingdom that night.

Once a woman in our neighborhood was going through a horrid and vicious divorce. She feared for the welfare of her children. She needed help moving her furniture. A group of us rushed over on a Friday night. She too became a welcome visitor from time to time. This was all perfectly normal because this table, though formed by Christians, would always be open to the world. It offered these folks a way to enter in and see what life in the kingdom looks like.

At the very beginning there were many hurdles to leading people together around a table like this. For more than a year we sought to invite ten people for a shared meal every Friday night where we would listen to one another and tend to the presence of Christ among us. Regularly, we were turned down for various suburbanite "I'm too busy" kind of reasons. Few could imagine making such a commitment to do this every Friday night. This was the suburbs after all. Nonetheless, eventually ten people responded to the invitation, and we slowly explored what it could mean to submit to one another in Christ's presence around the table. Once started, this table grew to more than twenty-five. We had to turn people away or split the group. We saw miracles happen around this table too personal and too dynamic for me to tell. I have since seen physical and mental healings, marriages mend, and people get saved around the table. We came to understand this table and Christ's presence around it as an extension of his real presence at the Lord's Table on Sunday.

The dotted circle is a group of Christians hosted by a Christian tending to Christ's presence around the table in the midst of everyday life. As so often happens in everyday life, the dotted circle finds itself in a crisis (as, say, the lack of food in Mark 6 or a shipwreck in Acts 27). It is a place of healing and reconciliation. The circle is hosted by disciples of Jesus and is always open to onlookers who have not yet followed Christ. And always, the presence of Christ, as tended to around the table, ministers flourishing, encouragement, and a rearrangement of life into the kingdom for all to see.

The Lord's Table in the half circle. The table however does stop here in the dotted circles of our neighborhoods. If the table begins around the close circle and extends into the neighborhood via the dotted circle fellowship, it extends further through the half circle into the world, where the hurting and broken people live their everyday lives.[14] Into these half circles Christians go, imitating Christ as he enters the homes of the marginalized, the publicans, and the sinners. Here, like Jesus, we go, not as hosts inviting people to our table, but as guests, submitting ourselves to the hospitality of others.[15] We no longer serve as hosts, ordering the affairs at these tables. Instead, we give up control, risking humiliation and even scandal. In all our weakness we submit to Christ's presence among us and allow him to work. We live vulnerably alongside our brothers and sisters in the world. We pay attention to what God is doing as we listen, tending to his work. This open half circle is a completely different posture from the other two circles for the Christian.

And yet something marvelous happens in this space. As we share the food and the coffee, as we sit across from one another around a table, Christ's presence is here too. The question in the space of the half circle is not whether Jesus will be present, but will he be recognized? Will Jesus be received? This is another reason why I call this space the half (open) circle.

In Luke 10, Jesus sends the Seventy into mission to "every town and place where he himself intended to go" (v. 1). He instructs them to enter a home and become present there ("remain in the same house") sitting around the table "eating and drinking whatever they provide" (v. 7). They are to take no money or extra clothes (v. 4), go needy and be present as guests, and be vulnerable, "like lambs into the midst of wolves" (v. 3), giving up control. They are to take the posture of receiving before offering anything. They were not to move from house to house but to be present long enough to discover persons of peace (v. 6), the ones who are seeking peace and are receptive to the gospel. In these postures then, around the table of the sinner, the space is opened for the presence of God in Christ to become manifest.

It is important to recognize that in Luke 10 Jesus taught his disciples to sit with people around the table before he mentions proclaiming the gospel. Verses 8-9 say, "Eat what is set before you; cure the sick who are there, and [then] say to them, 'The kingdom of God has come near to you.'" So, as we sit *with* people, the occasion arises when the gospel will be proclaimed. By word and deed the kingdom will be disclosed, and we will point to it and proclaim that Jesus is Lord, the kingdom has begun, and Jesus has come to set things in order.

Will he be recognized? Will he be received? For when we point to the kingdom and announce it is here, Jesus says, "Whoever listens to you listens to me, and whoever rejects you rejects me, . . . [and] the one who sent me" (v. 16). In essence, Jesus becomes present in these spaces in a special way. Similarly, at the end of instructing his disciples, Jesus says, "Whoever welcomes you welcomes me, and whoever welcomes me welcomes the one who sent me" (Mt 10:40). Through the half circle table then, the visible presence of Christ is extended. When Christ is received, when his lordship is submitted to, his kingdom becomes visible.

Jesus modeled these disciplines of the open table regularly.[16] He visited the homes of publicans and sinners throughout the Gospels. He famously went to Levi's home, where he sat intimately and ate with the tax collectors and sinners. The Pharisees were in an uproar (Mk 2:15-17). They could not imagine that a true rabbi would submit himself to the table of sinners. Throughout the Gospels Jesus is always sitting around a table, eating alongside and with the hurting, the sinner, the despised, the weak. He went to Zacchaeus in the tree and implored him to come down so that he could stay at Zacchaeus's house (not vice versa!). Many grumbled and said, "He has gone to be the guest of one who is a sinner" (Lk 19:7). Nevertheless, he was welcomed by Zacchaeus to share Zacchaeus's table. As a result, Zacchaeus's life was reordered, and he paid back four times anyone he defrauded. The kingdom broke in. Jesus said salvation had come to this house (v. 9). And so Jesus modeled the half circle for his disciples by going to towns and villages and becoming the guest of sinners.

We live in a world that hungers for Eucharist: the sweet fellowship people experience in the presence of Christ. There are countless places where people gather to seek Eucharist, and yet it remains unfulfilled. We must seek out these places and go as guests.

One time my friend Gordon and I were walking the streets of Westmont, Illinois, where we live. I had just moved to Westmont and, as is my custom, I took my regular evening walk through town, and Gordon joined me. As we walked the town's downtown streets, we stopped at the entrance to a bar and noticed the people gathered around tables drinking beverages; they were seeking communion. I was so struck by it I said to Gordon, "Look, there's Eucharist going on in that bar. It just hasn't been discerned yet." There was a need there to go and be among them as guests so we could discern his presence there with them. As we walked further, we noticed the same phenomena in the restaurants; the "Magic Gaming Store," where teenagers gathered to play games; Uncle Jon's music, where people were playing banjo together; and of course more bars. Each time we made the same observation, "Look, there's Eucharist going on in there; they just don't know it yet." Then we walked down some residential streets and saw people eating dinner together late into the night. Could it be any more obvious? People in all their brokenness were seeking communion throughout the town of Westmont. Most of them, however, did not yet know or discern the healing, forgiveness, reconciliation, and renewal of their lives God wanted to work in their midst, even now. It was our task to be present as witnesses to the kingdom among them.

In all these places we might be tempted to see only the signs of hunger and hurt. There was excess alcohol, narcissistic conversations, expletives, and anger at some of these tables. We easily recognized the brokenness because we see it and know it in our own lives. It was painfully obvious to Gordon and me how segregated the tables were. There were white people sitting with white people in the expensive restaurants, and Latinos sitting together in the Taco Express. There were few African Americans sitting in any of these places even though we had many black friends and acquaintances in the neighborhood. What was evident in all of these observations was the incompleteness at these tables. The fullness of Eucharist was missing at most of these tables.

The tragedy is, in many if not most of these places there is no one tending to Christ. There is no wherewithal to extend his presence through the practice of the half circle table. It takes someone who is there, who knows the stories around this table, who lives in Christ's presence, who knows his story, who can simply sit and be present, to recognize his presence. This is why the church must extend table awareness into the places of lost brokenness. Here, in the half circle, we go humbly and vulnerably, giving up all control, listening, waiting, tending to his presence, and letting Jesus work through this space between us and them across the table. This *presence* is what makes possible any and all proclamation of the gospel. This is what faithful presence is. This is what faithful presence requires.

THE CHURCH IS ALL THREE SPACES TOGETHER

The Lord's Table happens every time we share a meal together with people and tend to the presence of Christ among us. Granted the formal Lord's Table only happens at the close table. But that table extends from there. When Jesus said, "Whenever you do this, do it in remembrance of me" (1 Cor 11:24-26, my paraphrase), he, in essence, meant, in the words of theologian John Howard Yoder, "whenever you have your common meal," whenever you eat in everyday life with people.[17] And yet this table is shaped differently in the three spaces I call the close, dotted and half circles of life. The table is never merely *in here* or *out there*. It is the continual lived space *with* and *among* the world. It is the table on the move. It starts with the close circle, the ground zero of his presence around the table.

The three circles together are inextricably linked. When we practice the table only as a closed circle, we in effect close it off from the other two circles, and the table becomes a maintenance function of the church. In a similar vein, when we practice the table as only the half circle in the world, we in effect close off ourselves from discerning the presence of Christ in the world. Devoid of Christ's presence in the world, the church falls into exhaustion.

Last, when we no longer practice the table in the dotted circles of our lives, we lose the space to extend Christ's presence as witness to our neighbors. We lose the place where neighbors can be acclimated to the ways of the kingdom. In my experience, rarely can a new believer go from the half circle directly to the close circle (see appendix 2 for more on this). New believers must catch a glimpse of normal everyday kingdom life at the home in their neighborhoods. From there they will go to the close circle. And in the end, if one is not to fall into either maintenance or exhaustion, every Christian, new or mature believer, must live in all three circles. And so the church must always live in the three spaces as an integral unity of what the church is.

RECOVERING FAITHFUL PRESENCE AROUND THE TABLE(S)

Throughout history the church regularly defaults to maintenance mode. When the church gets overly comfortable in society, believing its place is secure in a Christian society, it is easy for a church to lose its mission and fall into maintenance mode. Likewise, when a church tries to defend its position against a society that is non-Christian, here too it can drift into doing the disciplines right and fall into maintenance mode.

The New Testament church, as best we can tell, practiced the table as part of their everyday life together ("from house to house" [Acts 2:46 KJV]). There was a regular eating of the agape meal, which was differentiated from a more intentional practice of a closely discerned table of the elements of bread and wine called the Lord's Table (see Jude 12).[18] These two practices together comprised the dotted table and the close table.[19] All through the first centuries of the church's existence, the church practiced the table via the two dynamics of the close circle and dotted circle. In addition, the early church was known for its excessive hospitality in the neighborhoods—eating meals with the poor, the hurting, and sinners,[20] and so we can conclude that the New Testament church, prior to Constantine, for at least its first two hundred years, functioned in all three circles of the Eucharist. And the kingdom of God was spreading throughout Rome.

In the fourth century, after Constantine had conquered Rome, the Christian church became not only tolerated but eventually sponsored (via emperor Theodosius) by the Roman Empire. Millions of believers were now entering the churches. The table had to be prepared in a more efficient manner. Somewhere along the line (we do not know when) the table was taken out of the home and put into the newly returned and built sanctuaries. The practice of the table was taken out of the neighborhoods and brought into the church buildings.[21] The leadership of the table shifted from the leaders among the people to the priest above the people. By the fifth century only the ordained priest could preside, because the church felt the need to order the table faithfully among so many people. We could say the table became managed for maintenance. Mission was lost. Paraphrasing the words of Catholic theologian William Cavanaugh, the Eucharist became a performance of a redemption already achieved in the past. The Eucharist as the in-breaking of the future kingdom of God in the present was now suppressed.[22]

Signs of maintenance mode appeared in fifteenth-century Europe as well. Most notably, at some point the only communicant allowed around the table was the priest. And he now faced away from the congregation, separated from the congregation by the rood screen. And he now "said mass" for the congregation.[23] The focus of the presence of Christ around Eucharist, as Catholic theologian Henri de Lubac has argued, moved from being in and among the community of the church around the table to being in the actual elements themselves on the table. The presence of Christ had been lost among the people and were transubstantiated into the elements themselves.[24] The tending to the presence of Christ at the meals had become sequestered into the church building, to that one moment in time between the priest and God around the table.[25]

Today, in evangelicalism, it could be said that the largest churches practice the Lord's Table as a maintenance function. In some cases the churches are so big that for efficiency sake, we hand out the bread and cup together in little plastic packages. It is individualized. We do it as a pious remembrance for personal encouragement. There is no awareness of the social reality where Christ is present between us and among us. And so we've lost the social reality that binds us together into the presence of Christ and the remaking of the world into his kingdom.

We therefore need to recover the table for the church's faithful presence in the world. Just as there have been countless other times when the church has fallen into maintenance (and exhaustion), only to find renewal around the table fellowships of its people, so we too can begin anew to intentionally reinvigorate the practice of the Lord's Table for mission in our churches today. Starting with the close-circle table, let us lead one another into the encounter with his real presence. Pulling from our various traditions, let's teach and practice the full presence and discernment of Christ. And then let's cultivate the practice of the table in our neighborhoods. Let us teach leaders how to tend to his presence at these tables by being present to one another. (See appendix 1 on tending to the presence around the neighborhood table). Then let us shape our people around the table to become guests among the tables of the hurting and lost. Let's lead people into a formative encounter with the living Christ at the table and then cultivate the extension of his presence into the rest of our lives. This is the beginning of faithful presence.

As we will see again and again, the three-circle pattern of the table characterizes all seven disciplines.[26] Just as with the table, in each one of these disciplines, a space is opened up for Christ's presence to come and manifest his rule among us as a community. The table, however, is the foundation. It is the basis for a new politic that witnesses to the compelling reality of the new kingdom of Christ, begun in his person and work, and extended into the world by the church until he returns. It challenges all other politics. It is never coercive. It resists antagonism. It sweeps over all of life. It is ground zero of faithful presence. And so to the next discipline we now turn.

4

The Discipline of Reconciliation

If your brother or sister sins against you . . .

Matthew 18:15 CEB

Ferguson, Missouri, a suburb of St. Louis, had a police force that was 94 percent white, while its population was 67 percent black. On August 10, 2014, an unarmed black teenage boy, Michael Brown, was shot dead by Darren Wilson, a white police officer. His body was left in the street for four hours. Protests emerged. The police gathered quickly, looking like a military unit enforcing crowd control. The town erupted. Vandalism and violence spread. There was tear gas and massive incarcerations. When the white district attorney, four months later, announced no indictment, more violence erupted. The ensuing riots and marches expressed years of black frustration from systemic racism, racial profiling, and the abuse of white privilege.

In the ensuing hours, Twitter lit up with people taking both sides. Tweets stereotyping young black men defended the white officer. Anyone who dared to defend the white police officer was castigated on social media. Fires were set and property was destroyed in downtown Ferguson. Of the hundreds of thousands now involved in the conflict through media, few were talking to anyone directly involved in Ferguson. At the actual site of the murder, many had come from outside Ferguson for the spectacle. Ferguson was about so much more than the killing of Michael Brown. The fury of years of racial injustice had erupted.

By now, the story of Michael Brown and Ferguson is well known. It birthed a massive new awareness of white privilege at work in the legal systems and the culture of the United States. It served as a national catharsis of black rage. But there were also new levels of hate against hate, pointing fingers, and racial stereotyping on both sides. Many of those who actually lived in Ferguson, who marched peaceably, including the immediate family of Michael Brown, pleaded for calm and peacemaking. Nonetheless, violence and division were incited to an unparalleled intensity in the media swirl that had become Ferguson. Many people wondered whether anything would come of this new awareness. Or would all be forgotten when the object of hate (on either side) had receded to the background?

THE WORLD RUNS ON ANTAGONISM

Amidst all that went on in Ferguson in 2014, there was a different story taking place on the ground than the one portrayed in the media. There were surprising acts of kindness and face-to-face acts of reconciliation. Neighborhood families provided hot dogs for both police and protesters. A woman with a milk jug treated tear-gas injuries. Neighbors lined up outside of neighborhood stores that had been vandalized, ready to work, clean, and restore. Neighborhood people were giving strangers a room for a good night's sleep. Clergy and concerned people of faith gathered (from all parts of the country) to be physically present to give witness to peace, to ask for things to slow down, and to foster discussion. People were spending time with each other, listening and caring, and asking how they could help, where they had done wrong, how they could participate in healing. There were acts of profound presence—giving witness to the unacceptability of the violence and requesting honest, face-to-face encounters.[1] Little of this was being reported in the mainstream media. Nonetheless, these acts in Ferguson bear witness to a reality that the world hungers for reconciliation.

The world runs on antagonism. It's always easy to stir up a crowd to hate an object or a group we are against than to gather both sides in one place to be present to each other. But the group that gathers in antagonism will not last long. And once the catharsis is over, it will eventually need another episode of rage to gather the troops. In its aftermath, some laws may be passed, but if there is no true reconciliation and setting things right, we will be back to where we started or even worse. We may even get cameras installed on police officers. But as theologian Willie Jennings said, a camera on a police officer is merely setting up things "to become a reality television video game, complete with weapon and target."[2] White people will still see black men with the same eyes, only through a television lens. Some black men's lives may be preserved from police bullets. Beneath the surface, however, the racism will go on, only in a deeper way because hearts and minds will not have been changed.

And so we weep for the broken relationships everywhere manifesting their ruin on towns, cities, neighborhoods, our children, families, marriages, businesses, school systems, and gang life. Though our laws might make prejudice and discrimination illegal, the oppressive relations simmer beneath. Though we might outlaw violence, it still seethes between us. We tolerate each other in the melting pot of antagonism while the world hungers for love. Meanwhile, the Bible says that God is working for the reconciliation of the whole world to himself in Christ. We are now ambassadors of Christ, entrusted with the message of reconciliation (2 Cor 5:18). The world hungers for a new space of mutual understanding and blessing of each other's uniqueness, gifts, and cultural heritage. The world hungers for God's people being faithfully present to this reconciliation work of God in the world. But how will this new world start? Where will this new world begin?

THE DISCIPLINE OF RECONCILIATION

Reconciliation is at the core of what God has done and is doing in the world in and through Jesus Christ. As the apostle Paul states,

> To all who are in Christ the new creation has begun, the old has passed away, behold all is becoming new. All this is from God, who reconciled us to himself through Christ, and has given us the ministry of reconciliation, that is, in Christ God was reconciling the whole world to himself not counting their trespasses against them, but putting in us the message of reconciliation. (2 Cor 5:17-19, my paraphrase)

Reconciliation is so central to the good news of what God has done in Christ that to see no reconciliation in our churches suggests there is no gospel in them. Reconciliation marks our presence in the world. It is so much a part of the gospel we bring into the world that the apostle Paul calls Christians "ambassadors" of his reconciliation (2 Cor 5:20). We are extenders of Christ's reconciliation.

And yet reconciliation is not merely an idea for Jesus. It is not even a doctrine. It is something we do as his followers. More than a status given to us by God through Christ's work on the cross, it is a discipline we practice together. This discipline shapes a space of reconciliation where God calls into being this new world he is creating in Christ Jesus.

The discipline itself is really quite simple. Jesus says, "if another member of the church [a brother] sins against you, go and point out the fault when the two of you are alone" (Mt 18:15). Go privately ("alone") and directly to the person who has hurt you. This encounter is to be face to face. We are to listen and be listened to. The question is, "Will he (or she) listen to the other's sin?" Do not triangulate. Do not go around the person to achieve your goal in the conflict.

The offense presented could be a sin or simply a conflict between us as we seek to discern life together as a community. Scholars have pointed out that the "binding and loosing" language of Matthew 18:18 was a rabbinic phrase used to describe discernment of multiple kinds of disagreement.[3] And so we must read the word *sin* in verse 15 to mean more than a grievous act of sin against someone. It could mean any issue of disagreement we are striving to make sense of. If we disagree on something important with someone, if we are in unresolved turmoil, we are told to go and express our grievance or disagreement and seek agreement. The most common approach should be, "I believe you have committed this sin against me" or "We disagree on this and I think you are wrong to do _____." Then we follow up with questions like, "Do you agree with me that this act is sin?" or "Do you understand why I disagree with you?" Next, we follow in acts of submission to one another under Jesus' name. We say, "I submit to you that the best course of action is _____. What would you have me do?" and similar questions.

If agreement or peace is not reached, Jesus instructs us to bring one or two more people into the conversation as witnesses. There is a space now being formed among *us*. By participating in this discipline of reconciliation, we are in essence opening up space for Christ's kingdom to take shape. Jesus promises to be present in this space. In this space we seek clarity and eventual agreement. This may include repentance or mutual sharing of peace. All the while this space is determined by the good news that Jesus as Lord is working for his will in this conflict. Furthermore, we are determined by his forgiveness and his promise to renew all things.

If agreement is still not reached, we take the disagreement to the community as a whole, which for some traditions means the elder or executive board, or perhaps a town hall meeting before all interested parties of the church (if indeed the matter affects the entire church). We will listen to the gifted ones, hear the gospel, and tend to each other and Christ's presence among us. We will say, "Based on Scripture, my prayer life, and what I know from last week, I believe God is saying _____, and I submit to you. Are you seeing what I am seeing?" We will use a consensus-based decision-making process guided by the Holy Spirit. We will stay at this mutual dialogue in mutual submission until all parties are satisfied that Christ Jesus has been followed and submitted to as Lord, and we can say, "It has seemed good to the Holy Spirit and to us" (Acts 15:28).

James 5:16 says, "Confess your sins to one another . . . that you may be [saved/] healed." The roots of the Greek word for confess are *ex–homologeō*. Translated those three syllables mean "out-same-word." The implication is that "confess" refers to the practice of getting our *words out* into a space where we can all agree (become one and the *same*) on them. We do this humbly in gentleness (see Gal 6:1). When we do this, his presence by the Spirit is unleashed among us, and he works to reconcile, heal, and discern the kingdom among us. We are healed. The salvation of God is revealed.

The goal of this discipline is not vindication or punishment. It's not that someone wins and another loses. It is restoration, healing, and renewed common fellowship. Even more importantly, it is the discerning of the future as the Spirit in Christ works among us. At the core of this discipline is the presence of Christ established between two people. The charge is to become present to this other person in a way that recognizes Christ's presence here among us (Mt 18:17). Listening grounds this discipline. And so *presence*, both my presence to the other person and my tending to Jesus' presence here among us, is central to this discipline. Reconciliation is fundamentally a discipline of faithful presence.

RECONCILIATION AS HIS KINGDOM

When we gather to reconcile, we come in and under his name ("in my name" [Mt 18:20]). Invoking the name of Jesus Christ in this way is no different than bowing to his reign or authority (e.g., Lk 10:17). He is recognized as Lord here in this place. As people enter into this place under his authority, they are stripped of all presumption of power, including any positions of power they hold in the world that may put one person over another. The kingdom is being birthed here. We do not live as "the Gentiles do," "lording it over" one another. There is a conscious act of submission to what is happening in this space between us where Jesus Christ himself has promised to be present.

This is not about being right or who will win this argument but about the future of the kingdom. And so just as Jesus inaugurated the Eucharist by denouncing all posturing for position, so too here there is implied a mutual submission to the one Lord. This place between us is sacred ground for the kingdom. Here, in this dispute, a way forward will be revealed. This place is holy ground.

In this space the kingdom is breaking in. Jesus makes it plain that whenever two or more people go through this process and reach an agreement, heaven and earth move, the authority and power of the kingdom of heaven is unleashed. The words Jesus used in Matthew to describe "the keys of the kingdom" (Mt 16:19) are used here: "Whatever you bind on earth will be bound in heaven, and whatever you loose on earth will be loosed in heaven" (Mt 18:18). And so this is not a contest to see who will win. We in effect give up our interest in winning for the sake of something much greater, deeper, richer, and profound to occur in our midst: the reordering of our world for the kingdom to come.

At Life on the Vine, the words "I submit to you" became all important in our discernments. No matter how firm our convictions, no matter how clearly we put forth where we believed God was leading, after we finished speaking, we looked into the other person's eyes and said, "I submit to you." Other words follow: "What am I not seeing?" "What would you do if you were me?" "Do you see it this way too, or differently?" As always, it is important for the one in perceived power to submit first to the one whose voice is being heard less. Make space for the other voice. As Jesus around the Eucharist went first in submitting to the others by washing the disciples' feet, the leader must always go first. "The first shall be the servant of all" (Lk 22:26, my paraphrase).

A month after the Ferguson shooting, I was asked to speak at a conference on the subject of racial reconciliation. I am a white male, so I started out my talk with an open confession: "I am a racist." I confessed that even if I wanted to, I could not with the snap of my fingers undo the habits formed within me as a white man raised all my life in a culture of white privilege that is hundreds of years old. So, I said, "Today, I confess, I am a racist." This, I suggested, was the starting point for Jesus transforming the world around me divided by race. By submitting myself to others in this area of my life, especially people who are different from me, I could, through his grace, learn the ways I am a racist. Then, piece by piece, God could change me. I have learned that the more I do this, even confessing this to myself, it fundamentally changes the posture between me and someone else of another color.

In essence, submission opens up a space for the Spirit to work reconciliation, growth, and learning what the future might look like. I can do this because I can trust that Jesus is Lord and is working over this space. I do not have to fear among Christians, because, as we do this together, submitting to Jesus as Lord and not our own devices, I can give up all violence or defense. I can submit to you and believe that you will not kill me. I can give up all defenses.

Submitting together to Jesus as Lord opens up the space for reconciliation. It is the start of a new community. We must give up ego and surrender to Jesus as Lord and his kingdom our right to be right. And, again, so very importantly, just as Jesus modeled around the table when he washed the disciples' feet, those presumed to be in power must go first. The fear of the oppressed is eased here, and a space is cleared for his presence. Christ's rule now begins to work for the future of the world. This is what faithful presence looks like.

Kingdom and Presence

The discipline of reconciliation, as with the Lord's Table, presumes there is more going on here than merely what happens between two or more persons in a room. If we submit together to his name, Jesus says, "I am there among [you]" (Mt 18:20). In this discipline of reconciliation, God extends Jesus' presence to be among us. Could it be any clearer? In this discipline a social reality is birthed where his presence is sacramentally made real.

In order for reconciliation to happen, we must acknowledge that we are being invited into the arena of the presence of Christ. The kingdom is breaking in. We need to understand that what is happening here will shape the church's destiny by what God is doing in the whole world. It is that sacramental.

As a pastor I have encountered numerous conflicts within church life. It is an inevitable part of life together. Sometimes when this happens, I am asked to mediate, make a judgment between the two people, and enforce it. What I've learned however is that I must openly reject this mode of operating. I must refuse this way of reconciling as if it were from the devil. Instead, I must see this moment as the opportunity to invite these persons into the Holy of Holies, the very presence of Christ. If I do mediate and make a judgment on the conflict, inevitably one person will leave the church and the other stay. If we submit together to what God is doing, God takes us together to somewhere new in our lives and the life of the church. Often we go where we could never have imagined.

One time a newly widowed woman, Emily, in our church was overburdened with taking care of her two children, homeschooling them, while also holding down a job. Sylvia, who was a social worker, offered to help. She sacrificially gave many hours to working with Emily's children. One of the children had special needs, according to Sylvia. She believed that Emily was not taking care of the children's educational needs. After a few discussions with Emily about this, Emily asked Sylvia to not visit her children any longer. Sylvia, in a huff, reported Emily to Department of Children and Family Services, charging Emily with neglect of her children.

The resulting breach of trust could not have been worse. When the pastors asked them to come together to mutually submit to Christ, we were refused. Emily told the pastors to get Sylvia "in line." Sylvia said it was her professional duty to report Emily to the proper authorities. She was an expert. She knew what she was doing. There was no need for further discussion. Two more times we attempted to bring them together. The third time the pastors sat with each one and asked what they were afraid of. We talked about the kingdom and the way God works through his presence coming into these spaces. Nonetheless both Sylvia and Emily refused to give up the authority of their positions as parent and social-service professional. They refused to put those claims aside. They both left the church. And our church body was poorer. All the pastors firmly believed God was teaching us much about how to care and be with our children and children in the neighborhoods. But this kingdom opportunity was foreclosed, never again to be revisited.

It is interesting to listen to my friends tell of their experiences marching in Ferguson or the Black Lives Matter marches in Chicago. They speak about the impact of these marches, when just by being present in the conflict with each other they were able to calm one another down and deal with their anger. They talk of being overcome by the presence of white people standing with people of color in the midst of injustice. These, I suggest, are the signs of Christ's presence in the confrontation to those who would be present to the other in the discipline of reconciliation.

If our churches are engaging in God's mission, we will encounter life situations like these regularly. Indeed, by definition, if we are in mission, we will encounter things we have no prior scripts for. Disagreements, conflict, and even oppression are signs that we are engaging challenging places with the gospel. If our church is self-enclosed, engaging no one outside our immediate circle, we can go on for years without a disagreement, doctrinal struggle, or situation that challenges the way things have always been done. Churches in mission, however, should welcome disagreements as signs that God is moving and that he comes to be present among us. They are opportunities for the kingdom to break in and change the world. They are signs of faithful presence.

RECONCILIATION IN THE THREE CIRCLES

As with the Eucharist, the discipline of reconciliation follows the pattern of being on the move. It starts with the close circle and moves into all areas of the community's way of life. And yet it does start in the close circle.

Reconciliation in the close circle. In Matthew 18 we catch a glimpse of the close circle of reconciliation. Jesus directs the offended person to go literally to "your brother." Jesus implies the person is a family member. In fact the prior verse (v.17) is one of the few times Jesus uses the word, *church*. And so there is little doubt that Jesus intended this discipline to be an intense part of the close circle of Christian life. The discipline of reconciliation was part of those discerning their submission to Jesus as Lord.

In 1 Corinthians 5 we discover some dynamics peculiar to the close circle of reconciliation. Evidently, a man is living in sexual relationship with his father's wife in the close circle among them. Paul calls for extreme measures. Just as with the Lord's Table, the close circle of reconciliation demands discernment. If anyone refuses to submit to one another under Christ's reign, this is to be made visible so that everyone within the close circle can see it and discern it. In both Matthew 18:17 and 1 Corinthians 5:3-5, the community is instructed to make visible the refusal of one's submission to one another in reconciliation under Christ's name. There is a very real social reality taking shape here. In 1 Corinthians 5:3-5 the apostle makes explicit that this is a communal act ("when you are assembled"), and as we are present with each other, we discern expulsion (Paul talks about being "present" with them—even in Spirit— as an essential part of any discernment of exclusion).

Outside the circle, however, Paul is clear that the community is not to assume this kind of discernment is possible. Inside the community (the close circle) he asks the Christians not to associate with those who are in rebellion against reconciliation (1 Cor 5:9-13). Outside the community, he asks that Christians not judge (v. 12). God will judge those outside the community (v.13).

Reconciliation in the dotted circle. And yet the discipline of reconciliation does not stay in the close circle. It shapes our entire lives as Christians, including our family life, our marriage life, the life between roommates, the life we share in workplaces, and the life on the streets in our neighborhoods. And so when we take up table fellowship in the neighborhood, we must assume that the discipline of reconciliation extends there as well. We submit to each other under Christ during the week in the same way as we do on Sundays or within church polity.

It should not surprise us then that the apostle Paul tells Christians in Corinth to settle their everyday disputes not through the court systems but with one another. In 1 Corinthians 6:1-8, he asks the Corinthian Christians, why, in regard to "ordinary matters" (v. 3), they go to someone outside the church? He cannot understand Christians taking their disputes to the local courts, because God has already given his people of the new kingdom the means to make such discernments. For Paul, the kingdom has broken into their lives (through reconciliation) and so the power to judge the angels is theirs already (v. 3). Why would we then resort to the courts? Paul is incredulous. He insists they are to come together before Christ in mutual submission with a third person and let God's kingdom break in (v. 5). This describes the ongoing extension of the powers of the kingdom in reconciliation into the details of our everyday lives.

Most telling is that the apostle appears to be concerned about unbelievers witnessing the conflicts before the law courts (v. 6). This is a sure sign that we have entered into the dotted circle (at least), where believers are gathered in a dotted circle (v. 5) and nonbelievers are witnessing what is going on. Paul implies that the way we resolve our conflicts under his lordship bears witness to the kingdom.

It was not uncommon on a Friday night at our house for a conflict to break out. We'd be eating around the large table, tending to one another and one thing would lead to another, and someone would burst out with an accusation against someone at the table. There would be a hush around the table. The tension was palpable. Nonetheless, we were able to submit and listen. There would be a nonanxious presence in the room. The aggrieved person would air out their struggle and pain. Some ugly assumptions would be hurled. Then slowly either the person voicing the conflict or the one being accused, or another person around the table would say something like, "George, I love you, and here is the way I see things. I submit to you. Does that make any sense?" or "I never saw that before. I repent of my pride. What can I do to show you I care and love you as a brother (or sister) in Christ?" And so over the months we saw some antagonisms unwind, some resentments disappear, some binding oppressions lifted, some people's lives healed. It affected more than personal relationships; it affected all of a person's life and health. It affected the way we lived as a social body. The kingdom was breaking in.

The discipline of reconciliation extends into everyday life. But it is always preceded by presence. Christians hosting other Christians are to see themselves as hosts of reconciliation in everyday life. And as we live this reconciled life before our neighbors, people begin to see how we deal with conflict, how we engage cultural and racial prejudices among us, how our marriages carry on and grow through conflict, how our lives with one another grow even though we are so starkly different from one another. And the neighbors down the street, those struggling with marital or racial conflict, those at war with their city or police, begin to see a new way of living. They become curious and ask how this is possible. They slowly become drawn into the world of the kingdom alive in their neighborhood.

Reconciliation in the half circle. Like the Eucharist, the discipline of reconciliation does not stay located even among dotted circles of our neighborhoods. It is extended by Christians into the places we live and intersect with non-Christians, the half circles of our lives, where indeed we are guests. As we seek to inhabit the places of racial injustice, violence and addiction, economic injustice, and family brokenness, we tend to Christ's presence at work. As we share meals around tables and inhabit other places of faithful presence, opportunities arise for Christians to offer the way of reconciliation as a gift from Christ to the world.

Every neighborhood, social gathering, and meeting place is a flowing stream of antagonistic broken relationships. As we sit and tend to Christ's presence among these various places of life, it is inevitable that the occasion will arise to offer the reconciliation of God in Christ for the whole world. We cannot predict whether the offer will be received. Instead, we sit humbly and vulnerably, listening with the compassion of Christ. We sit present as a guest. And as we do, Jesus becomes present. And the occasion comes to offer reconciliation in this excessively tangible way: "I believe I have wronged you" or "I believe my forbearers have wronged you." "I repent from these wrongs." "How can I work with you to make these things right?" As I have learned from many friends of color in the Black Lives Matter movement, sometimes the discipline of reconciliation can only begin with the confession that something was done very wrong and I have been a part of that.

In the midst of a broken relationship, the discipline of reconciliation can also offer something like, "I believe Jesus has forgiven all the wrongs in this room. You all are forgiven in him. He wants to come and be present here to reconcile. Can we seek forgiveness? Can the wrongs be set right?" Again Christ can be rejected. This is the nature of the half circle. But if we start with being present to each other and then to Christ's presence, Christ himself can be welcomed. The kingdom can become visible. People's lives are transformed. In opening this space for Christ, an entry ramp has been formed into Christ's kingdom. This is the nature of extending Christ's presence into the world. This is what faithful presence looks like.

Christ announces in the Sermon on the Mount, "Blessed are the peacemakers, for they will be called children of God" (Mt 5:9). He is describing life in the in-breaking kingdom via the half circle.[4] The beatitudes are blessings on those who live in the kingdom, and yet they also infer we are living in the world. The beatitude on peacemaking comes before the last two beatitudes, which decidedly refer to conditions of living in the world (i.e., being persecuted for righteousness [v. 10] and being reviled and having evil uttered against you [v. 11]). The verses that follow (vv. 13-14) infer that these beatitudes apply to the community in the world (i.e., being salt and light). These beatitudes then are blessings of the kingdom for those who practice the discipline of reconciliation in the world.

But this beatitude is not saying "blessed are peaceful," but "blessed are the ones who are at work making peace." The blessings of the kingdom are on those practicing the discipline of reconciliation in the world. Christians are therefore to live in such a way that the half circle of reconciliation is always open.

One time I was sitting in my booth at McDonald's grading some papers when John slipped into the booth across the table from me. McDonald's had become a half circle for me. I was sharing tables with many friends for over five years. John had been without a home for over three years. I had known him for at least two of those years. As we drank coffee together across from each other, my attention turned to his face. Something was stressing him deeply. I sat there tending to the presence of Christ in our midst. Eventually John shared. It was Christmas time, and it was going to be one more year of not seeing his children. John said he hadn't seen his children in ten years. The stories of John's broken past with his children came out, and it extended to his other family members and his ex-wife. He felt isolated; he was not even allowed by his brother to stay over at his mother's house. John's broken relationships had spread beyond his family as well. He was mad at a friend for not being paid on a job he did for him. He was mad at another friend for calling him out at a PADS shelter, and now he was banned from sleeping there.

A moment came where I felt led to say something like, "John, I believe God would have you reconcile with your family, beginning with your children and your ex-wife. What do you think?" John replied, "That will never happen. You don't understand. My wife hates me. She and her husband have banned me from the kids. If I approached her, she would get violent, swear a blue streak, and have the police arrest me." Slowly he unraveled the tales of twisted lives enmeshed in hate and vengeance. But finally I quoted 2 Corinthians 5:19-20 and declared that even in the midst of this mess God is working to reconcile him and his ex-wife and children. "Can you cooperate with him? Let him work?" I asked. "But she'll yell and scream!" "John," I said, "I believe Jesus is Lord, and he wants to overcome all that and heal these broken relationships. I've experienced it and believe it is true of you as well. Can you receive that for your life too?" John said yes.

We slowly worked out next steps. John became convinced his first step was to write a repentant letter seeking forgiveness from his wife and kids. The constant question was, how can we invite the presence of Jesus into these reconciliations? It started a string of developments in John's life. He started inviting Jesus into other reconciliations. I saw antagonisms gradually start to unwind in his life. It took a while, but John reported to me a year later that he was visiting the kids, that his ex-wife and he were talking. A year later, I was surprised to learn he got employment. (Everyone else in McDonald's said it would never happen). Slowly, all around John, God started to heal the world around him.

Everywhere in the New Testament we are told to forgive others as we have been forgiven. It starts with the Lord's Prayer but carries throughout the entire New Testament. Repeatedly, we are told, just as we have been forgiven in Christ and loved, so in return forgive others and share that forgiveness with others. The consciousness of the early Christians was saturated with the dynamic of forgiveness and reconciliation. It was not just a discipline they did on Sunday before the Lord's Table. It was an everyday discipline that extended into all the half circles of their lives.

Likewise today, this discipline is to be lived out in all circles of our lives. In so doing God reshapes our lives, our neighborhoods, and indeed the whole world. Let's look at a few examples.

SEXUALITY CONFLICTS

One time Herman, a church leader, called me from Ohio after I had met him at a conference. He was not a pastor at his church but was a devoted church member contemplating leaving his church. He called to ask me about my position on LGBTQ relationships in the church that I had discussed at the conference where we met. I have labeled my position elsewhere in talks and books as "welcoming and mutually transforming."[5] Herman was obviously distressed. He told me how a wonderful lesbian couple had become part of their church community two years ago. Over the ensuing months they grew to love and respect each other. They had become members of the church with seemingly little concern from anyone.

Then one of the women started to sing solos and lead music during worship. Next, she asked to teach Sunday school. Soon word got around that a few people were asking questions about her fitness for such leadership due to her lesbian relationship. Rumblings of discontent surfaced and the senior pastor decided he had to act. Without a congregational meeting, the leadership announced that the board of elders had prayed, discerned, and decided that the new policy of the church should be a "welcoming and affirming" posture toward all gay and lesbian believers in our midst. All lesbian and gay believers, practicing or not, would be welcome in all leadership positions of the church. This announcement came as a surprise. Herman, who had been discerning this issue on his own for several months, felt dishonored. He disagreed with some aspects of this decision. He felt now like he had no choice but to leave the church. A policy had been implemented with little or no discussion, and now it was either agree with the decision or you're out. There was no space opened for discerning the disagreement and reconciliation.

Instead of leaving, I suggested to Herman that he go directly to the lesbian woman and tell her his concern and in love reveal his heart to her. "Tell her what you told me," I said. "Say something like, I'm a father of a young girl. In my experience, I have been deeply shaped sexually by the people modeling sexuality in my life, including my parents and my Sunday school teachers. I believe generally that we are affected deeply by our role models at young ages. And so I'm worried about my daughter being influenced, even subconsciously, by the modeling of your sexuality as one given authority to teach her. I mean no disrespect, but I'm convinced lesbian sexuality would not be good for her. I submit to you, what would you do if you were me?"

I then conjectured, "The woman might respond, and say something like 'you're wrong on your assumptions about sexual preference. It is not a matter of modeling. The *Journal of the American Medical Association* has refuted this hypothesis.'" She might offer many of her own reasons out of her own life for thinking differently. And then I suggested the conversation might have him respond by telling a story of how he was deeply affected by someone in his life who modeled sexuality or how a close friend or his wife was affected too. I said he could tell her how real this experience was and the fear is. I said he could submit genuinely to her again and ask, "If you were me, what would you do?"

I told Herman that I suspect we might both be surprised at how sympathetic the lesbian woman would be even if she didn't agree with him. Some repentance and confession might take place. Antagonisms might unravel for both of them. Perhaps this one moment of mutual submission and reconciliation would open a space to discuss each others' sexual formation and unwind stuff going on that both parties were unaware of. Perhaps the resulting new understandings and agreements would completely surprise and afford healing like we never would have imagined. We cannot know for sure, but God might shape a whole community of healing from this one episode of reconciliation.

Too often, I contend, leaders foreclose the discipline of reconciliation in their need to take control, act from the top, and impose a policy they think will solve the problem. But we can see from this one example how God indeed transforms people's lives through the practice of his presence in reconciliation. In these ways, God can shape the close circle to be a community for mission.

ON RESISTING VIOLENCE AND COERCION IN THE WORLD

A community that is practiced in the discipline of reconciliation can sense Christ's presence at work in conflicts in the neighborhood. We can in essence become the peacemakers of the Sermon on the Mount through extending the discipline of reconciliation into the other circles of our lives.

One time, while living in Wrigleyville, Chicago, I was sitting in a meeting of our local house gathering. In the past week our friend Jannine in the neighborhood had gotten into a fight with her boyfriend. She had a history of antagonism with certain men in the neighborhood. She would play one guy's affections off of another. One of these gentlemen got violent and destroyed her watch and stole her computer in her apartment. We were all shocked. One of the men in our community took her to the local police station to file a warrant for the man's arrest. We sat around listening and a few of us thought the gospel was calling us to offer reconciliation before going to the police. We asked how to offer Jannine the reconciliation offered in Christ for this conflict between her and her boyfriend. We suggested sitting longer with her and being present to her, listening for the possibilities for reconciliation in her life. Could we ever support Jannine and go with her to her boyfriend and speak truth, saying, "You have sinned against me"? Could we dare to ask Jannine to start reconciliation by confessing sin and asking forgiveness from her boyfriend? (If this was in fact warranted.)

And so, as we inhabit dotted circles in our lives, we will see conflicts arise that often turn to violence. Whether it be a nasty divorce that turns violent, a domestic relationship that turns coercive, someone committed to act out revenge against an enemy in business, I have seen all these occasions become an opening for the gospel of reconciliation. For sure, we must protect the vulnerable from more violence. But before we rush to help a person file a warrant for someone's arrest, before we let a person walk away ready to commit vengeance, I believe we are called to offer the process of reconciliation, like I did with John that day in McDonald's. Nine times out of ten, it may be rejected. But we cannot let that stop us. Because the one time it is received, Jesus promises to be there and unwind the antagonisms and violence of the world and heal and renew. The kingdom will begin and spread in this one entry point. This is truly faithful presence.

RETURNING TO FERGUSON

Some may say that the discipline of reconciliation is too small of a strategy to make an impact on the systemic injustices of our day. We must fight through larger organizations and governmental strategies.

I would never want to discourage such larger efforts. But in order for such efforts to avoid becoming another bumper sticker or a T-shirt slogan, they must be shaped by the discipline of face-to-face presence that Jesus teaches us in Matthew 18:15-20. The various mass efforts for justice of the past century have shown a propensity to be absorbed easily into our societal systems. Civil rights legislation has at times become the means to institutionalize racism through other means. Injustice can so easily become justified by an ideology that enables the privileged to point to the injustice, make minor changes, control it, and move on.

And so Christians are called to be present in the half circles of injustice, broken racial relationships, the oppression of one person by another.[6] A public demonstration, done in peace, can orchestrate such a face-to-face encounter. The victims, as well as people standing with the victims, become present to the oppressor. The march puts real human faces on the injustice. A moment of presence then occurs, and it becomes extremely uncomfortable for those in privilege to turn their faces away and move on. A space is opened to dislodge the ideology and invite the oppressor to submit to one another. Repentance and reconciliation can begin.

Martin Luther King Jr. made his case for face-to-face, nonviolent encounters from his prison cell in Birmingham in 1963. White clergy were accusing him of being an "outside agitator" coming from Atlanta to lead the demonstrations against segregation in Birmingham. Rev. King wrote, "We had no alternative except that of preparing for direct action, whereby we would present our very bodies as a means of laying our case before the conscience of the local and national community." The idea of bodily face-to-face *presence* here is key. In Martin Luther King's words, it will be nonviolent with the goal of creating a "constructive non-violent tension" in the minds of the public versus a "violent tension."[7] This constructive nonviolent tension is presence. It is necessary and inevitable as we seek to bring the reconciliation of God in Christ into the world. It is dangerous. Christ was crucified and Martin Luther King was assassinated in this tension. But thus is the beginning of true reconciliation. It is the opening of space for the presence of Christ and the actual practice of reconciliation.

Here we go into these half circles of racial injustice to be present face to face. This is Matthew 18:15-20 in another form. Here in this space those in power (or perceived power) submit first, as Jesus modeled for us. As one of my white friends says about marching with black brothers and sisters in Chicago's Black Lives Matters protests, "I'm basically there to check my privilege and show my face." We become present to one another, and then Jesus becomes present in that space if we will just discern him. A space is opened up for the Holy Spirit to work. The twisted antagonisms of ideology can be unwound. We are in essence extending the presence of Christ from the close circle into the half circle.

As we go into the violence, racial oppression, and systemic injustice, we go humbly and vulnerably. We are not in control. We give up violence in subject to Christ's lordship over all things. We put our lives in danger. It is an example of moving as guest into a half circle.

In demonstrating we present ourselves as simply present, witnesses to injustice, and supporters of the oppressed. We go in peace. Antagonism always seeks to disrupt presence. Violence offers the privileged an excuse to turn their faces away. And in the end Jesus cannot inhabit the space of the perpetrator of violence. Reconciliation can begin and transformation can commence in the space of face-to-face presence, which can be afforded in a nonviolent demonstration. Carried out in this way, demonstrations can be a premier example of faithful presence. And it can lead to so much more.

As I have sat with friends who have learned the practice of presence in protest marches in Chicago, Cleveland, Baltimore, New York City, and Ferguson, I have heard stories of how presence has changed a neighborhood, stopped violence, and opened space for a reconciliation and change. I have talked to pastors and Christian-community activists skilled at cultivating faithful presence between Black Lives Matters leaders and local police. I know of meetings in neighborhoods where black pastors and local police gather to sit together at tables, sharing a meal and being present to one another. They share food, they share their pains and how they see conflicts. They listen deeply. They brainstorm over how to help and encourage one another. These pastors then pray for the police. As one man told me, "As I watch the confessions, the conversations, the honesty, the kingdom breaks in." A reordering of the community's entire social culture is taking place in Christ. This is what faithful presence looks like.

RECOVERING FAITHFUL PRESENCE IN OUR CONFLICTS

As inspiring as the discipline of reconciliation is, down through history the church has regularly defaulted to maintenance mode with regard to reconciliation. It is simply easier to manage conflict than to tend to Christ's presence at work in it. On the other hand, when presented with injustice and conflict in the world, the church has just as regularly defaulted to exhaustion mode. Examples of this abound throughout the church's history.

Vibrant reconciliation was everywhere in the life of the New Testament church. The *Didache*, a first-century document of the early church's life together, displays this. And yet, already by the third century, the local bishops were given sole authority to lead the practice of reconciliation, taking it out of everyday life.[8] Soon thereafter, after Constantine, the Roman church was dealing with huge numbers of Christians coming into the church. And so the Council of Nicaea (AD 325) formalized placing the forgiveness of grave sins under the authority of bishops. The discipline of reconciliation was well on its way to being taken out of the everyday lives of Christians and moved into the four walls of the church organization.

Over the ensuing centuries, in Europe the sacrament of penance became more individualized. Its communal context was lost. The Fourth Lateran Council (AD 1215) established the confession of sins for all believers "in secret to their own priest." And so we are on our way to sequestering reconciliation to the Roman Catholic confessional of the medieval church.

Space does not allow a full recital of the entire history of the discipline of reconciliation. I can only note that anytime the discipline of reconciliation has been extracted from the space of everyday life, it is a sure sign the church is slipping into maintenance mode. Perhaps the most egregious (and notorious) was in the fifteenth century when the rites of penance were used to raise money for the church by the selling of indulgences. What had been a place of Christ's presence had been des-ecrated, and Martin Luther among others rebelled against it. Anytime the church moves to locate the control of the discipline into the hands of hierarchy, this is not only a sign of maintenance mode but that Chris-tendom has taken over the church.

In similar ways, today's Protestant evangelical churches often relegate the practice of reconciliation to "conflict resolution ministries" with trained (in some respect) conflict mediation counselors. What is lost, in the process, is that the real presence of Christ comes in the midst of reconciliation.[9] Rarely, in these conflict mediation sessions, do we tend to his presence and one another in his presence. It often separates the two people in conflict from the church, so they cannot infect the rest of the congregation. Conflict is resolved from the top down and never moves from the bottom up. And rarely does the outcome of these con-flicts affect the church at large positively. In the process evangelicals lose the sacramental earth-shaking, future-forming social discipline of being with Christ faithfully in reconciliation for the world. This is why we must reclaim the discipline of reconciliation for mission as part of being his faithful presence in the world.

FAITHFUL PRESENCE AND THE RECONCILIATION OF THE WORLD

One evening in October, while sitting in front of the neighborhood ice cream shop, I met a Latino man named Jorge. He told me stories of the police giving him tickets for his car being parked over the sidewalk. This man felt it was a "white man's law" written for Westmont people living as single families. Because Latino people often live three families to a house, they had more cars. White people lived more often as single-family households. The sidewalk parking law was therefore a white man's law because it discouraged Latino people and other less affluent people from living in Westmont. That evening we talked about the built-in racism of our town. We pledged that day to work together for peace.

That began a journey for me to more awareness of the racial divides of my suburb of Westmont. Two African American women, aunts of a friend, lived down one end of the block. They didn't like white people we were told. They had had bad experiences as they had worked as janitors for a nearby white church. There was a Latino family who had moved two doors down from me. The first time I greeted them as a white man, Ernesto said, "We're only here for three months." Despite my attempt to welcome them, they seemed to fear not being wanted here by the white man. Up the other end of the block resides an African American family who we know has strained relations with another white family we have gotten close to. A few weeks ago, while writing this chapter, four police cars stopped one black man in front of our house. With a new awareness, I saw all these things happening and decided in all my white machismo to do something about it. So I called a meeting. I said to our leadership, "Let's bring our black, Latino, Asian, and white brothers and sisters together and have a meeting! Let's invite some police officers. Let's talk about this, listen to each other, work for peace." Let's open up space for the kingdom. Let's lead some reconciliation!

Jean, a woman leader in our church, looked at me graciously and said, "Dave, you're doing it again." I said, "What? Doing what?" She said, "You're doing your white privilege thing. You're inviting people of color to come to your church building to settle a problem. You are taking a posture of power. You are leading the meeting. You are enforcing your rule on them." She said I somehow needed to get invited to their turf. They need to invite me into these struggles. She was telling me I needed to be present long enough to be a guest, and offer, as opposed to impose, reconciliation. This is the way God brings healing. This is the way faithful presence works.

My knee-jerk response was, "That could take years." I thought to myself how much I would have to order my life differently so that I could be among these friends and spend time being present to them. I must sacrifice time, speaking engagements, nights watching hockey games (a very white Canadian thing to do). I must be present to them on their terms and watch basketball or soccer ("football" in Latino terms) games. I must be present regularly over time. When and if the time comes, I must offer to our neighborhood the reconciliation that God is working in the world through Jesus Christ.

This episode describes what faithful presence must look like in the half circles of our lives. As we enter, we bring the marvelous processes in place of God reconciling the world to himself in Christ. But we cannot enforce it. We cannot make it happen. We can only become present to our brothers and sisters who face this pain. I must quiet my ego, listen, tend to his presence, let him work. When the time comes we must submit to reconciliation. We must ask for forgiveness. We confess our sin. We must make things right. We must learn new ways to talk. We must seek inclusion. We must march and be present with our brothers and sisters who hurt and live under the oppression of racism. Then comes the changing of laws. We must pray for renewal. And in this space of faithful presence God's kingdom shall be born.

Imagine what could happen if churches everywhere inhabited their neighborhoods with Christ's faithful presence of reconciliation. Amid domestic disputes on the block, gang fights in the local school, racist police activities on my street, we bring a concrete practice of reconciliation that begins with presence. As we become present at local tables, protest marches, every conflict in our churches, with faithful presence, imagine what God might do. According to Jesus this is how the world will change. God in Christ is reconciling the whole world to himself (2 Cor 5:19), and we are his ambassadors (v. 20).

5

The Discipline of Proclaiming the Gospel

Whenever you enter a town . . .

LUKE 10:10

One wintry night in Palatine, Illinois, some leaders at Life on the Vine gathered in Jon's kitchen to address issues going on in the community. After the meeting, while we were sitting in the kitchen sipping some wine, the subject of our friend David came up in discussion. David had been part of our community for a year or so. A good friend, he had been without a home for himself and his three-year-old grandson, Jay, for over a year. His own son (the father of Jay) had left town with various problems related to addictions. David and Jay were now living in the basement of one of our family's homes.

After struggling with health issues and no income for a year or so, things were starting to come together for David. He had gotten a job. His health was improving. Little Jay was flourishing while experiencing life with other children in our church community. And so, as we turned to pray for David, we asked each other some general questions. Was it time to help David get an apartment of his own with Jay? His finances were not good. Can we help make up the difference? Was it time to urge him to offer up Jay for adoption since David's own son seemed to show little signs of overcoming a heroin addiction and reconciling the broken relationships that were causing so many issues for him?

The ensuing discussion brought forth a slew of doubts and unsettling questions. We heard questions like, "What if David is not ready for such a move?" "Could we be pushing him into disaster for himself and little Jay?" We heard sentiments such as, "David does not even know whether he wants to keep little Jay. Therefore we should not encourage him to make plans that include his grandson." "David doesn't want to make a six-month commitment to an apartment lease, because he wants to move back with family in his farm town where he grew up in Princeton, Illinois." "David's health might be pushed to extreme if he has to move now!"

Two problems became apparent to all of us. First, we were discussing David without David being present. We all knew we were called to discern the future *with* David, not *for* him. Second, there was the problem of the missing gospel. We were talking about all the things that could go wrong that we should be wary of. We were calculating missteps. Where was the proclamation that Jesus was indeed Lord over all these circumstances, that he, by the Spirit, was working for renewal? Why were we not seeing God at work in the very struggles we were dealing with? We were failing to proclaim the reality that Jesus is Lord and working in these circumstances.

In the midst of the discussion, I pressed on some different questions. Could it be that God is working in these very circumstances to bring forth something new for David and for God's kingdom? Could it be that God has brought David and his family into our community to teach us and heal us from our own selfish or control maladies that keep us from fully participating and knowing the fullness of his kingdom in our own lives? Could God be using all these circumstances to heal David's son's brokenness, his grandson's life, and indeed David's own life? Can we trust him and discern what God is doing?

These are gospel questions. They are based in the confidence that God has come in Christ to reconcile all these relationships, heal the brokenness, and set the world right. In the midst of a broken family, an uncertain future, can't we announce that God is working for his purposes in all of this if we will just be present to him? But of course this is the point: Had we become present enough in David's life to see what is happening and proclaim the gospel into the very heart of David's life among us? Faithful presence requires the gospel, and to proclaim this gospel requires we be faithfully present in David's life.

THE WORLD YEARNS FOR A NEW WORLD TO BE BORN

We are told daily, via media statistics, how few can escape the cycles of poverty. Socioeconomic circumstances dictate our future. Psychologists tell us people don't change. Addictions never go away; they can only be managed. Problems can only be manipulated by science, but never transcended. We've been stripped of the supernatural in our society. Social problems can only be changed through government, and the government is corrupt. As a result, most modern North Americans see situations in terms of either we make things happen or there can be no change. We must take control. And when there is no possibility for such control, we feel helpless. Our lives are traps we cannot get out of. The result is a world engulfed with depression in multiple forms.

And so, at the turn of the millennium, antidepressants are the best-selling prescription drugs of any type in the United States. Psychiatrists diagnose depression in 40 percent of their patients. And most epidemiological studies report the numbers are much larger.[1] People feel lost and trapped by circumstances. The cycles of violence and anger, abuse and pain, never seem to be broken. We are a society that yearns for hope. We crave good news. We long for the gospel, for a new world to be born.

THE DISCIPLINE OF PROCLAIMING THE GOSPEL

But how will this new world be born? How will the seeds of hope fund the imagination and space be opened up so that we can see God at work and join in with him?

In chapter four I recounted sitting in McDonald's with my friend John who was estranged from his children and ex-wife for over ten years. John, as you recall, saw no hope in the series of broken, hate-filled relationships he had left behind with his wife and children. He was caught in a chain reaction of vengeance trying to avoid the pain. There was no way of escaping the cyclic violence and hate in his prior family relationships,

except to leave and be alone in the confines of his 2003 Chevy van. As I
recounted in chapter four, after two years of living alongside John in
McDonald's, a space opened up for me to say to John, "I believe Jesus is
Lord over all these relationships, and he's working to heal them. Can you
receive that for your life too?"

Recounting 2 Corinthians 5:19-20, I revealed to John how much I believed that, even in the midst of this mess, "God is working to reconcile
you and your ex-wife and children if you can submit to his rule and let
him work." Starting with the words "I believe," I proclaimed the new
world made possible in Christ by the Spirit. Based in the story of God (in
Scripture), founded in my own experience, I announced this new possibility for John. By the Spirit, God funded his imagination (or conviction)
sufficiently to breed hope and enable him to respond and enter into the
kingdom. This, I suggest, is at the heart of what it means to proclaim the
gospel in the world. And I believe it is a discipline that Christians are
called to practice regularly among ourselves and in the world.

At first glance, it might seem odd to call proclaiming the gospel a
discipline. Isn't it something we do spontaneously? And yet, in places
where Jesus is not recognized as Lord, where everyday we are asked to
place our ultimate identity in the success of our careers, our economic
status, our bodies, the things we own or consume, the success of our
children, we cannot depend on self-expression to shape our lives into his
lordship. It takes hearing the good news regularly to live into the reality
that Jesus is Lord and working all things for his mission. Only then can
our minds be formed, our imaginations shaped, so as to live daily in this
reality. Proclaiming the gospel is the power from which God births salvation to those who believe (Rom 1:16). We must therefore regularly hear
the gospel, submit to it and faithfully respond to it if we would truly live
in the reality of Christ's power. The heart of the church's life together is
funded by the proclamation of the gospel.

WHAT IS THE GOSPEL?

What is the gospel? What then does it mean to proclaim the gospel?

As the apostle Paul defines it, the gospel is the announcement that

God has fulfilled the promise of Scriptures to make the world right in Jesus Christ (1 Cor 15:1-11). Christ has died for our sins. By his death and resurrection (and ascension), he has defeated the effects of our sins, including death itself. He now sits at the right hand of the Father ruling over the world. In Christ the new creation has begun. Old things are passing way. Behold, the new has begun (2 Cor 5:17). All who respond to this good news repent of the old ways, and make Jesus their Lord and Savior, enter in and become part of what God is doing to reconcile the whole world to himself (2 Cor 5:18-19), and receive power to become the children of God (Jn 1:12).[2] This in one paragraph is the gospel.

In the 1930s, British New Testament scholar C. H. Dodd famously outlined this gospel in a book called *The Apostolic Preaching and Its Development.* It still holds weight today.[3] Much like current New Testament scholars Scot McKnight and N. T. Wright, Dodd outlines the gospel according to the apostle Peter's four sermons in Acts. He summarizes it as (1) the age of fulfillment has dawned; (2) this has taken place through the life, death, and resurrection of Jesus Christ; (3) by his resurrection, Jesus has been exalted to the right hand; (4) the Holy Spirit is the sign of Christ's presence and power; (5) the messianic Age will shortly reach its consummation in the return of Christ; and (6) the gospel always closes with an invitation to repentance and the promise of "the life of the Age to Come."[4] The gospel then, as outlined in Acts, is the announcement that the kingdom of God has begun and has come via "Christ and him crucified." It is nothing less than the announcement of a new world being born.

Personal salvation is certainly part of this gospel. But personal salvation alone is not the gospel. Certainly, in Christ we are pardoned, forgiven for our sins, and restored to a new relationship with God as father. This is all part of the gospel: God reconciling the whole of creation. Certainly, in Christ we no longer fear death and know we will be raised with him. But the gospel is much bigger than that. The gospel is that God has come in Christ, who has been made Lord, and a whole new world (the kingdom of God) has begun. In Christ, God has begun to make all things right.

To proclaim the gospel is to do something akin to what I did with John that day in McDonald's. I announced the new reality of the gospel before an open listener. Out of a place of presence I proclaimed, "the kingdom of God has come" and is active over John's life ("come near to [him]" [Lk 10:9]). I told him how I believed Jesus was Lord over his circumstances and working to make them right. I proclaimed the gospel contextually (into his own situation) out of my own life with vulnerability.

But proclaiming the gospel goes beyond something personal. The gospel is a cosmic reality that supersedes being about *me*. If it's merely personal, the gospel would stop with me. I might share it with someone as something nice that really benefitted me and maybe the other person might like to give it a try too. But if it is cosmic, it is presented as a matter of fact that has reality regardless of whether I (or anyone else for that matter) have chosen to live by its news. Proclaiming the gospel therefore is the art of announcing to our neighbors that this new world has begun in Christ.

PROCLAMATION VERSUS TEACHING

Proclaiming the gospel is a different kind of speech-act than most of us are used to. It accomplishes something different from conveying information. Dodd therefore draws the sharp distinction between preaching (or proclamation) and teaching in the New Testament.[5] *Teaching* is moral instruction to Christians for how to live. It is the exposition of key beliefs. It may even be apologetics, helping the Christian to make sense of a belief in light of the world. But *preaching* is the public proclamation of the gospel. It is the announcement of a new world.

Proclamation is description. It is like painting a picture. The proclaimer describes the world as it is under Jesus as Lord and then always invites the person into it. Arguably proclamation must precede teaching. Proclamation does not explain the gospel or argue for it. Proclamation tells the story, describes the alternative account of reality it offers, and then asks, "Can you see it? Can you receive the news? Do you want to enter in?" The teacher then explains it by answering questions delving deeper into all its meanings. Christians need both proclamation and teaching.

Only after having seen the beauty of the story, the power of its description, being compelled by the reality of Christ's reign and "cut to the heart" by its goodness, can we ask, "What should we do?" (Acts 2:37).

Only after having entered into the gospel can teaching make sense of what we now believe. The imperative (what we must do) always comes after the indicative (the description of the way things are).[6] Our lives respond in faith, choosing to enter the world as it is under his lordship. We then must learn more about what this world means.

Because proclaiming the gospel does not immediately appeal to one's rationality but offers a new interpretation of events, it is an epistemological shift of sorts. It does not play on Western cognitive rational ways of knowing. Instead of putting my self forward as the control center of knowledge, it decenters my self. It decenters me from being the center of my world, and instead centers me before God and what he's doing in the world in Jesus Christ. The gospel does not come as "plausible words of wisdom," as a good teaching lesson. Instead it derives from "a demonstration of the Spirit and of power" (1 Cor 2:4). The authority of preaching does not derive from a person's expertise in biblical knowledge, reasons for believing, or rhetoric, although these skills may be of help. Proclamation is spoken from a place of weakness and humility (1 Cor 2:3). It tells the gospel from a place of having witnessed it, seen it, been humbled by it. It is unsettling. It calls for conversion (a response) every time.

In Luke 4, Jesus stands up in the synagogue and reads the famous passage from Isaiah, "The Spirit of the Lord is upon me." When he had finished all the eyes had fastened on him. His presence among them was riveting. He then proclaims, "Today this Scripture has been fulfilled in your hearing" (Lk 4:21 NASB). Luke takes notice of how "gracious" his words were (v. 22). His presence was gentle, not coercive. Nonetheless, this proclamation of the gospel birthed a new reality among them. More than a truth read or explained, proclaiming the gospel opens space for a new reality to be birthed among us by the Spirit. In our hearing and receiving it, it births a new reality in our midst.

The regular proclamation of the gospel makes possible the birth of a community living in the new world of his reign. It funds our ability to see God at work in all we're going through in our everyday lives. It brings us together to discern life in the new world under the one "mind of Christ" (1 Cor 2:16).

PRESENCE IN PROCLAMATION

As with the Eucharist and reconciliation, the discipline of proclaiming the gospel opens space for Christ to be present among us. It clears space for Christ to come, be present, and transform all people in that space. As Eastern Orthodox theologian Alexander Schmemann recognizes, "The proclamation of the Word is a sacramental act par excellence because it is a transforming act. . . . [It] is the eternal coming to us of the Risen Lord."[7]

Jesus states, after sending his disciples to proclaim the gospel of the kingdom into the towns and villages, that "whoever listens to you listens to me, and whoever rejects you rejects me, and whoever rejects me rejects the one who sent me" (Lk 10:16). In hearing and receiving, or hearing and rejecting, the gospel, Jesus is there. His power and authority breaks in by the Spirit.[8] It is nothing short of "a demonstration of the Spirit and of power" (1 Cor 2:4). In its hearing, judgment is set loose akin to that of Sodom and Gomorrah (Lk 10:12). And so, just as with reconciliation, here also the keys of the kingdom are unleashed and the future of the kingdom takes shape among us in the proclamation of the gospel. It is an event that opens space for Christ's presence. As with Eucharist and reconciliation, proclaiming the gospel shapes us into faithful presence in the world.

The preacher, therefore, at the Sunday gathering, must tend to the presence of Christ amidst the community, for it is in submission that the proclamation becomes the means of his power. The preacher must not stand over the community but must stand as one among the community being present to the people in the community's midst, for it is in this space that Jesus is found. From this posture comes the practice of proclamation. This is not a rhetorical performance. This is proclamation of the gospel for the people gathered in Christ's name in this space and in this time. In the words of Dietrich Bonhoeffer, "If Christ is not wholly present in the sermon, the church breaks down."[9] In this way, in the close circle of the gathered community, preaching is an exemplary act of faithful presence.

As the preachers at Life on the Vine Christian Community moved behind the preaching lectern on Sunday morning, we put a cross over our chests as a sign that we were in submission to Christ's presence in this place. We also wore black in any way that fit our regular clothes. Our intent was not to separate us from the community but to remind us that "I must decrease and he must increase." The black signified that the preacher was to recede into the background. Christ must be lifted up. It was all part of the process of submission and tending to his presence, which is the discipline of proclaiming the gospel over the community.

I remember one time in a leadership meeting when one of the newer leaders was surprised to hear about the practice of wearing black and a cross when preaching. Matt questioned the whole process, protesting that "the congregation doesn't know any of this!" But we were all right with that. Wearing black and a cross was for the preacher's spiritual formation. If the community knew or caught on, all the better.

SUBMISSION IN PROCLAMATION

The discipline of proclaiming the gospel therefore invites the participant to submit, not to the preacher but to Jesus as Lord. This space of his subjects, both proclaimer and hearer, in submission opens the space for his reign, and we are able to hear God. The kingdom breaks in. As opposed to a response of pondering the pastor's eloquent well-crafted words of wisdom (1 Cor 2:5), proclamation creates the conditions for either submission or rejection. Proclamation cannot be argued or debated, only accepted or rejected.

Often, evangelicals preach a gospel for control freaks. This gospel says, "You have a problem. You're going to hell. Do you want to take care of that problem? Receive Christ's provision for your condemnation." You have now taken care of another problem. You have also remained in control. But proclaiming the gospel is a profoundly decentering experience that places the hearer in submission to God. It is the opposite of being in control. Proclaiming the gospel starts with, "Are you hopeless? Are you caught in a world gone wrong? Have you become caught up in sin? Are you powerless? Are you being destroyed by the world, by injustice? The gospel is that God has come in Jesus Christ and defeated the powers. God has made Jesus Lord. He therefore rules and is working in all of your circumstances, personal and in the world. Will you give up control, submit to Jesus as Lord, and participate in this new world? Will you discern what it means to follow him (and join him) in his work of making the world right? Welcome to his kingdom."

PROCLAIMING THE GOSPEL ON THE MOVE

In *Apostolic Preaching*, C. H. Dodd asserts that proclamation (*kēryssein*) in the New Testament church was for non-Christians, while teaching (*didaskein*) was moral instruction aimed at Christians for their growth as Christian disciples.[10] Rarely was the gospel proclaimed by Christians to Christians. But Dodd overstates his case.[11]

Paul, for instance, was eager to come to Rome, an established church of Christians, and proclaim the gospel to them even though they had already received it (Rom 1:15). In his most explicit statement about proclaiming the gospel, 1 Corinthians 15:1-2, the apostle states that the gospel was not only received (past tense) by the Corinthian church at their founding, but it was also the means by which they currently "stand" together, and that by which they are continually being saved (future).[12] For Paul, the proclamation of the gospel is an ongoing part of the life of Christians and forms us regularly into the kingdom of God. Proclaiming the gospel therefore is not only for the people outside of Christ, in the half circle. It must be part of the whole of Christian life, including the worship gathering and everyday life in the neighborhoods. It must take place in all three circles of our lives: the close, dotted, and half circles.

Proclamation in the close circle. Proclaiming the gospel, as most of us know it, happens every Sunday in the close circle of the gathered community. The story is unfurled. Our minds are opened by the Spirit, and we are invited, right then and there, to live into this world where God is at work making all things right. And from there the gathering partakes of the eucharistic meal.[13] We enter the kingdom together. A new world is being born. Proclaiming the gospel each Sunday grounds the church in the world as it is under Jesus as Lord. As I like to say, I'm getting saved every Sunday morning.

During the first several years of Life on the Vine Community's existence, we reflected seriously on the whats, whys, and hows of preaching.

Why even have preaching? Few people remembered what we taught on any given Sunday anyway. Those who did rarely did anything with it. And I kept running into younger persons from the large conservative church ten miles away who were exhausted after a year or two of sermon application points. They were never able to catch up with all the things the preacher was telling them to do if they were to grow as Christians. During this questioning, I began to see the difference between teaching and preaching. This differentiation began to reshape what we did in those twenty-five or so minutes when we would preach. I saw how important it was to proclaim weekly out of Scripture what God had done and is doing in and among us and through Jesus Christ. I saw how important it was to declare all of Scripture: what God has made possible in the life, death, and resurrection of Jesus Christ.

Over the years at Life on the Vine, we slowly learned the craft of preaching as proclamation. We learned how to structure a rhetorical phrase to summarize a text and proclaim the gospel. We learned that it was important to say words like, "we proclaim," "we declare," "on the basis of what I've learned, what God has said (in a given text), we as a congregation stand in the reality that God is . . ." We'd start a typical sermon by describing a situation we were living in as a people, usually through a story. We'd open it up to the gathered community for discussion (two hundred of us!). Then we would proclaim the gospel over all these things we heard. Preaching for us was reading the text and then unfolding the story of God, his character, his promises, his ways, and how he is Lord over our lives and the world we live in. The text was unfolded as a reality we were invited to live in. And then we would ask, Will we follow him? Will we trust him? Will we submit to him? Will we confess our sin? Will we believe and walk in faith and hope? Will we enter the reality of his reign in his kingdom? Will we let Jesus be Lord? The sermon always ended with an invitation to live into the kingdom.

Proclaiming the gospel is always contextual. It is always grounded in our ability to be present with the people we are proclaiming it *over*.[14] We proclaim the kingdom because we have been sent to this place (Lk 10:1; Rom 10:15), and so it's always a discipline spoken out of where we have been called to live. So, as Life on the Vine community learned what proclaiming the gospel was, we discovered how important it was for preachers to stand among the congregation, present in their weakness (1 Cor 2:3), owning who they are, yet not making the sermon about them. From this posture we proclaimed the gospel for this people for this time. Then, instead of an application point, we offered the opportunity to respond. We offered sentence responses of confession, affirmation of truth, praise, submission to God, a step of faith, and obedience. We all bowed before his real presence, with each person offering a sentence prayer response that transported us into his kingdom.

Many times, sitting amid the congregation during those times of response, I felt the fullness of Christ's presence. I heard the responses around the gathering of people entering the kingdom. And the Eucharist followed. I could not help but explode with amazement. A new world was being born in our midst, the world of Christ's kingdom.

Years later, I am more convinced than ever that such proclamation of the gospel is essential to the founding of a community in mission. It forms a social reality that is the kingdom. As we learn how to be present as proclaimers and hearers in this close circle, Christ becomes present. A people is born in the midst of this gospel event. In this sense, proclaiming the gospel is truly a social sacrament. From here then we go out to proclaim the gospel in the world. Proclaiming the gospel is the lifeblood of a people shaped into faithful presence.

Proclamation in the dotted circle. But the proclamation of the gospel does not stay in the close circle. It happens throughout the week in our neighborhoods. The apostle Paul said his final goodbyes to the church leaders at Ephesus with the words, "Now I know that none of you, among whom I have gone about proclaiming the kingdom, will ever see my face again" (Acts 20:25). For the apostle these churches and their leadership are the product of the gospel being proclaimed as he lived among them. He implies that he proclaimed the gospel face to face in their presence. This is how these people were formed as house churches in Ephesus; Paul both proclaimed and taught "publicly and from house to house" (Acts 20:20). What is modeled in the close circle must also be lived in the neighborhoods, "publicly and from house to house." Just as we learn to hear the gospel proclaimed and respond to it in the close circle, we must now become proclaimers ourselves in our own houses and neighborhoods. The gospel must be proclaimed house to house in every context.

It all sounds so unnatural at first. It seems so foreign to proclaim the gospel to each other sitting around a table in a neighborhood. "Where is the pulpit?" someone might ask. But just as with the close circle, so also in the home, we must first tend to being present to each other and to Christ's presence among us. As we sit around a table and share our lives with each other, expose our sufferings and our joys, a moment comes that begs for the proclaiming of the gospel into our lives. And so we must wait and listen, and when the time is right, we might even ask humbly, "May I say something?" And then, as with the first disciples, the Holy Spirit guides us into all truth (Jn 16:13).

This gospel will not be the old standby we've known through the small booklets or tracts handed out at church. It will be contextualized in this space that is opened up in the neighborhood. There is no one, set gospel starting point. There are numerous entry points. To the one suffering fear and anxiety, Jesus is Lord, and he is working in that situation. Can you believe and take a step forward in faith? To the one angry at what has been done, Jesus is Lord, vengeance is his, and he is working to reconcile all things. Can you forgive in Christ? To the one suffering depression, God is working here, he alone has created you for purposes before the founding of the world. To the one who is lost in guilt and shame, he has taken your sin in the cross and forgives you unconditionally. He is Lord. Can you receive that? To the one who is broken, he heals; to one who is dying, we cannot be separated from his love. Christ's lordship over the world may be proclaimed over that addiction destroying someone's life. He is Victor. He is Lord in that broken marriage and the evil cycle of violence that has got ahold of our playgrounds in the neighborhood. And on and on. "Jesus is Lord" is the gospel. He is working for the renewal of all things. Can we enter in, trust him, and begin to participate and discern what God is doing, and be faithful to him?

We must remember that the gospel is so all-encompassing that there is not one aspect of life that it does not touch and transform. So the gospel for this time and place may not address the hearers' sin condition or their trust in Christ and his sacrifice on the cross (the most common starting point for evangelicals). Instead, as we sit together, long enough in each other's presence, faithful to his presence, we will be presented with an entry point. We must not translate our priorities into the lives of others.

Growing up in Canada (an intentionally bilingual country), I would eat breakfast before school reading the cereal boxes in both French and English, learning French in the vocabulary of breakfast cereal. It was an entry point into an entire world of French if I would just follow its discipleship (which regrettably I never really did). To this day I still remember more French from the cereal boxes than I do from the endless rote French classes I had from third grade on, because the French on the cereal boxes was contextualized. Cereal-box French illustrates that contextualizing the gospel is about finding an entrance point and being confident that any given entrance point into the gospel will always lead to the whole of the gospel if we will but follow Christ into discipleship. Breakfast cereal could have led me into becoming a brilliant French person if only I had been a better disciple (or had a better French teacher in the third grade). With the gospel, the entrance point always leads to the whole.

Every day in our neighborhoods, amid strife, broken relationships, and tragedy, whether we are Christians or not, we need the gospel. Christians must play host to spaces where the gospel can be proclaimed. As we gather around tables and the various meeting places of our lives, if we will be patient and tend to Christ's presence among us, the moments will *present* themselves for the gospel to be proclaimed contextually, humbly out of our own testimony. And in these moments Christ will be present, transformation will come, and onlookers will catch a glimpse of the kingdom. This is faithful presence.

Proclamation in the half circle. In Luke 10:1-16, Jesus gave to the disciples his most explicit instructions on proclaiming the gospel. He tells them to first go into the villages and be present with people. Go to be among them in their homes. Go without power, as lambs among wolves.

Go needy, without money ("Carry no purse" [v. 4]). As we've seen in this text before, the disciples go as guests. Don't move from house to house. Instead be present, submit, eat what is offered, be a guest, put yourself at the mercy of the order and relationships in this place. In other words, be present. Only after these many instructions on being present does Jesus then instruct his disciples to proclaim the gospel.

It is therefore important to get the order straight. Just as in the close circle and the dotted circle, the one who proclaims must first be present. Presence precedes proclamation. Our tending to Christ's presence in the world, and to each other's presence, makes possible the proclamation of the gospel into people's lives. It is at the heart of faithful presence.

Just as in the other circles, the gospel must be proclaimed contextually in and among a person's life. For many of us in the secular world, when someone speaks of God, we ask, "Which one?" If someone talks about sin, many have never heard of such a thing. When we say "the Bible says," some might respond, "I'm happy you have found something that works for you." And so now we must be present, listening long enough until a space opens up where we can proclaim the gospel in words that make sense in the same humble posture we learned in the other two circles.

Proclaiming the gospel opens space for the in-breaking power and authority of Christ's reign. If the gospel is received, disruptions occur, signs and wonders of this new world follow. In the book of Acts we see that miracles accompanied the apostles when they proclaimed the gospel. And many entered into the kingdom. In the words of the apostle Paul, "My speech and my proclamation were not with plausible words of wisdom, but with a demonstration of the Spirit and of power" (1 Cor 2:4). And so the proclaimers of Luke 10 reported to Jesus, "Even the demons submit to us!" (v. 17). And Jesus replies, "I watched Satan fall from heaven like a flash of lightning" (v. 18). Satan had been dethroned from power. Proclaiming the gospel opens up space which demonstrates the power and authority of Christ's rule. This too is faithful presence.

And yet as we learned previously, Jesus says, "Do not rejoice at this, that the spirits submit to you, but rejoice that your names are written in heaven" (v. 20). Don't think this demonstrates your power to control. Rejoice instead that you have been privileged to be participants in the power and authority of heaven itself, the seat of God's rule.

Despite these signs of the kingdom, when we proclaim the gospel in the half circles of our lives, where we live as guests, we always enter humbly, submitting to his presence. In submitting to the King, we open space for the kingdom. And so the apostle Paul makes it clear that in his proclaiming the gospel to the Corinthians, "I came to you in weakness and in fear and in much trembling" (1 Cor 2:3). He came not with brilliant words of worldly wisdom but in humility. This is the posture of the half circle. This is the posture that makes possible the proclamation of the gospel as a guest.

We sit humbly with our friends, tending to Christ's presence among us. We vulnerably open up ourselves to their every word. We submit to what God is doing. And when the hurt and pain is revealed, when we are prompted by the Spirit, out of our own story we speak softly the proclamation of good news in Christ. We tell our story of Christ's lordship over our lives, and then we say, "As with me, I believe Jesus is Lord over your life too." And this opens up space for the power and authority of God to rush in and do his healing work.

There are many half circles in our lives just waiting for the gospel to be proclaimed. These are the places we must go and be present as a guest, patiently awaiting the invitation to proclaim the gospel. These are the ways of faithful presence.

But as with all half circles, the question is, will Jesus be welcomed here? Jesus warns that we may not always be welcomed (Lk 10:10). The stakes are high. The authority of the kingdom is being unleashed. "Woe to you, Chorazin! Woe to you, Bethsaida!" (Lk 10:13). And yet this is not our work but God's. We cannot control. We are guests inhabiting the world as witnesses to his faithful presence.

RECOVERING FAITHFUL PRESENCE IN A WORLD WITHOUT HOPE

A pattern through church history is that proclaiming the gospel becomes less prevalent whenever the church gets comfortable in society. No longer seeing the world as outside of Christ's reign, the church turns its focus to teaching. It turns to deepening the knowledge of its parishioners. This is what Christendom does to the church. I have called this the maintenance mode of the church.

When the church became the recognized religion of Rome (after AD 378), historians report that the practice of proclaiming the gospel diminished.[15] The church was consolidating and organizing for the large populations coming into its membership. The teaching office was formalized to keep some control over deviant teaching. One cleric was now responsible for all the teaching in one parish. Proclamation of the gospel was moved away from the neighborhoods and into the homily at the Sunday gathering in the church building. In the process the church turned its focus to teaching what it meant to live according to the gospel, and proclamation was pushed to the sidelines.

Likewise, most of today's preachers teach on Sunday morning. The preaching often takes the form of word-for-word exposition of Scripture. The believer in the pew carefully listens, analyzes, and consumes the sermon, often taking notes. And the listening self is put firmly in charge of the impact the sermon will have. Individuals leave with a few things to work on and in general feeling better about themselves. The parishioners are reinforced in what they already believe. They feel confident that they have more of this Christian life figured out.

In the process, the gospel as shaping the new world among us gets lost.[16] Expository teaching (as just described) cannot fund imagination for what God is doing in the world. This is a sign that the church is living out Christendom habits, keeping existing Christians reinforced in their current version of Christianity.

Sometimes proclaiming the gospel can get replaced with rally speeches for social justice causes or self-help speeches on how Jesus can help us lead an improved and more fulfilled life. There is a sense we are trying to bring in the new world ourselves. We eventually grow tired of another pep rally. These are the signs that we have separated proclaiming the gospel from presence: both our presence among the broken and hurting, and Christ's presence with us. Exhaustion lies not far behind.

In order to avoid either maintenance or exhaustion, the church must recover the discipline of proclaiming the gospel in all three circles. This starts with Christians being present to one another in the close and dotted circles of our lives, and learning to proclaim the gospel into each other's lives. This will shape our preaching on Sunday morning and our table fellowships in the neighborhood. This will subsequently shape a faithful presence in what God is doing in all the circles of our lives.

6

The Discipline of Being with the "Least of These"

When you see the hungry, the thirsty, a stranger,
the naked, the sick, the imprisoned . . .

MATTHEW 25:37-39 (MY PARAPHRASE)

A group of missional leaders were sitting around a table one night sharing a beverage and celebrating relationships in the neighborhood. I was there as a coach to the group. I was nodding my head along with everyone else as we applauded the ways God had been working in the neighborhoods. They had hung out in the local coffee house. This led to a relationship with an elderly man struggling with the death of his wife and his own health. They helped paint his house orange and blue (his choice of colors). A homeless man in the neighborhood had found a job and an apartment through a local food pantry they served. A wall that lined the children's park needed a coat of paint and some repair. They rallied the locals to paint a beautiful mural. One of the group had been appointed to the zoning committee of the town and was working for positive changes. Many relationships had developed. People were intersecting with people. There was much to give thanks for.

Then, after a brief pause, the subject turned to what they were supposed to do next. What places of need, situations of distress, places where the "least of these" live would they devote our time and energy for the kingdom? How about the domestic violence shelter down the street—could they help there? How about the need for half-way housing for the town's homeless? How about a ministry for the moms whose husbands work late every night and need fellowship and babysitting?

After listening for a while, I felt prompted to say, "Maybe the best thing you can do is do nothing." Silence engulfed the room. I got some snarky looks, which in the past I have often deserved. Then I talked about some of my own mistakes in trying to find the next "justice-mercy project" in our ministry at Life on the Vine. I confessed how regularly over the course of my life I'd turned people into projects, which takes a lot of effort and resources, and ends up making us all feel better for about a week. In the end, I argued, we disempower people, doing very little in terms of real justice. Things stay the same. Even worse, the power structures at fault for the problems are stronger than they were before.

So I offered that maybe what we are supposed to do is—*do* nothing. As opposed to looking for projects, let's be *with* people in and around our lives long enough, years maybe, to listen and become friends, partners in life. Then we might offer who we are and what we have become in Christ as friendship and support for what God is doing in their lives. Let's simply be present.

At least some of the snarky looks turned pensive. And thus began a journey that led to going deeper into what it might mean to practice being with the "least of these" as a part of our everyday life.

THE WORLD LONGS FOR KINSHIP

The world operates by people doing things for and to people and then making them into projects. This is an overstatement, I am sure. But it speaks to the way American society (especially white male society) organizes whole systems to employ power efficiently, to get things done at a price. Corporations hire consultants to solve problems by recommending strategies to be implemented by managers. Money flows to put the solutions into motion. People are employed by the managers to do things for people at a price. As we all become part of the system, we become pieces in a system to make money. And we all become part of the power relationships of a society organized for efficiency and making money.

In this world, problems become projects. People become pieces to be managed within projects. And then people themselves become projects. Those who control the money control the power. By this process, we all get bonded into the system. The world, it seems, makes pawns of us all.

We experience this dynamic every day. We feel ourselves being categorized as we answer the questionnaire and then sit down for the job interview. We feel like a number as we wait in line and fill out forms to get food-stamp assistance at the local Department of Humans Services office. It's a dynamic we feel anytime we sit across the desk from our supervisor at work for our year-end review. We sense it when leaders get together in a room and there is this subtle pecking order. We agree that things like organization, accountability, and leadership are necessary, and yet something is missing. Even if we're at the top of the pecking order, we sense we're bound to this project-oriented system, and we long for something more. We imagine a world where each person is respected by every other person for what each one brings, where we all join together and share a kinship in an endeavor that is incredibly significant. The world, however, makes pawns of us all, and we persevere in the midst of it all, all the while desiring kinship.

The kingdom of God is life with God in a space where people join together as brothers and sisters. Jesus says as much when he tells his disciples, "I do not call you servants any longer, because the servant does not know what the master is doing; but I have called you friends, because I have made known to you everything that I have heard from my Father" (Jn 15:15). With a stunning sense of kinship, Jesus invites us to be *with* him. Elsewhere, he says, "Whoever is not with me is against me, and whoever does not gather with me scatters" (Mt 12:30). Here Jesus gathers people to be "with" him. He does not invite us to be his underlings but calls us to be part of something with him, a new politic of the kingdom. Those who leave, rejecting him, scatter amid the world's violence, with no true community. For those who come, the kinship is so close it's like family.

A little later, when Jesus is told at a gathering that his mother and brothers want to speak to him, he answers, "Who is my mother, and who are my brothers?" And stretching out his hand toward his disciples, he says, "Here are my mother and my brothers! For whoever does the will of my Father in heaven is my brother and sister and mother" (Mt 12:48-50). There is an inherent kinship in gathering people in the presence of Jesus. It is closer than a brother or a sister. In Christ's new kingdom no one becomes an object to or a project of someone else. We are invited to participate in life together with God. This is life lived in *withness*, kinship, faithful presence with one another.

This posture of being "with" is the signature mark of the way God has come to us in the world. "'The virgin shall conceive and bear a son, and they shall name him Emmanuel,' which means, 'God is with us'" (Mt 1:23). This is the posture we learn at the Eucharist and practice in reconciliation and proclaiming the gospel. But it is also a deliberate discipline we are called to practice regularly with the hurting, the impoverished, and the broken, those called "the least of these" in Matthew 25:40. In this posture, being with the hurting people in our churches, in our lives, in our neighborhoods, spaces are opened up among us for the in-breaking power of God in Christ. This is where miracles happen. This is his kingdom.

The Discipline of Being with the Least of These

Being with the "least of these" is a discipline that shapes whole communities into Christ's kingdom. It starts by coming alongside hurting persons. It starts with people being present to groups of people in need. This is something we do as a regular part of our lives as followers of Jesus. We offer our presence and who we are to the other person. We are present to the other person and tend to the presence of Christ between us. We are with each other. In so doing, a space is opened where no one is over the other person, no one is an object, no one is a project.

From this space of kinship, we share life. We pray together, confess sin together, proclaim the gospel into each others' lives, share resources as needed, reconcile, speak truth in love, encourage one another. Being with "the least of these" is the practice of opening this space of withness between us and the poor and tending to the presence of Christ there in that space. This space is like a clearing in the middle of a forest, where something new can be planted and new things can grow. And the authority of Jesus' reign comes rushing in by the Spirit. Being with the least of these is a discipline fundamental to shaping communities in mission.

The early Christians were known for this. They walked the streets tending to and being with the poor. In the first centuries of the church this practice became regularized in the church via the practice of almsgiving. They became known to the Roman authorities for the way they came alongside the poor, took them into their lives, and cared for their own orphans, widows, and poor. In early church history the church believed they were encountering the presence of the living Christ in the poor.[1] It drove their existence.

The early church understood the space between the disciple of Christ and the poor to be sacred. In being present to the poor, Christ himself would be specially present. This is why, later in church history, this discipline would evolve into the sacrament of unction. As the early Christians practiced being with the poor, a space would open up, Christ would become present, and they would pray for the sick, anointing them with oil. Miracles of healing took place. Lives were changed and restored in this space. Being with the poor spread Christianity like wildfire to every town and village. In many ways, being with the "least of these" is what faithful presence looks like in all its dynamics. If we would lead churches into a new engagement with God's mission, we might start with this discipline. The discipline of being with the "least of these" must become a part of the way Christians live.

In the early days of Life on the Vine Christian Community, I would invite young seminarians (people studying for the ministry) to join me on visits to the hospitals. For some of them visiting the sick was a terrifying experience. Imagine being in your twenties and for the first time visiting someone facing death. What would it mean to be face to face with someone facing death? What could anyone say? As we entered the elevator they would often pose questions: "What are we supposed to do?" or "What do you do or say when you go into someone's hospital room?"

My response was, "Just do nothing." What? "Yes, nothing. Say nothing. Do nothing. Greet the person and sit beside them and be present."

The hospital room is a sacred space where God in Christ becomes present. People who are sick are especially vulnerable. They are hurting. In many cases, they are afraid. They have lost control over their lives and are facing their mortality. They lie there open to everything and anything God would do in and around them and are often ready to submit everything to God. This makes them closer to God and his kingdom than those of us who visit them. It is therefore an awesome privilege to be invited into this space. The best thing we can do is be present. Tend to what God is doing. Tend to the presence of our Lord in this place.

And so we would enter that hospital room together and sit for minutes, sometimes hours, and say very little. We would sit by the bed tending to their face, their anguish. We would laugh at their jokes and cry at their sorrows. We would listen and ask questions. A space would be opened up. And many times I would experience the depths of the living God at work.

After a long while of being with the person in the hospital room, the Spirit often would prompt me to proclaim the gospel. This could be done by simply reading a Scripture passage, sometimes accompanied by a word God would give. I'd almost always ask first and then I would pray. I'd pray for Christ's kingdom to come into this place. I'd pray his lordship over this body. One time, I sat through the whole time saying very little, and at the prompt of the Spirit I got up, wrote on the physician's white board chart above the hospital bed, "Jesus is Lord," and then walked out, signing the cross over my brother's bed.

I believe it is my job as a minister visiting the sick to tend to the person and the presence of Christ in our midst. I believe it is important that anything I say or do is a response to what God is doing in Christ, it is never forced or coerced. This is what it means to give witness to what God is doing. This is what it means to be present. Regularly, in hospital rooms, I experience viscerally the presence of Christ, the lordship of Christ in the midst. And so I sometimes ask if I could verbalize it, declare, stand *with* the hospital patient. Almost always, I left the hospital room believing I had experienced God and his kingdom in ways not possible in ordinary, everyday life. I believe many people come to see Jesus as Lord of their lives for the first time in a hospital room. It is a holy meeting place with God.

Like going to the hospital, the church is called to make being with the "least of these" a discipline wherever the poor and hurting may be found. It is a discipline of community that opens up space for the presence of Christ to become visible. In these spaces we enter as people who come alongside. We come to be *with*. We come to discern. We come to be present. We come ready to give witness. We tend to his presence. The discipline of being with the "least of these" is at the core of what it means to be God's faithful presence in the world. And as we will see, it is how God changes the world.

NOT A PROGRAM

In the parable of the rich man and Lazarus (Lk 16:19-31), Jesus describes a scene where the poor man Lazarus, now in heaven by Abraham's side, is looking over the chasm at the rich man who now stands in the flames of Hades. The rich man begs Abraham to have Lazarus, who once ate the leftovers from the rich man's table, to come and relieve his suffering. Please, he says, "send Lazarus to dip the tip of his finger in water and cool my tongue; for I am in agony in these flames" (Lk 16:24). In *From Tablet to Table*, Leonard Sweet notes that at the beginning of the parable the rich man is "dressed in purple and fine linen" and "feasted sumptuously every day" (v. 19).[2] According to Sweet, he is the Bill Gates of his day.[3] He nonetheless allows Lazarus, a homeless person with an advanced case of leprosy ("the dogs would come and lick his sores" [v. 21]), to reside at his highly secured front gate to eat of the leftover food from his table. The leper, a pariah of his day, is allowed to sit comfortably at his front door where undoubtedly the movers and the shakers of society made daily passage. In so doing this extremely rich man was doing more to take care of the poor than most of us are willing to do. Sweet asks, "How many of you have homeless people living on your front porch?"

So what landed the rich man in hell? Sweet takes note that the poor man's name is Lazarus, the namesake of Jesus' best friend, whose home was Jesus' favorite place on earth. For Jesus, therefore, this story is about kinship. Note the detail Jesus gives in the parable concerning the rich man's five brothers. The rich man is urgently concerned for the damnation of his own brothers. But he was not as equally concerned for Lazarus, a man closer than a brother to Jesus. Sweet concludes that the rich man is in hell not because he didn't take care of the poor. He actually did take care of the poor better than most. In Sweet's words, the rich man is in hell because he thought he had five brothers, when God had actually given him six. While he helped Lazarus, he failed to see him as his brother. He failed to embrace him as family. As generous as he was, the rich man failed to invite Lazarus to his own dinner table.

Often we seek to make the poor into a program, someone we distribute resources to. We in essence make space for them at our doorstep. Churches dedicate whole ministries to do justice and mercy as programs for the poor. They organize the ministries so people can volunteer to help. Such ministries alleviate immediate suffering. These programs however, inevitably keep the poor at a distance, at our doorstep. They keep the poor from being a part of our lives. They prevent us from being present with the poor at our tables. In so doing, justice programs (done singularly) undercut God's work for justice in the world. They work against the new socioeconomic order God is creating in his kingdom.

In the parable of the final judgment found in Matthew 25:31-46, the Son of Man, having returned to gather his kingdom, separates the sheep from the goats, those who inherit the kingdom from those who don't. The sheep are welcomed into the kingdom based on the fact that they gave the Son of Man food to eat when he was hungry, a cup of water when he was thirsty, welcomed him when he was a stranger, clothed him when he was naked, and visited him in prison. Those who didn't do these things were sent into the eternal flames (v. 41). The righteous react with "Huh? When did we do that? We have no recall?" To which the King replies, "Truly, I say to you, as you did it to one of the least of these my brothers, you did it to me" (v. 40 ESV).

Jesus seems to be making the point that the righteous ones are unaware they were doing anything special when they were with the hurting.

It appears that being with the poor was part of their everyday life. No big deal. And so, with no pretention, no worldly power or mammon, simply out of their everyday life, these people gave food to the hungry, a cup of water to the thirsty. They were with them. They were doing things they would do naturally for any friend or relative. They were in essence with kin. This is what it means to become present to the poor in our lives.

The "least of these my brothers" (*adelphoi*) historically has been a controversial phrase (see appendix 4). Some have argued that since Jesus often referred to his disciples as "brothers," he must be referring here to his suffering disciples (the particularist interpretation). Jesus intends to say therefore that those in the world who respond favorably to the needs of his sent disciples, the suffering missionaries of the church, will be found righteous (inheritors of the kingdom). On the other hand, more recently, some interpreters see the phrase "least of these my brothers" referring to the poor wherever they are found (the nonrestrictive interpretation). In this interpretation Jesus intends to say that those of his disciples who tend to the poor are the righteous ones. This interpretation is defended based on the argument that Jesus wasn't consoling threatened Christians with this parable. Rather he was motivating "faithful discipleship marked by mercy and love."[4] Furthermore Jesus' use of the phrase *least of these* (Mt 25) is so different from the other places where he refers to his disciples as "brothers" that New Testament scholar Klyne Snodgrass argues something else must be going on here.[5] "The least of these my brothers" must refer to the poor wherever they are found, and Jesus is encouraging his disciples to recognize the kingdom where they become present to them in these ways.

The parable of the rich man and Lazarus helps us see another option for interpreting the significance of the use of *brothers* in verse 40. Jesus is emphasizing the relationship of the kinship God is calling us into with the poor. *Brothers* is about the family relationship (like Mt 12:49-50), being *with* the poor in such a way that we become family (for more on this see appendix 4). Our relationship with the poor is not to be organized as a program at our local church. Instead, in everyday life we are to come alongside, be present to the poor in a relationship of family. In this relational space something truly amazing happens. Jesus becomes especially present (when you did these things to one of the least of these my brothers, you did it to me—I was there [v. 40]). Antagonisms become unwound. Resources are shared back and forth. Healing takes place. Relationships are restored. And a new world is born. This is the discipline of being with the "least of these" that is to characterize our everyday life as Christians, as Christ's church.

There will always be times when the church offers strangers gifts of mercy to contribute to the preservation of souls. Church programs to alleviate pain and suffering, and to preserve the person through suffering, are important and should not be abolished! But the church must not be deluded into thinking these programs will redeem the world. If the church places its hopes and efforts entirely in these programs, it will be exhausted from unfulfilled expectations and the eventual dependency this kind of work cultivates over long periods of time.

More central to the church's life with the poor is the discipline of being *with* the "least of these" as part of everyday life. Through history the church has made its biggest impact when it has practiced being with the poor (whoever they are in our context) and resisted turning the poor into a program. In this way, being with the "least of these" disciplines us into the relational space of faithful presence with the hurting.

A NEW WAY OF DOING ECONOMY

Books like Robert Lupton's *Toxic Charity* help us understand why it is so important to resist making the poor into a church program. We should be careful whenever we distribute resources at a distance, apart from the space of being present. Lupton argues famously that most aid programs create dependency. They do not address the deeply unjust systems that have created the problem. Instead, all too often, they provide a means for the affluent to be distracted from the real work among the poor, assuaging their guilt while accomplishing little.[6]

In terms of money, the larger the amount of money that flows to the poor apart from a relationship, the more likely the givers are supporting systems that caused the injustice in the first place. It's a rule that once a sum of money gets large enough that its benefits cannot be distributed through relational means, it must by default go through the various structures already in place (e.g., food distribution centers, government programs, banks, etc.). These structures are often part of the system that caused the injustice in the first place. Our monetary help thereby often works to further prop up the power of the evil structures, the very same structures that produce and reproduce the cycles of poverty in the first place.

In various places in the New Testament (2 Cor 8:4; Phil 1:5, 7) the apostle Paul talks of sharing financially in one another's burdens as being a fellowship, a deep communion or, in my words, a kinship (*koinōnia*). In Philippians 4:14-15 Paul associates sharing financially in someone's burdens as sharing in their sufferings as well.[7] This all testifies to the ways giving and economy are not offered by Christians to the poor in a detached mode of assistance. They are part of a kinship we already share with one another.

A church in the Toronto suburbs decided to do a care ministry *for* the poor in a very impoverished urban section of the city. They drove several miles each way every Sunday afternoon, bringing food and clothing from their church. They would arrive at the building, set up the clothing to distribute according to need, and warm the food to be served. They would set up tables and arrange the food nicely on the tables. They would read a Scripture and then give thanks and say a blessing over the food. Then they would set up the food line. Those from the suburban church would serve on one side of the table, and the homeless and needy would line up on the other side to receive the food. The suburbanites would try to talk with those who were homeless or struggling. After a few hours, they would clean up and depart in time to get home, relax with their families, and prepare for their own upcoming busy week.

This went on for months until one Sunday afternoon a few people started to evaluate what was happening at this soup kitchen. They asked the recipients of the ministry what they liked about the program. Was the food or clothes enough? What would they change if they could? Surprisingly, the homeless and hurting said things like, "We'd like to bring food too. We have food stamps, we have gift cards, and we'd like to bring food and share it as well. We'd like to help clean up too. We'd like to serve you sometimes."

Stunned and surprised, these people from the suburbs changed the whole approach to their food pantry ministry. They now asked the homeless and poor if they could fellowship with them. The homeless and poor helped set up the tables the way they preferred. Those without homes and poor now served those from the suburbs, and they shared tables together. The ensuing dynamic reshaped everything that went on between the people. Soon, such deep relationships started to develop, that some twenty or so people moved to this deeply distressed neighborhood. A few short years later a church grew up in this place. People's lives on all sides of the tables were changed. Kingdom broke out.[8]

It is only through being present to the other, what I have called kinship, that God changes the world. In this relational space with the marginalized and hurting, God's authority and presence in Jesus Christ becomes real and can be tended to. Here an economy takes shape where each one's life has purpose, meaning, and a role to play. Here economic resources can be shared as family. Goods are shared out of an abundance from God, not as a charitable gift from one who has to the one who has not.

For all these reasons, people of privilege, people of means, people who have never suffered the brutalities of life must submit to the discipline of being with those who have. When we do this, a spaced is opened up that is beyond our own control. We who have never suffered see Jesus at work like we've never seen before. We encounter God in Christ in the flesh. In the process we see our own deficits, the ways we have never depended on God, the ways we have kept in control. A new world is born: the kingdom of God.

THE REAL PRESENCE OF CHRIST AND HIS KINGDOM

Remember once more the parable of the final judgment in Matthew 25. Those persons declared righteous ask the King, "When did we do those things? Give a cup of water to the thirsty? food to the hungry? When did we visit the sick?" The King replies, "Truly, I say to you, as you did it to one of the least of these my brethren, you did it to me" (Mt 25:40 RSV). Jesus tells his disciples in essence that he is present among them when they are with the "least of these." Using similar words elsewhere, Jesus says, "Whoever welcomes one such child in my name welcomes me" (Mt 18:5) and "Whoever listens to you listens to me" (Lk 10:16). Jesus in essence says each time, "I myself am present there." As in these other places Jesus makes it clear: his real presence is sacramentally located in the discipline of being with the poor.

This notion drove the practice of almsgiving in the early church. The patristic writings are filled with teachings on how giving to the poor made Christ mystically present to the almsgiver.[9] Historian Emmanuel Clapsis recites how the early church writers called the poor the "temples of God" because of the belief that Christ's presence was as palpable among the poor, as present as God was in the temple for the Jews.[10] As scholar Gary Anderson puts it, in the early church "the hand of the poor provides a privileged port of entry to the realm and, ultimately, being of God."[11] The early church lived daily with a clear understanding that being with the "least of these" was the opening of space for the direct encounter with the living Christ.

In both Matthew 18:1-5 and Luke 10:16, where Christ's presence is invoked in similar wording to Matthew 25, Jesus refers to the kingdom coming into our midst (Lk 9; 10; 11; Mt 18:4). The parable of Matthew 25 is about the Son of Man discerning who is in the kingdom and who is not (v. 32). In so doing, he is recognizing that when the righteous were doing these things, they were in essence already in the kingdom. The kingdom was breaking in.

And so we should expect the dynamics of Christ's reign to take shape here in this space we inhabit with the poor. As we are present, we become like kin. We share what we have as we would with any friend. Yet we never take on the role of caretaker or superior. Instead a new socioeconomics takes shape among us that is beyond the haves and the have-nots. We pray for healing and anoint as the Spirit moves. We proclaim the gospel. We share struggles and receive prayer. We share our financial resources. But in so doing, resources are not expended but multiplied.

There is a relational reordering of our lives in this new, wonderful, surprising space. The kingdom of God is being made visible. And a whole new world is born. It is the world of faithful presence.

While sitting in McDonald's studying, my friend Wayne came over and sat in my booth. The right side of his jaw was swollen twice the size of the other side. I was no dentist, but I knew one of his teeth was impacted and infection had set in. He was in great pain. I had known Wayne for two years. He'd been without a home this whole time and was living in his van. I looked at him, and in my own human frailty worried how much this extraordinary dental work was going to cost me. Nevertheless, the Holy Spirit pushed, and soon thereafter I wrote the phone number of my dentist on a napkin. I asked him to make an appointment, and if the dentist asked who would pay, Wayne was to have him call me and I would guarantee payment. Secretively, I thought my church would pay. (We had a large mission fund to help defray costs of people in mission.) The next day the dentist called, and I promised to cover all costs. I said I would do it for any friend in need like that. Wayne's teeth were treated and healed. Many weeks passed, and I waited for a bill. But I never got a bill. The dentist decided not to bill Wayne. Two months later, as Wayne and I were talking, Wayne thanked me again for paying for his dental work. I said, "Wayne, I never got a bill." Wayne was shocked. I said, "Wayne, I literally did nothing. God used me to facilitate the kingdom. What you experienced was the kingdom."

British Anglican priest and theologian Sam Wells lived among one of the poorer sections of London. He once wrote these words:

> Poverty is not primarily about money. It is about having no idea what to do and/or having no one with whom to do it. The former I called imagination and the latter I called community. To the extent that our neighborhood had imagination and community, we were not poor. But without imagination and community, no money could help us. . . . The role of the local church is to be a *community of imagination* [for the kingdom].[12]

These words speak to a reality I have witnessed time and again as I have practiced the discipline of being with the "least of these." Being with the poor rarely calls for a huge outlay of one's own bank account. I once tallied a whole year's personal expenses from being among those without homes in my local McDonald's. Excluding cash I paid some of my friends to work on my house (tasks I was not skilled to do), it came to $242.58. It was hardly a huge expense for me and my family. Instead, I discovered that in my coming alongside a hurting person, a space opened up for Christ's presence to work, realign relationships, and make new things happen. It rarely cost me money (but it sometimes did). It rarely cost my church missions fund money (but sometimes it did). Most of the time, if I waited long enough and tended to what God was doing, the kingdom would start to take shape in our lives together. I invited homeless people to my home only after they had become good friends. I shared money with people out of a relationship of kinship. Together we saw miracles happen (greater than the dentist's bill). The gospel would be proclaimed, and often people would confess Christ as Lord, if they hadn't already. Often it was the economically privileged in McDonald's who got saved. Often, I was the one compelled to deal with things in my life I'd never confronted before. And so the in-breaking kingdom appeared in unpredictable ways. This I came to recognize is what happens in the practice of faithful presence.

Being with the "Least of These" in All Three Circles

As with all the prior disciplines, being with the "least of these" is a discipline on the move. A close look at the New Testament reveals just how much this discipline was functioning in all three circles of the early church's life.

The book of Acts, for instance, describes the local church being present to the poor in their own close circles. Acts 4:34-35, for example, reads, "There was not a needy person among them, for as many as owned lands or houses sold them and brought the proceeds of what was sold. They laid it at the apostles' feet, and it was distributed to each as any had need." It is evident from this text how much the first Christians knew each other's needs. They gave as an act of submission and worship ("laid it at the apostles' feet"). We know that the first churches in Acts organized deacons to care for the widows among them. The whole community was pleased with this decision (Acts 6:5). Being *with* the needy started in the close circle of fellowship. Here, being aware and present to the hurting shaped the imagination and drove the way they organized their common way of life.

The apostle Paul, likewise, carried with him the same imagination as he organized the offerings from the Gentile churches to relieve the suffering among the needy of the Jerusalem church. In Galatians 2, Paul recounts how he and Barnabas were commissioned as apostles in their visit to Jerusalem. He then reports that "they asked only one thing, that we remember the poor, which was actually what I was eager to do" (Gal 2:10). According to New Testament scholar Bruce Longenecker, this text reveals a general principle that flowed throughout the churches.[13] This principle was "remembering" or being present to the poor among them, wherever Christians live as a community.[14]

The apostle Paul's own life bore witness to this principle. Bruce Longenecker contends that Paul voluntarily took on tentmaking as an occupation among his new communities in order to make "himself economically more vulnerable." In other words, the apostle practiced being *with* the least of these among his communities by becoming one of them in their economic struggles. He did this, according to Longenecker, out of "a conviction that Israel's sovereign deity was at work in Jesus-groups where the needs of economically vulnerable people were expected to be met as divine grace flowed through the lives of Jesus followers."[15] For Paul, there was a dynamic set loose in becoming present—to one another —with the poor. The opening of this space for the work of Christ set loose the kingdom. It was socioeconomic, not merely individualistic; holistic, not merely spiritual. Living this was essential to the close circle of fellowship, those submitted to Christ as Lord. It was a means of making space for his life-changing, real presence among them.

Being with the "least of these" must begin with the close circle. Here, Jesus is the host. Here, Christians learn to discern Christ's real presence among the poor, first by tending to his presence among the poor who are already part of the body. When, in Galatians, the apostle Paul urges the

Christians to "work for the good of all," but do it "especially for those of the family of faith" (Gal 6:10), he is giving a gentle nod to the priority of the close circle. Here we learn that which enables us to extend Christ's presence into the other circles in the world. Being with the "least of these" must therefore become part of every new believer's discipleship. It must become a way of life. And from here it can be practiced in the neighborhoods, the other two circles of life.

The early church followed the life and example of Jesus in the dotted and half circles of their lives. As Jesus walked the towns and villages of Galilee and Judea, he spent time with people, eating with them at their tables, being present in their neighborhoods, proclaiming the gospel— the coming of the kingdom. His very presence would gather people around him. The hurting and broken could not stop gathering into his presence. Spaces would open up around his presence. The poor and broken would wonder at his authority. Where there was faith, trust, and submission to him, miracles occurred. Where there was no faith, he could do no miracles (Mt 13:58; Mk 6:5). Faith in him was most often found among the sick, the hurting, the outcasts, and those who were despised. There, people were healed, sins forgiven, new life began. This is the way the New Testament church understood the meaning of being with the poor. This is the way they lived in the neighborhoods.

The early church of the first four centuries lived the discipline of being with the "least of these" in all three circles of their lives.[16] So much so that Roman emperor Julian the Apostate (361-363) famously said about the Christians,

> Atheism [Julian's pejorative term for Christianity] has been specially advanced through the loving service rendered to strangers, and through their care for the burial of the dead. It is a scandal that there is not a single Jew who is a beggar and that the godless Galileans care not only for their own poor but for ours as well; while those who belong to us look in vain for the help we should render them.[17]

Christian living among the poor famously undermined Julian's efforts to restore Rome's pagan religions over against Christianity (after Constantine).

Neither violence nor culture wars held him at bay. It was the faithful presence of early Christians among the poor that defeated Emperor Julian.

Recovering Faithful Presence
Among the "Least of These"

Even a casual review of church history reveals how a church, once known for seeing Jesus' healing presence at work among the sick, had moved the discipline of being with the "least of these" to a maintenance function of the church. By the thirteenth century, for instance, the sacrament of anointing the sick, once called unction, had become extreme unction—preparing people for their death. In the words of Catholic historian A. M. Henry, the church had forgotten the sacrament's "power to deliver from bodily ailments."[18]

As with all the other disciplines, once the church becomes comfortable in Christendom, it naturally organizes its functions to take care of Christians. Somewhere after Julian the Apostate, the church took healing from the streets and made anointing with oil an officially sanctioned sacrament available on request. There was now less focus on encountering Christ in the sick, the hurting, and the poor in the streets. The church instead focused on meting out the comforts of forgiveness, absolution, and dying in the peace of Christ to Christians. The encounter with the unpredictable presence of God among the "least of these" was lost. The church had drifted into maintenance mode.

When parts of the Reformation rejected Christ's presence at the mass, they also rejected his presence among the poor. Almsgiving was turned into a civic program in many parts of the Reformation. Much mercy was accomplished. Unfortunately, the loss of Christ's real presence *with* the poor profoundly changed the discipline of being with the "least of these." It turned it into a maintenance program.[19]

Today, most churches do similar things. We turn being with the poor into a justice program that Christians can volunteer for by signing up for a few hours a month. We build large justice centers on our church campuses and require the poor to come to us. We separate ourselves from being with the least of these. And the mission of God is thwarted.

In worship, Christians sit next to Christians in large sanctuaries, never knowing that someone next to them is struggling with poverty. Our financial and personal struggles remain hidden because we are too ashamed to talk about them in a church where everyone shows only their Sunday best. We know how to engage the poor only through a justice program. If we find ourselves poor, we are therefore shamed. So we ignore the poor among us and rush to start justice programs with the poor in our neighborhoods. But we do not practice being with the poor. As a result we miss the direct encounter with the living Christ in our midst and in our neighborhoods. In the process we risk our own damnation, not even knowing it (Mt 25:41).

We must therefore lead in a different way. We must lead our churches to a new experience of Christ's presence among the poor and the most vulnerable. We start with a posture of *withness*, in the close circle. We "rejoice with those who rejoice, weep with those who weep" (Rom 12:15). We learn how to be present with those who hurt. We gather as kin. Once we have learned to do this, we are better trained as a people to be present to the poor in the other circles of our lives. We then ask every Christian to spend regular time in hospitals, prisons, half-way houses, and homeless shelters to be present to the already faithful presence of Christ. Here, the fields are ripe for harvest, ready for outbreaks of healing miracles among the poor, sick, and hurting. We need witnesses, but the workers are few (Lk 10:2). This is the way God changes the world.

If we learn all this, then we have already learned some of the basics of the fifth discipline, being with children, to which now we turn.

7

The Discipline of Being
with Children

Let the little children come to me; do not stop them.

MARK 13:13-14 (MY PARAPHRASE)

In spring 2015, parents in a Washington, DC, suburb viewed children wandering alone in the local parks. These adults were not happy. Where were the children's parents? they asked. Didn't they know these children were in danger? They reported these children to the police.[1] On another day, some of these onlookers captured the young children on video walking home from school hand in hand, but again left unattended by adults. The onlookers reported them to the police. How dare their parents disregard the dangers of children walking home from school alone? A few days later, the *Today Show* did a story on police picking up children unattended in the neighborhood and giving them over to Child Protective Services until the parents could prove they were indeed responsible. The show called this phenomenon "free-range parenting." The parents protested the accusation. They had carefully thought through the dangers and decided to give their children some independence in going to the park and returning home from school.[2] They narrated how a practice that was common everyday life in the United States fifty years ago was now viewed as irresponsible parenting. Nonetheless, in order to get their children back, these parents had to prove to the authorities they knew the world was dangerous for their children. They had to show they were capable parents in a dangerous world.

The world has become a dangerous place for children. So we obsess about everything that could go wrong with our children. We obsess over their education and their ability to compete in the world marketplace for a job. We obsess about protecting them from the horrors of abuse, whether that abuse be sexual, physical, or emotional. We build sophisticated systems of surveillance for child abusers. We spend more per capita educationally in the United States than anyplace in the world. We fund more sports, art, music, and tutoring programs for children than any other society in the world. And yet actual parental time spent with our children might be at an all-time low.

To pay for the best sports programs, schools, household comforts, and surveillance systems, the average family must have two incomes. There are now more two-income households in America than at any time in history.[3] As a result, children are being shuffled from one thing to the next at breakneck speed. They are being told to do this or do that and vice versa. Families struggle to eat dinner together. Sixty years ago the average dinnertime was ninety minutes; today it is less than twelve minutes.[4] High divorce rates exacerbate this reality. The harder we work, the less space there seems for parent and child to be present with each other.

CHILDREN YEARN FOR PRESENCE

Every Saturday morning my ten-year-old son and I sit across from one another in a local greasy spoon eating breakfast. I direct my attention to his face. He struggles to sit still. He can barely stand it. He wants to reach around and watch the television hanging on the wall in the restaurant. So I diligently choose the one spot in the restaurant that blocks all such views of the television. Then he wants to play a video game on my phone or read a Calvin and Hobbes comic book. I quietly say no thanks and ask him for three topics. It's all part of the Saturday-morning ritual we've been doing for years. Nonetheless, he still grimaces and lets go an exasperating "Oh, Dad." He chooses two topics. I choose one. He says, "Dogs, airplanes," and I say, "School, let's talk about the highlights and lowlights of school this week." "Oh, Dad." And slowly, by making sure I never raise my voice, we begin the exchange. So much more important than anything I say, or he says, is my posture at the table. I sit peacefully. I cast my eyes on him and give him the entire focus of my face. I am intentionally trusting that Jesus will be present in this space that we inhabit together, and I am tending to what God by his Spirit is doing among us. Nothing affects my child more than when I take time to sit with him across a table and tend to Christ's presence. It is the epitome of faithful presence on a busy Saturday morning.

Our children are the casualties of a crazy, confusing, frenzied society. They are cast adrift from the moorings of their relationships at home, church, and in the neighborhood. The world can't be trusted, they are told. We therefore need certified programs for everything. Sports, music, tutoring, dancing, the arts, boy scouts, girls scouts, and gaming must all be programmed, and leaders must be screened for past crimes and sexual history. As the children shuffle from one scrubbed program to another, their souls are pushed and pulled, looking for the right path to direct their passions. They are waiting to be drawn in to a place worthy of their trust. They are longing to know and be known. The world is obsessed with its children. Meanwhile the children want presence. They yearn for face-to-face presence.

Being with Children

Historically, the practice of guiding children has always been a central fact of the life in the church. Even today, when new congregations form in North America, one of the first tasks the leaders pay heed to is teaching and guiding children, which is often called "children's ministries" in contemporary Protestant churches.

For much of Christendom, infants were baptized as early as possible, with parents and godparents the communal guarantors of the child's upbringing in Christ. Then, at the age of accountability, the child would go through a catechesis process and be confirmed by the laying on of hands and anointing with oil, signifying the giving of the Holy Spirit. Many times the child's first Communion would happen subsequent to confirmation.

Through its history the timing and necessity of confirmation has been controversial in the church. Early on, many saw no need for a separate confirmation of the Spirit after baptism. Receiving the Spirit was already complete within baptism itself. During the later patristic age, however, the practice of baptism and receiving the Holy Spirit were separated in the West.[5] Over the years, confirmation became the rite of passage into maturity. The appropriate age for confirmation has differed through the centuries and between various cultures. Between baptism and confirmation was the catechetical instruction of the church, which would lead the initiate into mature faith and life in Christ Jesus. During Christendom the infant was baptized with the understanding that the family spoke the vows of commitment for the baby, who could not yet speak. The family, godparents, and the church together committed to raising the child in Christ. This whole process of initiation was always a communal process. Confirmation signified a completion of that process into maturity.

Whatever one thinks of the various controversies surrounding infant baptism and confirmation, the church has usually considered these ways of being with children, together with the child's first Communion, as sacramental. As the church guided its children, this was special work of God by the Spirit whereby Jesus became present.

To this day the discipline of tending to children defines a people as coming together to be a church. Whether it is a flannelgraph, the Action Bible, or wooden figures, churches pass on the story of God in Jesus Christ to our children. In addition, all churches have ways of infant baptism or dedication (in the free church tradition), ways of confirmation or initiation into adult baptism (in the free church tradition). We have ways of grafting parents, godparents, and communities into supportive communal practices that, together as part of regular family life, allow us to pray, teach, read, and direct the young child's life. We have ways of initiating children into adulthood. All of these practices are inseparable from what it means to be the church. What we often miss, however, is the reality that Jesus becomes present in these spaces. As the adult becomes present to the child, the space between them becomes the place of faithful presence.

THE KINGDOM VALUE OF WELCOMING CHILDREN

Matthew 18 opens with the disciples jockeying for position again. The disciples are back at it, asking Jesus who among them will get the best post with the most power in the kingdom to come? It offers the occasion for Jesus to talk one more time to the disciples about power, the kingdom of God, and his presence. Jesus points to a child and says this is the way the kingdom will work. Unless you change and become like this child, you won't make it into the kingdom. The children, those with no status in this ancient world, will be the ones who have status in the kingdom.[6]

Then he says the all-important words: "Whoever welcomes one such child in my name welcomes me" (Mt 18:5). He uses the important word *welcome* (*dechomai*), which is used elsewhere for the way strangers receive missionaries sent by Jesus into their homes in his name (Mt 10:40). It is used to describe the patience one must have to hear Paul in the midst of his foolishness (2 Cor 11:16). It is used to describe the posture of receiving generosity and love (Phil 4:18). It connotes patience, embrace, openness, and genuineness. It communicates the posture of receiving someone into my very presence. Jesus says, when you do this with a child, you enter the very kingdom of God (Mt 18:3). When you receive a child into your presence, you also receive the presence of Jesus. A space is opened up where God can work. It is a space where God in Christ not only transforms children's lives but the adults in the space as well.

Very early on in the beginning of the Life on the Vine Christian Community, we decided to resist making children's ministries into a program. We wanted to lead the community into being *with* our children. From the very beginning, when we were but a small Bible study, we asked every member, young, old, single, and married, to spend time with the children during a Bible story time. At various times we would say that by being with the children, you were being prepared to experience the kingdom. If you refused, you might be refusing the kingdom itself.

When our congregation grew, we decided to have our children with us for as much as possible in the main worship gathering. They were with us for the stories of wonder, a time of telling what God had been doing in our lives during the week. This opened the beginning of our gathering.

As we bowed in silence, sometimes for as long as ten minutes, they would be with us. The children found silence strangely interesting. They were with us for the invocation, the call to worship, and the reading of Scripture, and then, right before the sermon, we dismissed them for their own time of hearing the story told and the Word proclaimed over their lives. We asked the appropriate age groups to head toward the doors, and as they did we raised our hands toward them and blessed them, saying, "The Lord be with you as you worship." The children responded, "and also with you." They returned after the sermon to gather with us again and be blessed around the table, sing praises to God, and receive the benediction.

This time, between the reading of Scripture and the table, when the children left for their own story telling time, was a special time with the children. We adopted storytelling methods based on the curriculum called "Godly Play."[7] We emphasized adults getting on the level of the child, inviting God's presence by the Spirit to be with us, then telling the story slowly, allowing space for wondering and questions, and above all being present to God. Adults spent time being with the children as they explored. This space between the adult and the child became sacred.

We asked everyone in the church to participate in this ministry with children. There were regular teachers rotating in and out, but everyone was asked to participate. All adults were asked to be in the children's ministry a minimum of once every eight weeks. They were asked to be present with our children, to know them, to be changed by them. This resulted in a community where our children could grow up recognizing Jesus not purely as a historical person and a doctrine, but as someone present to us in our daily lives. We recognized, in this screen-crazy society, the space for his presence would never be more available with our children than during these early years.

It was difficult to convey to our church community that Jesus was actually present in this space with our children. One time a member of our church community who contributed in so many ways to the life of the church approached me and said that he wished to be excused from children's ministry. We had asked everyone in the church, beginning with the leaders, to take seriously the duty to be with our children. We asked everyone to sign up for no less than one Sunday every two months to be present with the children. Doug said to me that "working with children is not my gift." This was not an uncommon response in our church when people were asked to serve with children. People could not grasp the sacramental reality that being with children is an encounter with the living Christ. I said to Doug, "Being with children in our teaching ministry is not a spiritual gift. It is never mentioned in the Scripture as a spiritual gift. Instead, the church brings all its gifts to the space of ministry with children. And all who can lower themselves to be present with a child will experience Jesus and his kingdom like nowhere else." Several years later, Doug looked back at his experience at Life on the Vine and said he experienced the renewal in his life with Christ first and foremost in his blossoming relationship with children.

At one point we had 70 percent of adults, in a church of two hundred, participating in our children's ministry. There was a sense of community with and around children like few had experienced. It was a foretaste of God's kingdom.

THE PRESENCE OF CHRIST WITH CHILDREN

Paul exhorts children to "obey your parents in the Lord, for this is right. 'Honor your father and mother'" (Eph 6:1-2). Then, immediately following, he exhorts fathers not to provoke children to anger but serve them by bringing them up in "the discipline and instruction of the Lord" (v. 4). Scholars have shown how revolutionary these words were in their first-century context. In a day when children were viewed as inferior and patriarchs ruled with an iron fist, Paul, contrary to the prevailing culture, calls parent and child into a space of mutuality in the Lord. The parent is not singularly over the child. The child is considered too. Parent and child come together under the one Lord in a mutuality between them that honors their respective roles. This text falls under the opening text of the Household Codes (Eph 5:20–6:9), where Paul says, "Submit to one another out of reverence for Christ" (Eph 5:21 NIV). And so the apostle is describing a revolutionary relationship of presence between adult and child under the Lord's reign.[8]

This speaks once again to the way the disciplines make space for his presence as each person submits to Jesus as Lord. Children are asked to obey their parents *in the Lord*, and the parents are asked to serve their children *in the Lord*. Parents play their role yet release control. Jesus is the one who works in this relationship.

Jesus concludes the Matthew 18:1-5 episode with the surprising words, "Whoever welcomes one such child in my name welcomes me." We immediately recognize in Jesus' words some of the same verbal patterns of the other disciplines. His words, "He who welcomes this child in my name welcomes me" are similar to the pattern, "He who listens to you, listens to me" of Luke 10:16. Except here there can be no mistaking this to refer to the emissary who speaks in the place and name of Jesus. There is no expectation that the child will speak in Jesus' name. Rather the focus here is unmistakably on the presence of Jesus being there and his authority coming and working in the space of being with children.

Just as it is in the discipline of reconciliation, "in my name" is used here as well. As with reconciliation, "in my name" marks off the space that gathers people into Jesus' presence under his authority as Lord and King. In this space the dynamic of Ephesians 6:1-2 is rehearsed. And so Jesus promises to be especially present here with children just as he does in reconciliation (Mt 18:20).

The stunning reality is that being with children is an encounter with the living Christ. Just as with our gathering around the table, so likewise here we gather around children. We set aside our striving and we quiet our need to control. We enter their space and tend to their presence. In their vulnerabilities, my own vulnerabilities are exposed. In so doing, a space is opened up, and Jesus becomes present and begins to work. As a result, the space for direction and care is opened up for his kingdom.

It is not surprising then that the church has viewed the process of initiating children as sacramental. But what we see now, in light of Matthew 18:1-5, is that being with children is more than the concrete physical act of baptism or the laying on of hands and anointing with oil at confirmation. Being *with* children is the entire process whereby we become present to children and together present to Christ as part of everyday life. The sacrament of being with children is a social sacrament that brings together the community in its *withness* with the child. This is what we have lost in Christendom. This is what we must recover for the mission of God in the world.

In the beginnings of Life on the Vine, a few married couples came to the leadership and said, "We're with our children six days a week. We're exhausted. When we come to church gatherings on Sundays we need some 'Jesus and me' time." It was clear that elements of (what I have called) exhaustion mode were at work here. We tried to open their imaginations for something more. We shared how God is at work in this space. That perhaps they could learn a new relationship with their children based not on control but in being with Jesus with them. Perhaps this could change the entire rest of the week they spend with their children. Perhaps various sports and arts programs during the week might become less important. This was the inertia we had to overcome in fostering a community that would be present to their children.

Years later, after leading our community in this way, we discovered that some adults (and teens) went to the children's ministry classrooms even when it was not their week to be with the children. They had experienced the real presence of Christ there and wanted to return. As one adult said to me, I go there "not because of what I teach them, but because of what they teach me." The experience of being with children was rich with discovery, love, and being deep in the presence of Christ.

One time a six-year-old child voiced his disbelief: "I don't believe in God anymore." The adult stayed present, asking, "Can you tell me more about that?" The child was able to voice how we cannot see God, especially when everyday things don't always go well. Together they explored how God is seen in these episodes. In simple but powerful ways, Christ was revealed. Typically the children's questions in these spaces were simple yet serious and would challenge adults. Often the answers to their questions would not come from the adults but from the children.

Because children are not yet jaded, they can often more easily be open to Christ's presence. So at Life on the Vine we discovered that children sometimes led the adults into tending to Christ's presence. Thus, learning went way beyond the rote memorizing of doctrine or Scripture, beyond the cognitive lessons or even storytelling. Together children and adults learned to tend to Christ's presence in their lives.

WHERE THE KINGDOM TAKES PLACE

As the Matthew 18 episode begins the disciples wonder who among them will get the positions of authority in the new kingdom. How will life be ordered in the kingdom, and who will have power over others? Jesus, just as he did around the table in Luke 22, must reorient their understanding of how the kingdom of God works. This time he orients them around a child.

He calls a child and "placed the child among them" (Mt 18:2 NIV). The text emphasizes the space Jesus opens up among them around the child. He then says that unless you change and become like this child, "you will never enter the kingdom of heaven" (v. 3). This is the space of the kingdom. The one who becomes humble like this child enters the authority of the kingdom (v. 4).

There is more going on here than Jesus merely using the child's humble posture as a metaphor for what is necessary to enter the kingdom (although it is that). Jesus is saying that in entering the space of the child, his presence is here, and to the extent one can submit to his presence, as this child did, a reorientation of the world will begin. Here, in this space of the child, the kingdom will take shape.

Presence is the dominant theme of God's relationship to Israel and precedes the emergence of the monarchy in Israel (see chap. 1). Where the presence of the Lord is, there is always a reordering of life: forgiveness, reconciliation, peace and renewal. This is his kingdom. It makes sense then that Jesus responds to the disciples' jockeying for authority by pointing to the child and saying this is the way his authority and power will come into the world. Jesus will govern the world through his presence. There will be guidance and order in this space. Here is where children will be trained into the kingdom.

Most parents know instinctively that when the adult becomes truly present to the child, guidance and direction can happen. It is important then that the exhortation for children to "obey your parents" (Eph 6:1) and the challenge to do this because "this is your acceptable duty" (Col 3:20) include the qualifying phrase, "in the Lord." This correlates to "in my name" in Matthew 18:5. It is a phrase that does more than simply provide legitimation for parental guidance. It qualifies the obedience that is taking place between parent and child as happening within the larger framework of one's relationship to Christ.[9] In essence, this text speaks to the way that being with children opens space both for the love and the authority of his lordship to be fully recognized by children. And here heaven and earth can move. Children will be oriented to the kingdom.

The stakes are high. Jesus follows his exhortation in Matthew 18:5 with the statement, "If any of you put a stumbling block before one of these little ones who believe in me, it would be better for you if a great millstone were fastened around your neck and you were drowned in the depth of the sea. Woe to the world because of stumbling blocks!" (vv. 6-7). This dramatic statement is reminiscent of the judgment announced by Jesus in Luke 10:13 after the proclaimers of the kingdom returned from their missionary journeys. It has the same tone as Paul's warning of the seriousness that attends the Lord's Table (i.e., people get sick and die because they do not discern his presence [1 Cor 11:30]). This same sense of seriousness attends being with "the least of these," where God is ordering the world, separating the righteous from the unrighteous (Mt 25:33-34). This statement reminds us that in his presence heaven and earth are moved, just as they are in the practice of reconciliation (Mt 18:18-19). The only other place Jesus shows anger beside the clearing of the temple is when the disciples speak sternly to the children, keeping them from Jesus (Mk 10:14). Critical things are at stake in the spaces we open to be present with our children. And we must tend to these spaces and discern them carefully.

Therefore it's important to tend not only to the child's presence but to Christ in the midst of this sacred space. Both being present to children and tending to Christ's presence becomes real in this space between us and children. In all the practices, we have become used to this pattern of faithful presence.

Parents therefore must invite children to tend to the presence of Christ as we worship, as we share the table. First be with them, and then guide their (and your) sight to the presence of Christ among us. In this space God will do great things.

I have now been sitting in worship with my ten-year-old son for years. It has always been a twofold struggle to tend to him first and then, together with him, to the presence of Christ. Like many parents I have often been tempted to allow my son to become the center of my attention, especially during his younger years. During worship I discovered the more I centered my attention on him, the more others' attention would be drawn to him. So I encouraged him: "Can you give your attention to God? Can you give thanks to God with your singing? Can you use your music to give God praise for all he's done for us? Can you sense God's presence in the room this morning?" At night before bed, after reading either the Bible or another story, before we'd pray, I'd ask, "Can you sense God's presence here in the room with us?" Around the dinner table together we would pray for sensitivity to God's presence among us. I learned to both model my own tending as well as direct his tending to the presence of God in Christ. This kind of direction can only happen after I myself have established being present to my son.

We must constantly balance between being present to our children and directing their gaze and ours jointly to the presence of Christ. Loving our children in this way is so important. By together tending to Jesus in the space between us, we avoid idolizing our children. There are times when admiring our children affirms them and gives them rightful confidence. But we must resist centering our lives around our children and instead center our lives together with them in Christ's presence. When we worship, eat, or pray, or when we are with the poor, we have occasions to guide their attention and senses to Christ's presence. Being with our children offers the space to discipline our children into the ways of the kingdom. We do not stop the kingdom while we wait for our children to grow up. We bring them with us on this journey to follow Christ as Lord. In the process our children are saved from narcissism and lack of direction. This discipline opens the path for our children to know the presence of God and be ordered by his purposes. This is what faithful presence does.

BEING WITH CHILDREN IN ALL THREE CIRCLES

Most churches think of children's ministry as a church program, particularly on Sunday mornings. Children's ministry happens during church services or the church's boys or girls clubs on a weeknight, or Vacation Bible Schools during the summer. With few exceptions, children's ministry takes place in and around the church building. The discipline of being with children, however, moves children's ministries into our everyday lives. It disciplines us to be with children in all three circles as an entire way of life.

Being with children most often begins in the close circles of life because it takes Christians to practice it. We discern Christ's presence with children just as we do around the Lord's Table. In the circle of Christians we have the confidence to believe that Christ's presence will come to be with us and our children. As Christians, we can navigate the tension between being present to our children and guiding our attention jointly to his presence. If we can do this in the close circle, we will be able to do the same in the other equally important circles of life.

We often lose this discipline of being with our children in a growing church. We find ourselves expanding children's ministries too quickly into programs in order to keep up with the demands of all the new people visiting our church. Ironically, as I have planted churches, I've had many acquaintances say to me, "Dave, we would so love to be part of your new church plant. We love the closeness, the friendship, the community, and the encounter with Christ we experience as we gather. But we need programs for our children, which you don't have. We feel as if we have such a short time with our children, so it is important for us to have the right programs for them."

I would give these parents books like Mark Yaconelli's *Contemplative Youth Ministry: Practicing the Presence of Jesus* or *Hold on to Your Kids: Why Parents Need to Matter More Than Peers* by Gordon Neufeld and Gabor Mate, a book about the psychology of adults being present with their children versus the damage done by peer-group attachment.[10] Nonetheless, whatever I tried, I would be rejected. I was amazed they did not see the value of small communities where the close circle of adults could practice being with children. They did not truly understand how Jesus comes to be present in the guidance of their children. Instead they chose entertaining children's ministries and large youth groups with glitzy programs.

We must lead well the discipline of being with children in the close circle. Ironically, I have met some of these same parents years later who were struggling, as so many parents do, with their (now) teenagers walking away from the faith when they go to college.[11]

Of course, being with children must move beyond the close circles of life. It must become part of our everyday lives. The place of presence between adult and child must become the trusted place our children know they can go anytime they have questions during the week, struggling with beliefs, doubts, and confusions of our day. Here they can find guidance via the trust built up in the real presence of Christ. Here they can safely go to be heard. Here they can seriously discern the goodness of God and come to know Christ's presence and rule over all evil. Here, every day, they will grow into their identities in Christ. As we practice this discipline together in our families, our neighborhood house gatherings, or wherever we hang out with children, neighbors can look on and see the kingdom. The dotted circles of our lives provide the theater for our neighbors and friends to understand the way the kingdom works through our children.

This then also means that being with children must move into all the half circles of our lives as well. Far from children being a hindrance to mission in our neighborhoods, being with children is actually an important way we discern and give witness to God's kingdom coming in the world.

I have often heard parents of little children say they are too busy for mission. When our child, Max, came into our lives, I remember my wife and I going through adjustments. Rae Ann (my wife) was used to going to work every day, being with people, being out with friends. Now she was a stay-at-home mom. Out of her need, she reached out. She started getting together with other moms who were going through similar adjustments. Out of mutual need, my wife was meeting more people outside the faith than I ever could have. Moms groups were popping up all over the place. She got to know many women struggling with raising children and with marriage itself. To this day, Max has been one of the best means ever to connect us to hurting people. When I and other dads were invited to the get-togethers, we would sit together stunned at the community these women shared. As my wife and I tended to Max, we would tend to other children. Connections were made. We met people of all faiths, and atheists as well. Max opened up a world where witness to the kingdom could happen naturally and unimposed.

I have seen parents entering worlds where people are paranoid of other adults being with their children. We as Christians must therefore come into these spaces on invitation only. This may take shape as we are invited to other people's homes for play dates, for moms (or parents) groups, or neighborhood birthday parties. We may volunteer for cafeteria duty at the local elementary school. We may become tutors at the local schools. As we enter, we come to be with children. We reject the competitive practices of today's parenting. We resist the idolatry of children. We are present to children as we tend to the presence of Jesus working among them. Children are transformed by love and presence. As strangers take notice, spaces are opened for healing the abuses and pains of families. Here, in these half circles of our lives, being with children becomes another mode of the church's faithful presence in the world.

The world's children are a field of God's mission. Amid all the pressures to achieve certain test results, schools have become more behaviorally oriented (some theorists have argued). Under these pressures, many teachers lose the wherewithal to be present to the children. As a result, many of our public schools are devoid of presence. Christians who practice being with children fill this gap. Through volunteer programs, tutoring, recess monitoring, and of course teaching, the public schools can be half circles for our lives. We can be witnesses to the real presence of Christ in the public schools. Without breaking any of the state's rules against religious proselytization, we witness to the reconciliation, the gospel, and the renewal of all things in Christ. This is faithful presence.

Over the years I have heard of churches renewed singularly by a group of twelve to fifteen people being present to children. Amazing neighborhood ministries spring up organically in neighborhoods around stay-at-home dads. Whether it be grandparents committing to be present to their grandchildren and friends, or a group of moms present to the needs of a local elementary school, by tending to their own children they meet other children. Slowly they are invited into other parents' lives through their kids. As they become present to the neighborhood's children they become magnets. Parents notice their children behaving differently for the better. Soon whole neighborhoods of children come to their backyards. Presence and ministry become possible with the parents in ways these churches never could have organized through a program.

This kind of presence with children should lead Christians to be the leaders in adopting and foster-parenting children into our families. As adoption becomes more difficult, more costly, and more regulated by misconceived motivations and agendas, Christians can establish homes for adoption that give witness to another way. We can come alongside pregnant women who have no family support and care for them, their new babies, and their future. We can help women see that their children are loved by God and that he has a plan for them far beyond what they can think or imagine. The many crisis pregnancy centers and adoption agencies cared for already by Christians bears witness to the presence of Christ with children. These are some of the half circles of our lives where God is calling us to be present to children.

This testifies to the fact that being with children makes possible the presence of Jesus in the world. The world's children starve for his presence. When they see it, they do not yet know it is Christ at work. But through the world's children God is drawing the whole world to himself. This is the way of faithful presence and mission.

RECOVERING FAITHFUL PRESENCE AMONG CHILDREN

In its first three hundred years the early church was renowned for being with children in the streets. Across the Greco-Roman world, Christians took children off the streets where they had been left to die (a practice called infanticide). They adopted children into their homes and cared for them. The early church's convictions about children led to their singular stand against the common practices of infanticide and abortion in their day.[12] This stunning witness of the early church can be directly tied to its practices of being with children in and among the neighborhoods.

And yet the church has regularly defaulted to maintenance mode when it came to caring for children. With the official sponsoring of Christianity by Rome via Constantine, there were now crushing numbers of infant baptisms coming into the church.[13] The bishops could not get to all the baptisms, so confirmations now (following the baptisms) had to be delayed. Slowly confirmation became a regimented process enforced over the Roman church.[14] We can see in this history the struggle of the church to maintain the presence of Jesus in the discipline of being with children. We can see the tendency to take the discipline of being with children out of the neighborhoods and put it under the sanctioning presence of a professional. Our churches must work hard to resist taking the practice of being with children out of everyday life.

When Max was young, and our family budget was meager for babysitting, Rae Ann and I would drive to the megachurch in our area on a Saturday night. There was a large children's ministry there. We would go into the large foyer of the ministry, sign Max up, get a printed bar code with adhesive, which would be stuck to his back. We'd get a number for him that would be displayed on one of the large video screens if Max needed us. We would then take him to the entry into the Children's Wonderland, where he would be mesmerized by a stunning array of play areas akin to a local mall. Children could use a slide to descend into this play area. Once on the slide, within thirty seconds, Max would be so distracted by everything that he would forget we even existed. Rae Ann and I could go off to the large cafeteria and have a snack and spend some quality time together, confident that if there were any problems we would see his number on one of the screens.

It's important to note the role that distraction played in this children's ministry. I'm not merely talking about the distraction of the slide but indeed all the toys and play areas that Max was initiated into that night. We can all understand the value of such distraction. But much of a child's life in our current culture can be taken up with distraction, and if children's ministry becomes all about entertainment, moving objects, and distraction from the absence of parents or adults, it is in effect moving our children away from presence. This becomes dangerous if we elevate it as an important time for our children's education. Children's ministry becomes dangerously close to being a stumbling block keeping our children from the kingdom.

We must therefore lead in a different way. We must resist defaulting to maintenance modes of church where we seek to keep busy Christian parents happy and coming back to church. We must work hard against extracting children out of worship and out of our lives in order to control their behavior. We must make space for adults to be with children and for them to be with us in worship. Then from here, once the presence of Christ is truly experienced and we've learned how to tend to his presence among our children, we can enter the other circles of our lives with our children. We can be faithfully present to Christ's presence among the children of the world.

8

The Discipline of the Fivefold Gifting

When you come together to share his gifts . . .

1 CORINTHIANS 14:26 (MY PARAPHRASE)

In the early days of Life on the Vine Christian Community, I remember sitting among a group of seven or eight men in a men's group on a Wednesday night. It was maybe our fourth meeting. We were forming a men's group to "work out our salvation in fear and trembling" with one another. We later transformed these groups into triads because we learned that the work of listening to each other, confessing sin, speaking truth in love, and praying was better done in threes. I was the "lead pastor" of this church plant (as the denomination liked to refer to me). I had already invited a few of the men in that group into pastoral leadership. Others were there simply because they wanted to have a place to sort out their lives in Christ. The fact that the group was all men is due to the fact we felt safer talking about all of our issues, including sexual ones, with men.

That night, as we went around the group introducing ourselves to each other and why we were there, I put a question to them: Is there anything about myself, any issue of sin or character that they had recognized in me, that they really wanted to tell me but were too afraid to do so? I asked them to trust me enough to just go ahead and tell me.

A guy named Mark, a struggling alcoholic in recovery, looked at me and said, "Whoa, are you out of your mind? Are you serious? Who would do such a thing to themselves? I mean, you're the leader of this church. Aren't you?" I replied by asking, "What's worse? You thinking it and not telling me, and me living in delusion? Or you telling me, and me having sufficient trust in Jesus as Lord that I can handle it and grow with it?" I talked about how I wanted my life to practice submission to their lives as the basis of how we will live together and gather a community. That night one of the guys revealed a resentment that was building toward me. He pointed out the ways I had been manipulative. I thanked him for having the courage to tell me. He said he was grateful for such a space to tell me. We proceeded to process what was going on with me for the next hour. I confessed some sin in my life and asked forgiveness. And I thanked everybody for telling me what was hard for them to tell me. I grew from that. And we grew together.

I learned the posture of submitting myself to others in the men's group from some earlier experiences in men's groups. I will always be grateful to the men who taught me those things. Because of that history, I experienced something that night that was freeing and transformative in Christ. I felt vulnerable yet real, free from defensiveness and yet free to fail and be told about it. I also noticed how people treated me with more care and trust after that. That moment shaped me and the leadership of our church for years to come. It was a highlight of my walk in leadership in the entire founding of Life on the Vine.

I can't say I have always done that well in welcoming other's criticism into my life. But those kinds of experiences still drive how I think about leadership. I have learned that it is essential to lead out of the posture of submitting myself to others in a community where Jesus is Lord. It is a posture both of vulnerability and of confidence in what God is doing in my life and where he has led me, and that he is also at work in this community I am sitting in as well. This posture opens the space for Jesus to work. Participation in the Spirit with one another makes faithful presence possible, which shapes a community. It is the opposite of coercive leadership.

THE WORLD ACHES FOR MUTUALITY

Nobody loves a bully. This is true even in American business. Yet we don't know how else to lead except by dictate. As a community of people, we want accountability, we need authority, and yet we desire mutuality. But we don't know how that is possible.

Most North Americans have experienced managerial coercion at one time or another. It could be a boss threatening our paycheck if we don't do something, an expert consultant evaluating our work in a heavy-handed manner, or a police officer stopping us and issuing a ticket for a debatable infraction. It could be something much worse: racial profiling, violent threats, vicious accusations. To some degree, these are common to everyday life. The world runs on coercion. Despite our best intentions, as courteous as everyone tries to be, when all else fails we default to negotiation by position. The threats are subtle. The use of influence and position is indirect. You over me, me over you; you against me, me against you.

Churches in North America, it appears, have taken on these bad habits. In Seattle, Minneapolis, and other places, several high visibility pastors of major evangelical churches or denominations have been forced to resign or take a leave of absence of their own volition. These did not occur because of a sexual failure or financial impropriety, but because of abusive behavior toward people working with them. One leader stepped down because of "various expressions of pride, unentreatability, deceit, sinful judgment and hypocrisy."[1] Another leader stepped down when a former highly respected elder stated publicly, "This is without a doubt, the most abusive, coercive ministry culture I've ever been involved with."[2] In the years 2014 and 2015, Internet conversations arose concerning the prevalence of narcissistic personality disorder among senior pastors of large churches. Christians are increasingly wary of pastors' abusive leadership practices when they appear to be imposing their will on a congregation.

Nonetheless, hierarchy still dominates Christian thinking about leadership. Despite the new popularity of participant management styles in the business world, despite the rise of agile software development bringing people together to develop collaborative work environments, most Protestant churches are still led by a senior pastor or lead pastor at the top of the organizational chain. So, whenever I speak in church settings about multiple leadership, about having no senior pastor, about being led by several leaders operating together as a group, people push back: "How will anything ever get done this way? We need a leader at the top, where the buck stops." Like the nation of Israel in 1 Samuel 8:6, we shout our pleas to God: "Give us a king!" We need someone at the top who we can all look to and understand where this place is going.

No group of people can exist for long without authority functioning well in leadership. And so the world tentatively accepts, and the church defaults to, hierarchical systems. We work and organize beneath the heavy hand that governs us. But we are tired of the abuse. We want something more. The world may operate on coercion, but it aches for mutuality.

The Discipline of the Fivefold Gifting

As Jesus and the disciples headed into Jerusalem on Jesus' last fateful trip, the disciples started clamoring (again) for their place at the top of the pecking order in the coming new kingdom. As Jesus talked about the coming suffering he would face, James and John asked to sit at Jesus' right and left side in the kingdom. They were saying, "Put us in the best position to be over the people." Upon hearing this, the rest of the disciples were indignant. Jesus calmed them down and replied,

> You know that among the Gentiles those whom they recognize as their rulers lord it over them, and their great ones are tyrants over them. But it is not so among you; but whoever wishes to become great among you must be your servant, and whoever wishes to be first among you must be slave of all. (Mk 10:42-44)

For Jesus, authority in the kingdom would be exercised in no other way. There would be no hierarchy, no coercive power, no one person ruling over and above another person. His model, as we will discover, is mutual, shared leadership under one Lord.

But how can this be? How would this actually work in the community of the new kingdom? How could a people of God function without hierarchy? How can we be led into the challenges of being a Christian community without someone at the top? The answer is the discipline of the fivefold ministry. The answer is recognizing those among us who are gifted by the Holy Spirit to lead in their respective giftings and enabling them to exercise those gifts in mutual submission to one another.

The clearest outline of the fivefold gifting is laid out in Ephesians 4. The chapter starts with Paul challenging the Ephesians "to lead a life worthy of the calling to which you have been called" (v. 1). Paul is not speaking to individuals here. He is picturing a group of people brought together under the mutual worship of one Lord. They were to lead a worthy life together in "humility and gentleness, with patience, bearing with one another with love" (v. 2). There will be conflict, for sure. This is to be expected. But in these conflicts, we will make "every effort to maintain the unity of the Spirit in the bond of peace" (v. 3). Because through one baptism we all participate in "one Lord, . . . one God and Father of all" (vv. 5-6). This is a picture of a people gathered under the authority of one Lord, working it out mutually.

Paul then quotes Psalm 68, starting with "When he ascended on high . . ." Interpreting this as an enthronement psalm, Paul pictures Jesus as enthroned at the place of ultimate authority, the right hand of the father.[3] From this place of his ascension, as if an extension of his reign, "he gave gifts to his people" (Eph 4:8). Paul then recites the five gifts: "some would be apostles, some prophets, some evangelists, some pastors and teachers." They are given "to equip the saints for the work of ministry, for building up the body of Christ" (vv. 11-12). The five gifts are given directly from the Lord in power. The gifted people are to lead in dependence on that same Lord, who is the source of the gift. And yet all this takes place within a community of mutual participation in this trust and authority.

There isn't space here to provide an extensive description of each of the five gifts. Suffice it to say that (1) *apostles* initiate, gather, and pioneer new works, calling people to live now in the kingdom; (2) *prophets* speak so as to reveal the truth and call of God into a situation, especially the injustice and neglect of the poor; (3) *pastors* tend to and sustain people's souls, especially the hurting; (4) *evangelists* bring the good news to those who are hurting; and (5) *teachers* help explain and deepen people's faith. Much has been written about the validity of these descriptions and the priority of this list of gifts. There is significant controversy over whether "apostle" in Ephesians 4 refers to the original apostles only or a gift given continually by God to sustain the church. For important reasons I am convinced "apostle" is an ongoing gift in the church.[4] I encourage you to read more on these issues.[5] For our purposes here, though, let's focus most immediately on how the fivefold gifting functions as a discipline that opens space for the presence of Christ among us. This space becomes the place of his authority and direction for the community into mission.

THE MUTUALITY AND INTERDEPENDENCE OF THE LEADERSHIP

The gifts in Ephesians 4:8-12 are multiple, and they are interdependent. No one person can carry out all the gifts in the community. Each person is to stay within the boundaries of their own giftedness as "according to the measure of Christ's gift" (v. 7). Elsewhere, the apostle Paul makes explicit that "to each is given the manifestation of the Spirit for the common good" (1 Cor 12:7). The Spirit allots these gifts to each person "individually just as the Spirit chooses" (1 Cor 12:11). No one can say to another, we have no need of your gift (1 Cor 12:21). The gifts cannot function on their own. We are all inextricably related to one another and must always lead within our respective gift in mutual submission to one another. It appears then that these gifts open up a space socially where people become interdependent, and the Holy Spirit works in that interdependence. Opposed to the striving, competition, and violence of the world, this community is formed by the opposite, the mutual participation in the presence of Christ, who is at the core.

In another letter Paul says, "We have gifts that differ according to the grace given to us: prophecy, in proportion to faith; ministry, in ministering; the teacher, in teaching; the exhorter, in exhortation; the giver, in generosity; the leader, in diligence; the compassionate, in cheerfulness" (Rom 12:6-8). He says that we have these gifts "each according to the measure of faith that God has assigned" (Rom 12:3). He could not be more clear. No one can do all things. Apostles have to depend on pastors for the pastoral role. Teachers have to listen to the prophets. We not only depend on the Lord of the gifts, but we are forced to depend on each other in a relationship of mutuality. In the words of the apostle Paul,

> Those who are unspiritual do not receive the gifts of God's Spirit, for they are foolishness to them. . . . Those who are spiritual discern all things. . . .
>
> "For who has known the mind of the Lord
> so as to instruct him?"
>
> But we have the mind of Christ. (1 Cor 2:14-16)

The last sentence could be just as well translated "but we, together, have the mind of Christ." So, in this amazing way Jesus becomes present to make his authority present. He works for the direction of the community in this space. The gifted leaders, together in mutual submission to each other's gifts, discern the mind of Christ for each situation. This is collaborative leadership. This was the way God worked through history through the nation of Israel.[6]

When Life on the Vine was starting, I took whatever support funds we had for the first few years and distributed them among multiple leaders. I kept my marketplace job, and instead of using all of the funds for my own support I redirected those funds to help people free up time for ministry. These funds, not even enough to support one pastor, were split between four pastors. I would say, "I see you excelling at doing this work in our community. Do you see the same? If we could find $1,000 a month to help you, could you free up ten to fifteen hours a week to give to the shaping of our church with your ministry?"

As a group of leaders, we worked through a gift inventory from time to time. This was a quick multiple-choice type test that could be taken and scored in fifteen minutes. We each got an assessment of our strengths and weaknesses among the five giftings.[7] It was irrelevant whether the test was accurate, because the object of the exercise was to discuss the results of the test for each person. We would ask each other questions like, Have we all experienced this person's strengths and weaknesses in the same way as the test did? How have you experienced this person's gifts? What emerges is an idea of what each person's giftings are (there can be more than one) and what strengths and weaknesses each person possesses. Recognizing our weaknesses makes us more readily dependent on everyone else. Our job descriptions were refined each time, and a wonderful mutuality developed out of this process. We learned how to trust and challenge each other in the joint leadership of the community.

Often as leadership develops, mutuality can be mistaken for a kind of passivity. But this is a mistake. We expect each leader to lead within the domain of their recognized gift. As an issue arises in the community, the leaders will meet to discern it. Each leader gives their opinion from within their own gifting. Sometimes leaders assume that all we need is conversation in order for things to get sorted out. But I learned along the way to encourage the one who is bringing the issue to the table to make a proposal. If the evangelist brings up an urgent need in the neighborhood, I ask the person, "Do you have a proposal?" This usually is enough for us to get going. Then it's up to the evangelistic leader to submit a proposal to the group. We don't take a vote. We discuss it out of our giftings. The pastor speaks to the needs of the individuals involved and how they will be affected by such a proposal. The apostle speaks to the proposal's urgency, and so on. Gradually the proposal takes a deeper shape, and we become of one mind. Sometimes the proposal is ditched entirely for something else. If everyone agrees, or those who disagree only disagree on a minor issue, we present the proposal to the whole church. The leadership group is not a democracy. It is a pneumatocracy (governed by the Spirit). Each person must lead out of their gifting and submit their proposals to the rest of the body for further development and eventual mutual assent.

In meetings like this, I have become deeply aware of my need for my friends' giftings that are different from mine. I, as an apostle, can be overzealous, quick to move, and not take into account the effect my proposals might have on the souls of people. I need to listen with special care to the pastors in our midst who so often speak in ways that challenge me. I must trust this space between us where Jesus has come to dwell. I must submit myself to his presence at work in this holy space of his gifts. By so doing, every decision that comes forth becomes a communal decision that moves us deep into the center of his will and his mind. This space becomes the center of his faithful presence.

THE PRIORITY OF THE FIRST LEADER GROUP

In Ephesians 4:12 Paul says the gifts are for the equipping of "the saints for the work of ministry, for building up the body of Christ." The fivefold gifts appear to be given priority in the ministry of the whole body. Yet this does not diminish the fact that the entire church is in ministry. The purpose of these five gifts is to "equip" the rest of the church for ministry. We locate these five gifts first, which set into motion the rest of the gifts.

A similar priority is given to three gifts in 1 Corinthians 12:27-28. Here the apostle says, "Now you are the body of Christ and individually members of it. And God has appointed in the church first apostles, second prophets, third teachers." Following these three gifts Paul uses the word *then* to continue with "deeds of power, then gifts of healing, forms of assistance, forms of leadership, various kinds of tongues." The three gifts given priority here overlap with the five gifts given priority in Ephesians 4. Nonetheless, in both texts more than one gift are at the top. There is a multiplicity of gifts functioning together at the beginning of the leadership train. Establishing this group of gifts sets the rest of the gifts into motion in the body as a whole. This is why Paul says to the Corinthians, who are overfocusing on the sensational gifts, especially the gift of tongues, that they should together "strive for the greater gifts" (1 Cor 12:31). They should locate and recognize the first gifts, which set the rest in motion and guide the other gifts into their rightful order.

When planting a church I have noticed that when the leadership is functioning well, the rest of the church community becomes a fully orbed gifted community empowered for mission. When the first three to five leaders are functioning well as a team, they know how to recognize the gifts in others in the wider community. They model mutual submission before the community. They are used to recognizing the gifts and boundaries in each other. They then do the same as they live in the broader church community. In turn they set loose the full gamut of gifts at work in the community by recognizing and facilitating them. They mobilize the power of the kingdom.

Each member of the founding leadership group at Life on the Vine recognized other gifted people in the community. Each in their own way affirmed what they had seen in other individuals. I sometimes pushed for someone to play a teaching role too quickly. The teacher in our midst had a word of caution. The pastoral figure engaged the person's whole life. Together we worked to mobilize leader after leader. But all of our voices were needed. Many times a recommendation would come to us from a local neighborhood group concerning a leader. Our combined voices helped to discern this new leader and facilitate that new leader's recognition before the whole community. Surely many tools, such as a gift inventory or Enneagram or StrengthsFinder assessment tools, help people to locate their role. But in the end, most leadership was put into motion by the overall guiding leadership group. This was important to the functioning of the community.

At Life on the Vine (and our church plants) we believed the ordination process worked well to facilitate the ordering of these first gifts. It served as a starting point to initiate a group of leaders for a community. It provided the testing grounds for the fitness and commitment of these leaders. Neither our denomination nor the process itself was perfect. But it tied us to the people who went before us and those who preceded them. It grounded us in history. Indeed, there is a sense that this is what it means to be the first leaders in the sense of the fivefold gifts of Ephesians 4. These leaders are set in place in continuity with those who have gone before. They walk in line with that authority as apostles, teachers, pastors, prophets, and evangelists. But this doesn't mean these leaders are now over the others in the community.[8] Each leader serves under the community, not over it. Each leader's gifts still had to be recognized within the community (or there would be no community).

In summary, recognizing the fivefold ministry is the first order of every community. But they too must then release the rest of the community's giftedness or all will be lost. This founding group of leaders sets the blueprint for the rest of the church's leadership culture. But they are never to be above the other gifted leaders. Everyone operates in mutual submission to one another and to the whole congregation. As the fivefold ministers are present to one another, they in turn become present to Christ at work among the community. They themselves become a model of practicing faithful presence.

EXERCISING AUTHORITY IN CHRIST'S PRESENCE

It is stunning to realize that the authority and power of the risen King comes to reside among men and women in the gifts of his people (Eph 4:7). But lest anyone think they can gain control of this authority, as soon as they seek to control or manipulate the authority of the King, his authority and presence departs. Gifted leaders therefore must always exercise their gifts in total trust and dependence on the Lord.

This is emphasized by Paul in Romans 12:1-3, where, in setting up his presentation of the gifts, he says, "Present your bodies as a living sacrifice" (v. 1); "Do not be conformed to this world" (v. 2); and do not "think of yourself more highly than you ought" (v. 3). Each is to exercise their gift "according to the measure of faith that God has assigned" and not one mite more (v. 3). Through worship, submission, trust and dependence on the Lord, we can exercise our gift as a participant in his authority on earth. As we lead, these postures of submission to the one King in turn open space for his presence and power among us.

Something special happens in this space among leaders when they practice the fivefold ministry. Paul says the goal of the gifts functioning together is to "come to the unity of the faith and of the knowledge of the Son of God, to complete maturity, to the measure of the fullness of Christ" (Eph 4:13, my translation). This is where the gifts together lead the community. The word Paul uses for fullness (*plērōma*) overlaps in meaning with the *Shekinah* presence of God in the Jewish temple. It is a word peculiarly chosen by the apostle to refer to Christ's "full and real presence" in his body, the church.[9] For Paul, ultimately, this is the goal of mutually submitting to one another's gifts—his presence.

When Christian leaders are present to each other and present to Christ's presence working among them, they experience the fullness of his presence. Likewise, when all gifts are functioning, they lead the rest of the church to be similarly present to each other and Christ's presence. Paul likens the result to the *Shekinah* presence of Christ dwelling among us. The discipline of the fivefold ministry is the basis for leading a church to be faithfully present to Christ in the world.

I have experienced this presence among a group of leaders. It isn't instantaneous. It happens over time as we submit to Christ and to each other. We grow to trust and love each other, and to trust Jesus as Lord at work among us. It is holy ground. Christ's presence comes to this space in a special way akin to a sacramental social presence. We often miss the mark. Outbreaks of pride are inevitable. Leaders are hurt by truth. There are ups and downs. But by continually, mutually submitting to each other, we grow. We ask and receive forgiveness regularly. We pray for the future and submit to Christ's rule over it all. And those moments arrive when Christ's presence fills all in all and heaven and earth are moved as we lead in concert with the Lord, who rules the world.

THE FIVEFOLD GIFTING IN THE THREE CIRCLES

Given what we've examined so far, it is obvious the formation of the fivefold gifting starts in a close circle, in the space of mutual submission to Jesus Christ as Lord. Because these leadership gifts are an extension of Christ's lordship, they are impossible apart from discerning our submission to his reign and presence by the Holy Spirit.

But it is a fallacy to think that the fivefold ministries are only for leading within the church's close circle. We already know that once they are set in place, they help recognize and facilitate all the other gifts in the close circle. But they also do the same in the dotted circles and half circles of our lives.

Nowhere is the fivefold ministry needed more than in our neighborhoods. Indeed, it's hard to imagine how the dotted circle fellowships could be possible apart from the fivefold ministries. For instance, the house gathering in the neighborhood that gathers weekly to share a meal requires an initiator to gather people together and commit regularly for a meal. This initiator will most likely be an apostle. When a church seeks to develop house fellowships in the neighborhoods, it should probably start with locating the apostles in our midst.

Likewise, there will be times when an evangelist is needed in the house gathering. As we gather in homes in each neighborhood, an evangelistically gifted person will need to be present, calling attention to needs in the neighborhood and then to lead engagements in response. Pastors will also be needed to respond to the soul care needs of everyday life. The entire fivefold ministry is needed in every neighborhood, which in turn mobilizes all of the gifts among us. This is essential for the kingdom of God to break out in our neighborhoods. Thus every dotted circle in the neighborhood should locate the apostles, prophets, teachers, evangelists and pastors in their midst.

This kind of activity is evident throughout the New Testament church. New Testament scholar Robert Banks says the primary context for Paul's discussion of gifts "is not the 'church' but the 'body,' not the large gathering of Christians together but the local Christian communities in the houses. Though gifts are certainly, even pre-eminently, exercised in the largest of church gatherings, they are also exercised on other occasions when Christians are in contact with one another locally."[10] They are part of the continuous ministry of the church into everyday life.

We know that almost all the churches of those first hundred years were located in homes in neighborhoods of some sort. So we should not be surprised that Paul is always recognizing gifted leaders working in these churches. In Romans 16 he recognizes twenty-five of them at various churches. He refers to them as coworkers (v. 9), relatives (v. 11), those chosen in the Lord (v. 13), a minister (v. 1) and famously (of Andronicus and Junia) apostles (v. 7). He may not use the fivefold ministry labels specifically to reference all of them, but given his reference to coworker and fellow apostle, we can easily see that he is working to reinforce the recognition of the founding first leaders in all of these houses.

In my travels I often encounter churches struggling to form missional communities in neighborhoods. My first question is whether they know who the apostles are in the neighborhoods and what have they done to locate, affirm, train, and send them out. Of course, these apostles eventually will need around them pastors and teachers and the other gifts. But apostles most often are the ones who get things started. We need the fivefold ministry in every neighborhood—in both dotted circle and half circle settings.

The discipline of locating, recognizing, and submitting to the fivefold ministry will push ministry into the half circles of our lives as well. From their location in the dotted circles, these leaders will inhabit places where there is great need. The apostle will mobilize prayer and resources where needed. The evangelist will tend to the gospel. Where someone's soul is in pain in the neighborhood, the pastor will tend to them and teach others how to do so. The pastor will teach people in the dotted circle how to visit the hurting ones in the local hospital. The fivefold gifting (and all the other gifts) will flow into the world. The only difference will be that in our pastoring, teaching, evangelizing in the half circles, we can only offer the authority, reign, and power of Jesus to our neighbors. We can't assume beforehand the authority of Jesus will be received.

Lindsey, a woman in one of our churches, was present in the half circles of her neighborhood. She volunteered a couple nights a week at a domestic abuse shelter. Being present there, she observed great things happening. Women at the shelter asked for a Bible study. There was a great need for counselors and families to take in women. Lindsey's house group, a table fellowship of Christians in her neighborhood, recognized her gift and what was happening. They appealed for resources and help from the wider church community. From Lindsey's dotted-circle fellowship, gifted people then flowed into the half circle of her life.

If Lindsey's church had been hierarchically organized, and this ministry had not fit the vision of the senior pastor, the request most likely would have been rejected, or perhaps Lindsey would have been urged to bring the ministry into the church building. But her church community was not structured like that. Instead, she was blessed by the church, and her ministry flourished with the help and coordination of others in her church. Three other people who had a passion for women in domestic abuse came alongside her. One of the women, an apostle, helped galvanize a vision for the church to get behind this work. One of the women—a pastor—came alongside Lindsey to minister healing. Some much-needed funds helped the organization take on more victims. The ministry flourished, and the church saw people added to the kingdom.

The gifted structure of the church therefore is meant for all three circles we live in as the church. Whereas hierarchy tends to centralize authority and push power in and up to the person at the top, a church based on the Spirit's gifts, as founded in the discipline of the fivefold ministry, decentralizes authority, pushes power down, and disperses it out. The fivefold ministry empowers people on the streets to do the ministry of the kingdom. Thus Christ's authority and reign flourishes in all the circles of our lives.

RECOVERING FAITHFUL PRESENCE AMONG OUR LEADERS

Through its history the church has regularly tried to centralize the fivefold ministry. Some say we can see this starting in the Pastoral Epistles. I nonetheless suggest there are many signs the fivefold ministry was functioning well in the Pastoral Epistles, including elders who labored in preaching and teaching (1 Tim 5:17; Tit 1:9) and pastoral care (1 Tim 3:5). But there is no denying that a massive change happened between the New Testament church and what some have referred to as the Constantinian church of Rome.

Whether for good reasons or bad, sometimes out of exigency, sometimes out of comfort, the Roman Church organized itself into a hierarchy.[11] Episcopalian historian Dom Gregory Dix describes how the priesthood, "which had formally been the function of all members of the church with the bishop as 'high-priest,' becomes a special attribute of the second order of the ministry." The presbyters (elders) became the priests empowered to preside over the Eucharist, and the practice of the laity participating in the ministry of the church disappeared. And the Eucharist turned into something "said" by the priest instead of an act of the whole congregation.[12]

Whatever version of these events we accept, it is evident the church gradually removed leadership from the neighborhoods and house churches and moved it into a clerical hierarchy once it became dominant in Rome. One could argue this move was necessary for sustaining the church in the midst of huge growth. Nonetheless, I would argue, an intensification of hierarchy in the church is a symptom of the maintenance mode. Hierarchy almost always works to take leadership out of neighborhoods and center the church in a building. It organizes the church for efficiency, not for mission.

In most evangelical Protestant churches, we function as hierarchies. We follow business gurus whose foundational assumption is that a good leader successfully guides an organization to a predetermined goal. And no matter how servant-driven the leadership might be, there's an assumed distance between the leader and those being led, between the driver's seat and the back seat. For most evangelical Protestants this understanding of leadership drives how we organize and lead churches. It is leadership that runs on efficiency—the maintenance mode—as opposed to the presence, power, and authority of Jesus Christ in our midst.

Of course, there are leaders in Christian justice ministries who are just as guilty. The same distance between leaders and the subjects of leadership operates here as well. And the poor are made into projects as opposed to being invited to mutually participate in the renewal of the world under the presence and reign of Jesus.

When we forfeit mutuality and tending to the presence of Christ among leadership, we forfeit the discipline of the fivefold ministry as well. We forfeit dependence on the Spirit and God filling and using our gifts (as well as the church community's manifold gifts). We in effect lose the authority and power of Christ to reign among us. We lose the centrifugal force pushing the authority and power of ministry into the neighborhoods. When we reach this point, the church defaults into either maintenance mode or exhaustion.

Throughout the history of the church in the West, attempts have been made to recover the fivefold ministry and the multitude of the gifts. For instance, in the Middle Ages monastic orders arose to fulfill one or more of the giftings of the Holy Spirit in the world as the church lumbered on in maintenance mode. During the Radical Reformation, many Anabaptist and Brethren groups sought to return to the priesthood of all believers. And John Wesley organized society meetings of laypeople in the Second Great Awakening. True renewal, it seems, always starts with local communities of pluralized leadership fostering grassroots movements. This points to the urgency of recovering the discipline of the fivefold ministry throughout all the circles of life, which will shape the church's faithful presence in the world.

9

The Discipline of Kingdom Prayer

When you pray, pray like this . . .

Matthew 6:9 (my translation)

At the beginning of Life on the Vine Christian Community, a group of leaders met once a week. I started every meeting with a prayer, asking for God's guidance. Then we'd get right to the agenda. Admittedly, it felt perfunctory. I was all business back then. A young seminary student, Geoff, who was just beginning to work with us, called me on it. He challenged me to slow everything down and take some time to lead everyone into the presence of Christ. I questioned him. Soon thereafter I started reading about listening prayer.

A few weeks later I asked him to open in prayer. He invited everyone to pray. We spent more than a few minutes in silence before God. We took a few deep breaths. We prayed to submit all things into God's presence, care, and enabling. I realized that something special was happening in this extended time of presenting ourselves to God in Christ. We were posturing ourselves before the Ruler of the universe. We were letting go of our egos, agendas, and personal issues, if only for the next hour or two. We were opening up space for God to work. Then we prayed for our church, offering up our church to be his church. We gave all of the issues that lay before us to God for his work. We invited the Holy Spirit into this space, our church, and our neighborhoods to transform and renew us. I look back on those times now and realize that I was learning about kingdom prayer.

At the time, this went against most of the impulses in my body. My inclination was to get things going. Let's pray and get moving. Our culture ingrained in me the need to get things done. I discovered that a lot of what we call church is run on this kind of self-generated energy. God can even use us in this mode. Nonetheless, this way of operating produces human effort with little cooperation with God. Praying as Geoff taught us to pray quieted our souls in submission before God. It forced us to tend to his presence among us and open our lives to cooperate with his power. We first submit all things to God. Then a place opens for us to submit to one another and listen for God. It opens space for God to work and for us to cooperate. It opens space for the inbreaking of the kingdom of God. It changes the entire nature of what goes on here. This is kingdom prayer.

THE WORLD CAN'T STOP ITSELF

The drive for control is at the core of the human condition. We live daily with overwhelming uncertainties. Anxiety is the air we breathe in the Western economies. Most people live isolated, vulnerable lives, and so we strive as individuals to secure our existence in every way. We strive to make our finances, our health, our family, and our future predictable. Most of us live under the delusion that we are in control of our lives. As a result, endless striving characterizes our existence. Most of us are not aware of how much it's affecting us physically and emotionally.

God can't work amid our striving. Certainly he works around us and despite us. He still gets things done. He is still ultimately sovereign and in control of the world. But as for actually using us in his power and authority, he will not oppose our grabbing and pushing for control. He refuses to steamroll our wills in order to dictate his will in our lives and in the world. God is love. God is patient. God's power can only work through us as we submit to him, let him work, open up space for him. As we gather in his presence, submit to him, and tend to his presence, he then works in all his power.

The apostle Paul challenges the Philippians, "Do not be anxious about anything, but in every situation, by prayer and petition, with thanksgiving, present your requests to God" (Phil 4:6 NIV). Prayer is the opposite of striving and anxiousness. Therefore, in everything we are to resist striving and instead present ourselves before God in prayer. Paul actually separates prayer from petition, putting it first. Prayer, as we will discover, is the profound act of giving up control of a situation, turning it over to the reign of God. Only after we have entered this space can we ask for things. Prayer opens space for his kingdom and for us to participate in his kingdom. I call this discipline kingdom prayer.

Striving is at the core of life in the world. Prayer dislodges us from the striving and opens up space. Then his kingdom is able to move in.

THE NEED FOR KINGDOM PRAYER

Kingdom prayer is the last of the seven disciplines. Though in this book it's the discipline appearing last, it is really first. It is the foundation for all the other disciplines. It initiates all the other disciplines. Through prayer we approach the Lord's Table, begin reconciliation, proclaim the gospel, be with the least of these, and do all of the other disciplines. It is ubiquitous. And so some might wonder, *Should it be treated as a separate discipline that shapes us into his faithful presence? Shouldn't it be integrated into all of the other disciplines?* I suggest otherwise. It is so important that we must separate it from the other disciplines and treat it all on its own. We must locate what it is, what it does, and how singularly important it is to the entire life of church on mission.

Kingdom prayer gathers us into Christ's presence. It creates this local space for God's kingdom to come "on earth as it is in heaven." Historically, it has initiated (in some way) all the sacraments. It sets the stage for Christ's presence to become visible. In this way it's a social sacrament, even if it has not been named one historically by the Roman Church.

THE DISCIPLINE OF KINGDOM PRAYER

The discipline of kingdom prayer is given to us by Christ most directly and obviously in the Lord's Prayer (Mt 6:9-13). Here Jesus teaches us how to pray by starting with the address, "Our Father." It is not an individualist "*My* Father." It joins people into a social group in submission to God together with "Our Father." It gathers a circle of subjects in submission to God's reign. Right upfront we learn that kingdom prayer is a social practice to be done with a group of people.[1] "Our Father" alerts us that to pray the kingdom prayer is a profoundly political act, joining us together as a group ready to disrupt the forces of evil in the world.

"Our Father" therefore resists the propensity in the modern West to reduce prayer to something intensely personal only. In praying this prayer, we are diverted away from focusing on the things *I* long for and desire. We must cease this striving first before we petition God.

We address God as our Father who is "in heaven." We bow before him as the one sitting at the seat of all authority in heaven and on earth.[2] This prayer gathers *us* to be with him in submission to his authority, not only over our lives but the entire world.

Jesus then instructs us to say, "Let your name be holy." By praying this we not only acknowledge God is sovereign (in heaven in authority over all things), working over the whole earth, but he can be trusted to be perfect in every way. By praying "let your name be holy," we are submitting to him so space can be opened for his perfect ways to be made manifest in our midst.

The next words, "Your kingdom come, your will be done, on earth as it is in heaven," guide our hearts, minds, and souls into a joining together in order to submit to the King. We are in essence pledging to cooperate with God. Our hearts are purified before God. Our attention is guided by this prayer to his power, majesty, grace, and authority. And a space is opened up for him to work. This kind of kingdom prayer is the most foundational of all disciplines for our faithful presence to God in the world.

All our other concerns for provisions and safety and forgiveness flow from here. As we are formed by his will over our lives, all of our desires become shaped by him. We are able to see the needs before us with trust in him. We are able to become part of something so big, we ourselves become enlarged. We see ourselves as part of God's mission. We then are able to pray for needs, including our own, like we never have before.

This is what kingdom prayer does. Together we bow before the King. We become his subjects. We submit our lives, resources, and situations to his reign. His reign becomes a social reality. It creates the social space for his presence. It opens the way for his kingdom to break in. It enables us to participate in his work. It shapes us together for mission. It is the founding discipline that constitutes his people into his faithful presence.

CHRIST'S PRESENCE

Missionary Vincent Donovan asserts that "when we pray 'thy kingdom come, thy will be done' we not only open our lives to God's in-breaking presence creating anew, we are saying we ourselves are willing to be involved as the participant in his presence, indeed as part of the something new God is bringing into the world."[3] Kingdom prayer makes way for Jesus' presence. This in turn makes possible our participation in his work and resists our doing anything out of our own effort.

Romans 8:15-17 also teaches us to pray, "Father." Here, however, in the most intimate of ways, the apostle uses the word for "Daddy" as our address to the Father. Paul, most likely using Jesus' very own word for *father* in the original Aramaic, says we cry "*Abba*, Father."[4] In so doing, Paul says the Spirit himself bears witness with our spirit that we indeed are children of the Father, "heirs of God and joint heirs with Christ" (v. 17). In prayer, we are joined with the Spirit. It is the entry way into his presence.

But in this text prayer is more than an individual ecstatic experience. Theologian Sarah Coakley uses Romans 8 to describe prayer as drawing us into the center of the triune God (vv. 26-27). She discusses the posture of vulnerability that enables us to submit entirely into the workings of God. Prayer is not just a contemplative kind of prayer that extracts us out of the world.[5] Rather, in prayer, we are joined with the whole work of God as all of creation is being taken up into this flow of his presence (vv. 21-22). For Coakley, submission to God through prayer incorporates us into the presence of God at the center of the triune fellowship, but it does not stop there. The triune God is at work in the world. Being shaped into his presence therefore shapes us to be in his work in and for the world. This is why I call it kingdom prayer.

We practice it in all situations of life. When we encounter a domestic violence issue in the neighborhood, race and hatred at the town hall, or a sick family struggling with multiple ailments, we gather around this space, join hands, and pray, and we in essence submit this social space to Christ's presence. The kingdom is not only subjects, it's space and time, systems and realities that shape how we live. By joining together in these spaces and praying "Your kingdom come," we are opening space for his presence to become visible. Where his presence becomes manifest, violence is resisted and sickness is covered by his lordship. We now become free and present to join in God's work to reconcile this situation to himself. The Spirit is invoked. People are healed. The dying are emboldened. Violence is dissipated. Evil is defeated. Far from only personal and contemplative, praying "your kingdom come, your will be done" opens up social space to participate in what God is doing.

In 2010 a group of eight people from two Sacramento churches felt called to the Detroit Boulevard neighborhood of Sacramento. It was known as one of the most notorious crime-ridden neighborhoods in all of Sacramento. Gang violence, prostitution, and drug arrests were regular occurrences. Each house in that neighborhood was a place of danger. Nonetheless, this group of eight decided to walk through the neighborhood praying over each home and praying for the presence of Christ to reign over violence, addiction, and satanic oppression. One of the eight, Sacramento street detective Michael Xiong, reported that "each time we prayed over the houses, we felt the weight of oppression becoming lighter." A woman from one of the houses confronted them. When she discovered they were praying for the community, she asked for healing, and God healed her.

The group soon physically moved into the neighborhood and started what they called Detroit Life Church. A couple years later the *Sacramento Bee* (the city's main newspaper) reported that there were no homicides, robberies, or sex crimes, only one assault, in Detroit Boulevard between 2013 and 2014. Michael Xiong reported that a neighborhood once known by the police as a "carnival" for its multiple arrests every night was now considered boring. Detroit Boulevard, a neighborhood once glorified for its violence and gangster lifestyle, had been transformed by a small group of people who began their ministry in the neighborhood by praying around houses, streets, and parks for the power of Satan to be vanquished.[6] Kingdom prayer made space for the kingdom to come to Detroit Boulevard.

Kingdom prayer brings people together around places, circumstances, and social structures, and opens space for Christ's presence to become real. In the space of his presence, we can now respond to God as witnesses. We invite people into the resulting fellowship, reconciliation, proclamation of the gospel, economic sharing, and flourishing that comes when people submit to the King. Our presence tending to his presence undermines the systems of violence and resists the powers of the enemy. Kingdom prayer embodies what it means to be faithfully present to his presence in the world.

THE ORDERING OF THE KINGDOM IN PRAYER

Order always comes with the kingdom. The kingdom is the flip side of the coin of God's presence. In this space of kingdom prayer, God reorders lives and the world by his lordship. As in Detroit Boulevard, this ordering begins when, in prayer, we have given up control and submitted ourselves to his lordship, and prepared ourselves to participate in his work, not ours. As theologian Karl Barth once wrote, "It cannot be for those who pray for the coming of God's kingdom to accomplish with their own deeds the act for which they pray."[7] Kingdom prayer disciplines us into giving up control and cooperating with what God is doing.

Nowhere is this better illustrated than in a few texts from the Gospel of Mark. In Mark 9:14-29 Jesus is descending the Mount of Transfiguration with three of his disciples. When they arrive at the bottom, they discover a commotion. A man in the crowd tells Jesus that he brought his son, who was robbed of his speech by a spirit, to the disciples. He reports that the disciples failed to heal the boy. Jesus sighs, calls the disciples "faithless," and then heals the boy. Later, after all the commotion is over, the frustrated disciples ask him, "Why couldn't we drive it out?" to which Jesus replies, "This kind can come out only by prayer" (vv. 28-29 NIV).

Here we see that the disciples were still under the spell that the kingdom is something humans can bring in. They asked, in essence, how come *we* couldn't cast out this spirit? They believed it was within their power and authority to do so. After calling them faithless, Jesus refers them to the posture of prayer in which they submit this situation to God's reign. This is the foundation of faithful presence. Only in kingdom prayer can we truly prepare ourselves to participate in what God will do. When we try to take a situation upon ourself and do it ourself, we are impotent in the kingdom. The authority of the King will not be present. But submit to God in this profound way of kingdom prayer and the space is opened for his power and authority to break in.

A few chapters later, as Jesus approaches Jerusalem, he curses a fig tree. He says, "May no one ever eat fruit from you again" (Mk 11:14). And when Jesus entered the temple in Jerusalem, he cleansed the temple because it had become "a den of robbers." It appears that Jesus is pronouncing judgment on the unfruitful tree of Israel and its temple religion.[8] Israel had rejected the kingdom of God as Jesus was bringing it in. They wanted the kingdom in their nationalist way. And they aspired to control the kingdom.

Passing by the fig tree the next morning, Peter sees that it was withered. And Jesus points his disciples toward the way God will bring in his kingdom, saying, "Have faith in God. Truly, I say to you, whoever says to this mountain, 'Be taken up and cast into the sea,' and does not doubt in his heart, but believes that what he says will come to pass, it will be done for him. Therefore I tell you, whatever you ask in prayer, believe that you have received it, and it will be yours" (Mk 11:22-24 RSV). He likely is pointing to the Mount of Olives when he is saying these words,[9] and is alluding to the prophecy of Zechariah 14 about the Lord splitting the Mount of Olives in two (v. 4) and the land being turned into a plain (v. 10) as preparation for the final victory of God and his coming kingdom.[10] He in essence is saying, if you can trust God in all he is doing and follow him, the kingdom will come, but not in the way the Jews were expecting.[11] He then describes prayer to them saying, "Therefore I tell you, whatever you ask for in prayer, believe that you have received it, and it will be yours." The RSV translation suggests that the last phrase might be also translated, "believe that you are receiving it." And so it appears

Jesus is challenging them to submit all things to God's work, trust him, and walk in that. In so doing, God will not only accomplish the kingdom but enable us to participate with him in bringing in his kingdom. It is a startling statement of just how much prayer brings us into the center of his kingdom and makes the ground we stand on sacred ground for God to work. It describes the dynamics at work in kingdom prayer.

As we walk through our neighborhoods, as we see the struggles and strife in the hallways of our schools, as we engage the hurting people around tables in McDonald's and other restaurants, as we face racial conflict on our city blocks, as we feel the resistance to God's ways and his kingdom in all these things, we should first gather with someone and pray. Submit these places and situations to the kingdom for God's work and then participate faithfully as the Spirit manifests Christ's presence. We should discern how to respond, realizing that we have been invited into the presence of Christ's work in reordering the world. And even though suffering and pain might ensue, we know that as God has used the cross to rearrange the world, so too he will use us (and our walking through the suffering) to rearrange people's lives—and whole towns and villages—as visible realities of his kingdom.

I once heard Charles Galbreath, a pastor of Clarendon Road Church in Brooklyn, tell the story of a black man gunned down by police in his neighborhood. Anger seethed in the neighborhood. Frustration from years of racial oppression was about to erupt in violence. Many people lined up to march down the main street while police gathered, expecting violence. Charles and a group of pastors rushed to the gathering place and found themselves caught in the middle between the police and the people. Tensions were rising. Insults were being hurled across the divide. One side picked up rocks, the other side clutched their guns.

The pastors feared for their lives, fearing bullets would fly at any moment. He says that some of the pastors bowed in the middle of the street and began to pray. They implored God to visit this place. As Charles tells it, slowly the tension died down, the people put down the rocks, and the police took their hands off their holsters. Those who cared stayed. And without a shot fired or rock thrown, conversations began and God's presence appeared that night in that community. It was the beginning of something new God was doing to bring justice and reconciliation to a street corner.[12]

Kingdom prayer does not remove us from the world but places us firmly in the middle of it. Even in the most violent, awkward, and hopeless circumstances, kingdom prayer opens space for God's presence and strengthens those praying to walk faithfully in that presence. His presence calms human striving, anger, violence, and the urge to control. And then, with the way made clear, we can cooperate with God's work to realign human realities. We can participate in bringing the kingdom, whether through reconciliation, the gospel, reorienting economic realities, or any of the other seven disciplines of faithful presence.

After praying "Your kingdom come," we can begin the work of responding to and joining in with what God is doing. Just as the petitions of the Lord's Prayer ask for horizontal needs like forgiveness, daily bread, and shelter from the evil one, so too we can pray for these things as we stand in the middle of life's circumstances with others. Kingdom prayer prepares space for this work. It disrupts evil and makes space for reordering life. In the words of theologian Karl Barth, "To clasp the hands in prayer is the beginning of an uprising against the disorder of the world."[13]

IN ALL THE CIRCLES OF OUR LIVES

We most easily learn how to pray kingdom prayer together with Christians. In the close circle we gather together intently as one people submitted to one Lord and one table. We are already committed to discern the kingdom.[14] But of course kingdom prayer must not be sequestered among Christians in our church meetings. We must continually practice kingdom prayer as groups in our neighborhoods and as individuals representing our communities wherever we inhabit the half circles of our lives. Prayer is a natural response to the struggles and pains we engage together as a people in everyday life.

Jesus' introduction to the Lord's Prayer start out with "When you pray, say . . ." (Lk 11:2). New Testament scholar Scot McKnight suggests this should be translated "Whenever you pray, recite this."[15] Jesus in essence is telling us that whenever and wherever we pray, we should pray, "Your kingdom come." We are to follow this pattern into all the circles of our lives.

Following McKnight, I suggest we should allow the exact words of the Lord's Prayer to shape our prayer together in the world. The first two petitions, which I have focused on in this chapter, set the stage for the rest of the petitions regarding daily life. In teaching the Lord's Prayer this way, Jesus is urging us to start off every prayer with the submission of our life and desires to the kingdom, from which our prayer life and petitions flow. The vertical sets the stage for the horizontal.[16]

As McKnight and others note, it was common for Jews to pray at regular intervals throughout the day.[17] Prayer was to be part of everyday life, not just early mornings or on the sabbath. In the modern world we may no longer pray at set hours. Yet what drives the practice of the hours applies to today. Kingdom prayer penetrates all the situations and encounters of our daily lives. We need to practice it in all the circles of our lives. We need to live within the frame of kingdom prayer. We should continually gather and submit all these into the space of God's inbreaking kingdom.

Every Friday night in my home, our gathering in the neighborhood would end with us joining in the living room with our children to submit all the things we had shared to Christ's reign. Even with strangers in our midst, we would pray, though we would sometimes ask their permission. As onlookers, they saw the kingdom breaking in. This was kingdom prayer in the dotted circle.

Likewise kingdom prayer shapes our presence in the half circles of our lives. I once listened to a group of pastors speaking on the topic of evangelism at a small conference. One pastor told us how the simplest and easiest thing to do when he meets someone in the midst of struggle, pain, uncertainty, or need is to offer to pray. Even if this person is a stranger, this pastor said the invitation to pray was rarely turned down. For him, prayer was the door that opens space for a conversation, an encounter with God, and opportunities to proclaim the gospel to those who are hurting and in pain.

In the case of being with a stranger, however, we must always offer kingdom prayer as a guest in that person's life. In the half circles of our lives we must always be ready to offer kingdom prayer, but never coerce it on someone. We must not be too quick to offer kingdom prayer. To simply spring prayer on someone as a tool to get them to an evangelistic moment is a mistake. There must be a connect. We must be present to the other person and to Christ's presence at work. Prayer is not contextless. True kingdom prayer demands we know and are involved in a situation concretely enough that an actual space is formed by our joining in prayer together. Here in this space we submit real situations to his lordship. Social media has promoted the sense that anybody can pray for anybody apart from any social or spatial location. Kingdom prayer demands a location and presence.

It is striking how often the early church prayed the Lord's Prayer. Because most of the early church practiced the hours, they prayed it throughout the day. The early church's *Didache* prescribes this.[18] Tertullian prescribed no rule about the time and place to pray, "except of course to pray every time and place."[19] According to Tertullian, rehearsing the Lord's Prayer served as the foundation from which petitions for all other needs could flow.[20] The Lord's Prayer dominated the average Christian's everyday life. It was a discipline for all the circles of their lives.

RECOVERING FAITHFUL PRESENCE THROUGH KINGDOM PRAYER

Throughout its history the church has been tempted to limit corporate prayer to within the four walls of the church building. For example, in many churches the pastoral prayer is prayed *for* the congregation instead of *by* the congregation. Some may point to the weekly prayer meeting as an example of this. Although started in the nineteenth century to spur revivals, sometimes this well-meaning program took prayer out of the neighborhoods and sequestered it in the four walls of the church on a Wednesday night.

Whenever the church relinquishes prayer to the professionals, or whenever the church removes prayer from the places of tension, need, and struggle in all three circles of our lives, kingdom prayer is in danger of becoming a maintenance function of the church. We must guard against this.

Life on the Vine practiced kingdom prayer in Sunday gatherings by asking the people to audibly voice their prayers to God in two to three sentences. Everyone was asked to end their prayer with "Lord, in your mercy." When the congregation heard that, we would all join in unison with, "Amen." This was our way of submitting our needs to the Father's care and then agreeing on it together as a community. We were continually and intentionally led into the concrete submission that is kingdom prayer. And so this space became sacred space for the kingdom. It was training for kingdom prayer in our daily lives.

When there is no kingdom prayer in the half circles of our lives, this raises red flags that perhaps the church has slipped into exhaustion mode. If prayer opens us to what God is doing among us in these various places of our lives, our entrance into these places should be prepared for by kingdom prayer.

Today many churches are learning the value of prayer walks in their neighborhoods (much like the church in Detroit Boulevard). Walking our neighborhoods and going to places of strife and then joining hands in solidarity and praying "Your kingdom come" opens space for Christ to be made visible. In similar fashion, I know friends who marched arm in arm in the midst of violence in Chicago, praying "Your kingdom come." Kingdom prayer is spatial and social. It opens spaces and extends Christ's presence into our neighborhoods. In these spaces, when people submit to Christ's presence, Christ's power is unleashed. Healings, reconciliation, and peace breaks out in Jesus' name. And the world looks on in wonder, asking what has made such happenings possible. These things are not possible by human effort.

Too often we come to prayer believing the more we pray the more results we will see. This too is a sign the church has slipped into exhaustion mode. Even with the best of intentions, we can gather merely to pray for the implementation of our own quick solutions to a situation of social injustice, for instance. Prayer has become in effect a quick-fix means to exhaustion. Jesus counters this propensity before he introduces the Lord's Prayer by instructing, "When you are praying, do not heap up empty phrases as the Gentiles do; for they think that they will be heard because of their many words" (Mt 6:7). Our God is sovereign, holy, and firmly in charge of the world. He is waiting to invite us to participate in his work. So prayer's primary task is to align us with God and his purposes. It brings us into a relationship in which we become participants in his work to change the world.

From this space we offer our needs, desires, and prayers for protection, just as children do to their parents. Then we add our deepest desires to our prayer. Likewise, we respond to the injustices that so anger our souls. We plead for God to make things right, and space is opened up for Christ's kingdom to break in with power and authority.

It's just as true with kingdom prayer as it is with all the other disciplines, both maintenance and exhaustion are a denial of Christ's presence. They fail to open space for God to work. The discipline of kingdom prayer undercuts both modes. Kingdom prayer is the ground of all the disciplines. Recovering it is the foundation of the church's faithful presence in the world.

Epilogue

How God Changes the World

One evening I was hanging out with three students from Northern Seminary, where I am a professor. We were at one student's apartment in one of the poorer neighborhoods in Chicago. Each of these students was an activist of some sort working for justice in the world. We were talking theology, justice, and their struggles to make sense of Christianity in difficult places like this. Toward the end of the evening I asked if any of them could see themselves as a pastor when they finished seminary. Every one of them looked at me with horror. They all said "no way," with some expletives mixed in. The thought of being a pastor was repulsive. I let the reaction die down a little, and a few minutes later I asked, "What about being political organizers for the kingdom?" Their eyes grew larger, and many positive comments came forth. This was something they could buy into. Somehow it never crossed their minds that to be a pastor of a church is to organize people to live in the kingdom. I have never quite forgotten that exchange.

This is the challenge of being a Christian today. We have forgotten how to live together in Christ's kingdom and invite the world along. Our collective imagination has lost the new possibilities for the world in the life, death, resurrection, and reign of Jesus Christ. Instead, within the comforts of Christendom, we set up churches as organizations for maintaining Christians. When people like those three students think of *church*, they think of large buildings where people gather to hear well-dressed men (mostly men) talk for an hour, usually from behind a pulpit. As a result, many of our sons and daughters cannot stomach the thought of becoming a pastor in these churches.

Nonetheless, this is the task the church faces: political organizing for the kingdom. To be clear, this has nothing to do with national politics. It is the work of gathering people into God's presence, living together under the one reign of God in Christ. This way of life doesn't stay within the walls of a church building but bursts out into the world through all the circles of our lives. The task of church leadership today is to gather people into Christ's presence in all the circles of our lives. This is what faithful presence looks like. This is church.

DEFAULTING TO MAINTENANCE OR EXHAUSTION

But we are ever distracted.

In response to the dwindling, aging church of the West, most churches scurry to either work harder to please an existing group of believers or organize justice projects exterior to the church that somehow make us feel we are doing something positive and relevant in the world. The first strategy I have called maintenance mode. This is the church of the parents of the Northern Seminary students. This is the church the students were rejecting. The second strategy I have called exhaustion mode, and it is the church that leaves the church behind. This the church the Northern Seminary students were implicitly accepting. I hope I have made it clear how important it is, at this crucial time in the church's history, to reject both of these impulses. Either strategy, I contend, draws us away from being the church. Either one, I fear, ends in a slow demise.

The church of maintenance will die a slow death as it focuses on the close circle, providing goods and services as efficiently and relevantly as possible to the already existing aging Christians in the church. It cannot help but fail to engage the world. The church of exhaustion, on the other hand, eventually runs out of resources and inspiration. It somehow separates the half circles of our lives, where we meet the broken and hurting, from the encounter with the living, resurrected Christ. As a result we are present in the world with no means to discern his in-breaking presence.

We are left to ourselves to do the work of the kingdom. And this church dies the death of exhaustion. Both kinds of churches ultimately fail to engage Christ's presence in the world and are doomed to wither in the years that lie ahead. Those of us in these churches are at a crossroads.

We have no choice, therefore, but to become political organizers for the kingdom. As Christendom wanes and the old ways of attraction fail to bring in new church members, and our resources for doing good in the world dissipate, we have no choice but to lead our communities into being present to Christ in all the circles of our lives. We have no choice but to practice his kingdom as an entire way of life.

So let us begin. Jesus has given us the seven disciplines to shape us as a people for all of life, not just Sunday mornings. Jesus has given us all we need to lead his people beyond maintenance or exhaustion and into his faithful presence. Let us start with table fellowships in our homes. Surely this kingdom starts in the close circles. But it will always move out as we tend to the tables of our neighborhoods. In every conflict, in every place of racial strife, in our homes, at the bars, and in the parks, let us inhabit the places where broken lives intersect in our neighborhoods and make space for God's kingdom to break in. Let us make space among us for a new proclamation of the gospel and the kingdom to become visible.

It matters not whether we are a megachurch, a church of less than a hundred, or twelve people meeting in a house. We are all called to faithful presence. As Alan Hirsch once said, "God can do more with twelve disciples than twelve thousand religious consumers."[1] And so it is incumbent on churches, large or small, to organize religious consumers into small groups of disciples to sit around the tables of their neighborhoods. The possibilities are endless. Faithful presence knows no particular size or location.

FAITHFUL PRESENCE: WHERE GOD IS TAKING THE WORLD

The book of Revelation tells us that the destiny of the world is "God with us." As pictured in Revelation 21, in the new heaven and earth there will be no temple, for its temple is the Lord God himself dwelling among us (Rev 21:22).

Behold, the dwelling place of God is with man. He will dwell with them, and
they will be his people, and God himself will be with them as their God.
(Rev 21:3 ESV)

The world will be restored fully to God's faithful presence. This future is
already assured in Christ, who now rules as the lamb of God.

And yet this future awaits completion. The lamb of God rules humbly
and patiently, opening one seal at a time, allowing all that must happen
to unwind for the restoration of the world. But it is through Christ's
presence already among the churches that he will work. The risen Christ
himself "walks among the seven golden lampstands" (Rev 2:1), bringing
forth a witness to his in-breaking reign.[2] For those faithfully present to
him, the lampstand of his presence won't be removed (Rev. 2:5). He
promises to be continually with us. And it is through his presence among
a people that God will change the world. The book of Revelation paints
this wonderful picture of his faithful presence.

God therefore has not called Christians to change the world. God already has changed the world in Jesus Christ. He now seeks a people to be
faithfully present to him and his work in the world for the completion of
all things—humanity united with God to live forevermore in his presence.

WILL WE PRAY "COME, LORD JESUS"?

So as we walk forward in this challenge, we can take heart that none of
this will be our own doing. Faithful presence is cooperating with God
where he is already present. It is living where the rest of the world is already headed. They just don't know it yet. So the closing question of this
book is, Will we be his faithful presence in the world?

Revelation ends with this prayer of the church: "Come, Lord Jesus"
(Rev 22:20). This prayer traditionally prays for Christ's future return and
the culmination of all things. But is there more to this prayer than that?
Is this prayer only waiting for the future? Or is it also a prayer for his
presence to come among us now? Like kingdom prayer, does "Come,
Lord Jesus" open space for Christ's presence to be among us here today
for the in-breaking of his kingdom, a foretaste of where the whole world
is going?[3] I contend yes.

I believe this prayer embodies that posture of prayer we gather in at every meal, in every conflict, while proclaiming the gospel, while sitting with the marginalized, and being with children, while exercising his gifts. "Come, Lord Jesus" is the posture we are to live as Christians together in all seven disciplines.[4] This prayer shapes us to live together as his faithful presence in the world.

Let's pray this prayer, suffer and flourish in this prayer; let's live all of life in this prayer as we learn to walk as a people called to be Christ's faithful presence in the world. This is the way God will change the world.

Even so, come, Lord Jesus.

Acknowledgments

This book has been a long time coming. I cannot begin to remember all the places I've discussed the ideas of this book and put flesh on them with groups of pastors, church boards, academic lectures, doctoral seminars, pub groups, seminary classrooms, and especially with my own church. Nonetheless, at the risk of leaving some people out, I want to give thanks to some people.

I give thanks to my present church community, Peace of Christ Community (Christian and Missionary Alliance) in Westmont, Illinois, and my former church community, Life on the Vine Christian Community (C & MA) in Long Grove, Illinois, which planted Peace of Christ. These two churches have played a huge role in putting flesh on the disciplines described in this book. Then there was the Friday night table fellowship in our home in Arlington Heights and all our friends at McDonald's in Rolling Meadows who invited me regularly to sit at their tables. I thank you all. I thank the breakfast table fellowships of Peace of Christ. I thank all the pastors I shared leadership with previously at Life on the Vine and those I currently share leadership with at Peace of Christ.

I thank all the people who read parts of this book's early manuscript and offered some comments or just a word of encouragement. Among these are Mandy Smith, Keas Keasler, Jon Berbaum, Scot McKnight, Anthony Bradley, Aaron Gerrard, Kurt Frederickson, Pierre Keys, Ben Swihart, Josiah Daniels, Aaron Niequist, Stanley Hauerwas, Cam Roxburgh, Michael Frost, and Todd Hunter.

Sam Cocar was my teaching assistant while I was writing this book. He did much research for me on the historic development of these disciplines as sacraments. Much of his work did not make it into the final edit, but it nonetheless helped shape my convictions shared in this book.

Thanks to Aaron Lindloff who designed graphics in the book. Catherine Lindloff (Aaron's wife) painted seven paintings of the seven practices for our church. Thanks to her for the inspiration her paintings have been in the writing of this book.

To Northern Seminary faculty and board, I thank you for supporting my ministry, providing me a sabbatical to get things started on this book, and prodding me on. Northern Seminary has been a blessing in my life.

Helen Lee has been my editor for this book. She and InterVarsity Press have been great partners in getting this book out. I thank Helen and IVP for all their great work.

Over these years I have seen and heard many stories of wonder from many different places and churches. I have told some of these stories in this book. To everyone whose lives and ministry have intersected with mine: Thank you for letting me be part of your lives and churches. You all have made this book possible.

Most of all, I thank my wife, Rae Ann, and my son, Max, for supporting me in my work and the writing of this book. There have been many late nights and some significant travel. But somehow God has woven us together in this life in ministry. And I praise God for you and how you have sustained me and my life in our ministry together. I love you. You have especially made this book possible.

In all these things, to God be the glory.

Appendix 1

What Formation Looks Like Around the Table

W hile speaking in North America on the table and the three circles, I have often been asked to describe in more concrete detail what formation looks like around the table, especially in our homes and in our neighborhoods. How can one lead that? How does the table on Sunday shape us to discern Christ's presence around the tables of our neighborhoods, where we eat throughout the week?

Every time we gather here around our Lord's Table we are being trained (disciplined) into a discerning posture that trains our eyes, minds, and hearts to discern the real presence of Christ among us. As we are being led to partake of the Lord's Table, we are being shaped to discern his presence here first and then in the world. We are being shaped to see Jesus, recognize him, and join what he is doing around the various tables of our lives. But how actually does this actually work? I offer four things in this regard.

First, we are shaped into a posture of *submission* at the table. We can't come to the Lord's Table apart from submitting to his presence and all of what is happening around this table. Jesus illustrated it in Luke 22, when the disciples were posturing for power and position he said, "not so with you" (vv. 24-26). He then inaugurates the table with the words "As my Father has conferred on me, so I confer on you a kingdom" (my translation). He in effect announces that a new kind of authority will be manifest around this table, and it will be manifest in submission to one another (vv. 25, 29-30). Indeed, he models this by washing the disciples' feet around the table. Only in this posture can the kingdom, his presence, function.

God will not coerce us. He will not force himself on us. He is careful not to overwhelm us. God is love, so he comes to be among us. This means that by surrendering to his presence we open up space for him to work and to discern his work among us and in the world. This is the way God works in Christ. The table teaches us how to submit to his presence and then to do the same when we sit at all the various tables of our neighborhood. It relieves us from trying to control or to coerce the neighborhood. This posture is foundational to discerning Christ's presence among us.

Second, we are shaped at the table into a posture of *receiving*. At the beginning of the Lord's Table, we always give thanks. Thanksgiving is fundamental to the act of coming to the table. It's the first thing we do as we gather around the table and is why the historic church has called the table *Eucharist*, the Greek term for "thanksgiving" or "gratefulness." Every time we give thanks before we eat at a table, we are enacting this tradition of the Lord's Table.

Giving thanks opens us to receive from God. It opens space for the blessings of the kingdom. In many of the ancient liturgies we must cup our hands in order to receive the bread. The wafer is placed in the open hand (or sometimes an open mouth). We must *receive* the bread, not take it. It is the same for the cup. In many ancient liturgies we are not allowed to take hold of the cup, only receive it as poured into our mouth.

I believe this posture of receiving is essential as we go into the world to discern Christ. As we sit, listen, and be present with our neighbors, we release control and open our lives to receive the ever-surprising works of God. We open space to receive from God what he would do instead of imposing our expectations on him and others.

Third, we are shaped at the table into a posture of *ceasing* to strive. Similar to submission and related to giving thanks, part of tending to Christ's presence at the table is quieting our egos. All of us must release the urge to control and to solve problems. We instead become present to Christ in this space among us.

I take this to be the dynamic exposed in Luke 10:38-42, where Jesus comes to the home of Mary and Martha. The text reports that "Martha was distracted by her many tasks" (v. 40), trying to get things in order and under control. In her busyness Martha becomes perturbed and asks Jesus to admonish her sister, Mary, to help Martha. Jesus replies, "Martha, Martha, you are worried and distracted by many things; there is need of only one thing" (vv. 41-42). Cease the striving and be present to me. Around the table there is a presence that puts my own concerns on the back burner as I tend to the other person before me.

When eating at a table in the neighborhood, especially when I am the host, I must learn to quiet my ego. I must also gently point others away from their own self-absorptions. We must tend to the presence of Christ in our midst, what is happening with the other person. We must not draw attention to ourselves. Trust builds from this, which in turn opens a space for Jesus to work. I learned all of this at the Lord's Table. This is essential to discerning Christ's presence among us.

Finally, at the table a *social dynamic*—forgiveness of sins, reconciliation, and renewal of all things—is set into motion, and this goes with us into the neighborhoods. The Lord's Table rehearses (Greek *anamnēsis*) Christ's death and resurrection. It is Christ's body broken for us: the forgiveness of sins. The cup we share, Jesus says, is the cup of the new covenant in his blood, the new relationship we have with God the Father, the renewal of all things in the Spirit. And so each time we take the bread, we open ourselves to his forgiveness anew. This forgiveness governs our life together. Each time we receive the elements, we are rehearsing our reconciliation with God and one another in Christ. Reconciliation governs our relationships. Each time we receive the cup, we open ourselves to receive the new covenant in his blood, the new relationship with God the Father through the Son by the Spirit. All that has been made possible via the Holy Spirit is opened to us anew.

This space around the table therefore shapes us into the logic of Christ's forgiveness, reconciliation, and renewal of all things. It opens up space for the work of the Holy Spirit to forgive, heal, reconcile, and to share grace and miracles of renewal. In the Spirit unimaginable things can now happen. And when we leave this table, this way of relating goes with us into the world. It shapes our discerning of what God in Christ is doing in all our relationships.

We should therefore sense in profound ways when God is working to forgive, to reconcile, to renew. We should see the yearnings and the stumblings, and the grasping and the violence that arise as occasions for God's work in the world through Christ. We can in essence discern Christ at all the tables of our lives and invite people into his work.

These four ways, then (I am sure there are others), are ways that the table shapes us in Christ by the Spirit to discern his presence in the world.

Appendix 2

The Indispensible Role of the Dotted
Circle in the Disciplines

When the church focuses on any one of the three circles to the exclusion of the other two, distortions happen in the church. When the church focuses on the close circle, cutting it off from the half circle, the church lapses into maintenance mode. Likewise, when the church focuses on the half circle, cutting it off from the close circle, the church becomes exhausted. In both of these cases distortions occur as well in the dotted circles.

When the close circle is the sole focus of the church (maintenance mode), the dotted circle is closed off from mission. The home fellowships of the neighborhood (the dotted circle) become affinity groups focused on themselves. The dotted circle becomes another version of the close circle. On the other hand, when the half circle becomes the sole focus of the church, dotted-circle fellowships lose their calling to extend Christ's presence into their neighborhoods. They devolve into support groups for social justice. Separated from discerning the real presence of Christ among us, these groups fail to reach the depths of the reconciled and renewed life made possible in the kingdom of Christ. They devolve into neighborhood block parties with a cause.

Distortions also happen when a church focuses on or even starts with dotted-circle table fellowship. Ideally the dotted circle should be the in-between station through which traffic travels between the half circle and the close circle. Rarely does a new entrant into the kingdom in the half circle go directly into the close circle. There must be an in-between stop on the journey from the half circle to the close circle.

Likewise, there are occasions when Christians, sitting as guests at the half-circle table of those who do not yet know Christ, become witnesses to the kingdom breaking in. When this happens, leadership and discipleship is needed. This best takes place next in dotted circle settings. Along the Emmaus road (Lk 24) and at Cornelius's house (Acts 10), both Jesus and Peter started out as guests in a home and later became the host.[1] When we lose either the close circle or the half circle however, the church loses the possibility of being on these journeys.

It was common practice in the New Testament church to have a general meal prior to the Lord's Table. In 1 Corinthians 11 this connection was evidently breaking down. There were divisions and disregard for the poor. Christ's presence was not being tended to at the general meal (or the dotted circle). Paul therefore accuses them of desecrating the Lord's Table (v. 27). He declares that they are not eating the Lord's Supper (v. 20). For Paul, there must be an unbroken connection between the dotted circle and the close circle.

Many megachurches of the last twenty years have organized weekly gatherings (most often on Sunday mornings) that welcome onlookers. The meeting place is carefully staged to make visitors comfortable in their anonymity. With no commitment or discernment, the onlookers can participate as little or as much as they prefer. Through the sermon, music, and other means they are presented with a taste of what Christ can do for them. Theoretically, this space looks most like the dotted circle. This kind of church often fails to develop a close circle either in homes or at the church building, and discipleship lags. These churches notably have trouble keeping people from flowing out the back door. And since there is little time to be in the half circles of people's lives, these churches become introverted and consumerist.

Jesus seemed to disdain those who stayed forever in the dotted circle. For instance, after the feeding of the five thousand in John 6 (what I call the dotted circle in chap. 3), Jesus seems upset that the crowds following him are only looking for more of the same (v. 26). Jesus tells them that they need more than that. They need to know him, "the bread of life" (v. 35). The discussion then escalates among his questioners and he ends up declaring, "Unless you eat the flesh of the Son of Man and drink his blood, you have no life in you" (v. 53). Those who do will live forever. This is offensive to many, who subsequently leave (v. 66). Jesus, I suggest, is telling the crowds (and his questioners) that the dotted circle is never enough. It must lead to the close circle that gathers people in the very presence of the risen Lord.

The dotted circle is therefore essential to the life of the church among the world. Just as with the other two circles, whenever it is either isolated or cut off from the other circles, it gets distorted and the church ceases to be the faithful presence of God in the world.

Appendix 3

Extending the Presence: An Alternative Basis for Ecclesiology and Mission

The missional movement has understood the church in mission (what is often called "missional ecclesiology") via the two doctrines of (1) *missio Dei* (the mission of God) and (2) the incarnation. And yet these two ways of relating the church to mission have often diminished the role of the church as less important for mission or left us with few ways to organize the church so as to see its role as central to mission. In what follows, I briefly outline these two problems and propose an alternative way to understand the church in mission, which alleviates these problems. The result is a way of understanding church (ecclesiology) that lies at the foundation of the what I call "faithful presence."

MISSIO DEI AND INCARNATION

Beginning in the late 1990s the missional church movement migrated to North America. Several North American theological leaders, following the influence of British missiologist (and missionary) Lesslie Newbigin, wrote *Missional Church*, which challenged the North American church to see itself and the world differently.[1] They spawned a new movement called the missional church. Two dominant themes emerged from this movement: *missio Dei* and incarnation. The first theme, *missio Dei* (the "mission of God" in English), asserted that God is at work beyond the church, reconciling the world to himself. The church therefore is called to go beyond its own walls and join with God in his mission. The second theme, incarnation, asserted that just as God has come into the world via the Son to be *with* humanity in everyday life, so too Christians are called to inhabit our neighborhoods to be with people.[2] Based on these two themes, missional church leaders pushed for Christians to move to where people are and be present in the surrounding contexts of our lives. These themes drive the various streams of the missional church movement to this day.[3] And yet they produce problems when it comes to ecclesiology.

The first belief, *missio Dei*, affirms that the triune God is a sending God. The Father sends the Son who sends the Spirit into the world to reconcile the world to himself. Mission is what God is doing, not what the church does. In theologian Jürgen Moltmann's words, the church does not have a mission to fulfill in the world, "it is the mission of the Son and the Spirit through the Father that includes the church."[4] In this way, *missio Dei* shapes a wider imagination for God working in the world beyond the church. It inspires us and emboldens Christians for mission, because it turns the burden of mission back onto God. Now all we have to do is cooperate with him in his power.

No one can deny the power of this theological insight. But, by itself, *missio Dei* presents a problem. God's mission is so big—he is at work everywhere—how do we discern where we are called specifically to join his mission? Surely God is at work in that homeless shelter in the neighborhood or the community park where moms gather with their children. God is surely at work in that broken person's plea for help, in that foreclosure across the street, in that Black Lives Matter march for justice, in that domestic abuse shelter, and in the struggle for immigration reform. While we are inspired to get outside the boundaries of the church to work for God's mission, we are overwhelmed by all the mission possibilities around us. We feel like the church is caught in a wild goose chase. There are so many places to serve, but our church has only so many resources. We soon get exhausted. What are we to do?

In addition, there are many different versions of justice out there. If we listen long enough, we might discover that some food pantries do things to keep homeless people as clients in order to keep their system going that pays their large salaries. Much of what we end up doing is providing temporary relief that in fact sustains injustice. We might discover we have become mere cogs in the machinery of federal social services. Isn't there more to justice than this? For sure, acts of mercy that sustain the poor among us are acts of righteousness. But isn't there more to God's vision for justice than mere preservation? Doesn't God want to reorder the world toward renewal of all things? Is there something unique I bring as a Christian to these places of service?

We need to be able to join what God is doing not on the basis of our own effort, power, or ego. We therefore need disciplines that can help us discern these questions. In short, we need to discern his presence.

The second belief, the incarnation, teaches us that God has come into the world as one of us. In the words of *The Message*, "The Word became flesh and blood, / and moved into the neighborhood" (Jn 1:14). Alan Hirsch says the incarnation teaches us that God came into the world "not only with humanity as a whole, but with a particular group of people." This is how God works, "from within a particular culture, in ways that people can grasp, understand, and respond." For Hirsch this is the primary biblical model of engagement.[5] We should go into neighborhoods, give up power, become present, listen to our neighbors. This is the incarnational way. Ecclesiology (or the form the church takes) must come afterwards. It's always something birthed brand new for each specific context. In the words of Hirsch, ecclesiology must come out the "back end" of missiology.[6]

But when living incarnationally among people and neighborhoods, we naturally fear imposing any kind of organization on those it makes no sense to. We rightfully resist the histories of European colonialism. We fear becoming a maintenance organization for the propagation of our own flawed religion. So by default incarnation avoids organization. The church must be an event, a breaking in of the kingdom anew for each new place we inhabit.[7] We struggle to take shape as a cohesive social reality as a people. We tend to stay as a group, individuals. We see ourselves as "little Jesuses," entering our neighborhoods incarnationally, from which God will birth his new kingdom.[8]

Again, I applaud the power of this theological insight. But there is a problem here as well. A socially visible community that witnesses to what healing and reconciliation look like never takes shape. We do not gather regularly in ways that shape us into his presence. The fear of maintaining an organization leaves us with no visible social presence that God can use to change the world. Whereas *missio Dei* was too big, it almost seems like incarnation is too small. And just as with *missio Dei* communities, communities based on incarnation often fail to land as well.

It is through a visible social life (i.e., the dotted circles) that people can see what the reconciled, forgiven, and renewed life of the kingdom looks like. We need a discerning presence that comes from the close gatherings around the table and proclaiming gospel (i.e., close circles). Without such communities, God's witness will be limited to private, subjective, individual experiences. We need regular disciplines that shape us into God's presence in all three circles, beginning in a close circle and extending to the dotted and half circles of our lives. It is therefore essential that individuals doing mission form organized communities of the kingdom in the world.

Missio Dei Plus Incarnation Equals Witness

The disciplines of this book illustrate that the church is a product of the twofold movement of the Son (from the Father by the Spirit) into the world.[9] Here, in this space of the church, shaped by the disciplines, the *missio Dei* meets the incarnation of God in the Son to produce the witness of the church.

The first move is God sending the Son into the world. In him, God accomplishes his victory over sin, death, and evil. Then God the Father, at the ascension, exalts Jesus as ruling Lord over all things (Phil 2:9-11). "He must reign until he has put all his enemies under his feet" and then comes the end (1 Cor 15:25). And so God continues to work in and through Christ's reign for the consummation of all things beyond the church. This is God's mission in and over the whole world (*missio Dei*).

The second move is God, in and through his Son, sending the Spirit into the world. Jesus says to the disciples, "As the Father has sent me, so

I send you." After he says this, he breathed on them and said, "Receive the Holy Spirit." Then he promises that the keys of the kingdom will go with them (Jn 20:21-23). The authority and power of his reign go along with them.

In this second move, God is extending the presence of the Son into the world.[10] In the Farewell Discourses, Jesus says, if I go, the Advocate will come in my place (Jn 16:7, my paraphrase; see also Jn 14). The Holy Spirit proceeds as Jesus ascends. He takes Jesus' place on earth. Far from being absent from our lives and residing in heaven (as my evangelical Sunday school taught me), Christ extends his presence with us in his church. The Greek word for Advocate, *paraklētos*, means "one called [to come] alongside." The word itself carries the idea of being *with*.[11] Jesus says the Spirit comes as "another [*allon*] paraclete" (Jn 14:16), a second paraclete, who comes to take my place. Jesus therefore extends his own presence through the giving of the Spirit to the disciples. The Spirit extends Jesus' incarnational reality into the world through his disciples.[12]

So, after the sending of the Son, the first move, Christ's ascension and cosmic reign, comes the second move, the extension of Christ's real presence with his church. Within these two moves the church lives until the consummation.[13] We go confident that God in Christ is at work in the whole world. Yet as we go, Christ's real presence goes with us, becoming visible in power whenever we are reconciled to one another ("I am there among them" [Mt 18:20]), whenever we proclaim the gospel in the villages ("whoever rejects you, rejects me" [Lk 10:16]), whenever we are present with "the least of these" ("you did it to me" [Mt 25:40]), or whenever we are present with children ("whoever welcomes one such child . . . welcomes me" [Mt 18:5]). Here God's cosmic reign in Christ (*missio Dei*) is made visible by Christ's presence via the church (incarnation). What God is working for in the world takes on flesh in the midst of these disciplines. This is witness. This is church. This is faithful presence.

Witness means we can point and say, "Behold, look what God is doing to change the world."[14] This is when we know witness has happened. It happens at the intersection of God's cosmic reign and God's particular presence in Christ in a specific people, a specific place, and a specific time. When God's people become present to God's presence in the world (*missio Dei*) by making space for Christ's presence to be among them (incarnation), witness happens. In mathematical terms we might put it this way: *missio Dei* + incarnation = witness. This is faithful presence.

THE POSTURE NECESSARY FOR MISSION

Surely this is dangerous to say the church is the extension of Christ's presence into the world.[15] Doesn't this idea align the church too closely with God's kingdom? Doesn't this put the church in control of the kingdom? Aren't we making the same error Roman Catholics make when they claim there is no salvation outside the church or that the pope is infallible?[16] Aren't we one step away from the Crusades of the thirteenth century all over again? Aren't we on our way to being another Westboro Baptist Church? These are all scary episodes in which the church oversteps itself, takes God's power into its own hands, and sometimes commits heinous acts. We should fear privileging the church over all other people and religions of the world. We should fear becoming presumptuous that we have cornered the market on God.

So it is important to reiterate: the church does not own or control Christ's presence or reign. Rather, his kingdom takes shape in our submission to Christ and his reign together as a people. When Christians gather together and tend to his presence in this way, Christ promises to be present. His reign becomes visible among (and in) us by the Holy Spirit. Any attempt, however, to take control of Christ's power and claim it as our own subverts this same power. Where there is no submission to Christ, he is absent. Any sense of hubris or lack of humility should set off red flags that Christ's presence is not here. We can only be vehicles for Christ's authority, neither owners of it nor arbiters of it.[17]

SENTNESS EXTENDS CHRIST'S AUTHORITY (NOT OURS)

A quick look at Luke 10 reinforces how important this posture is for the church's missionary task. It is at the core of what it means to be sent.

When Jesus sends the Seventy to proclaim the kingdom in the villages, he gives them a series of instructions: "Whoever listens to you listens to me, and whoever rejects you rejects me, and . . . the one who sent me" (Lk 10:16). This stunning extension of the presence and authority of Christ goes with them. When the disciples return, they are shocked by the experience of Christ's authority among them. They report, "Lord, in your name even the demons submit to us," and Jesus responds, "I saw Satan fall like lightning from heaven. I have given you authority to trample on snakes and scorpions and to overcome the power of the enemy; nothing will harm you" (vv. 17-19 NIV). Jesus pronounces unambiguously that the Lord's authority extends through the disciples sent into the villages.

But again, we must recognize the danger here as well. There is the potential in this sending to presume that this power is *ours*. The disciples fall into this trap throughout the four Gospels. So Jesus says, after the sensational reports, "Nevertheless, do not rejoice at this, that the spirits submit to you, but rejoice that your names are written in heaven" (Lk 10:20). Jesus says, in other words, do not presume that this authority is yours. Rather focus on the fact that you are citizens of the King, participating in the kingdom, that the rule and power being exercised is from heaven (the seat of God's authority). This in essence is what it means to say, "Your names are written in heaven." So this power is not yours. Rather, in your proclaiming the kingdom, you are making space for people to submit to the reign of God. In your submission, you create the social space for the authority of the kingdom to be unleashed in his presence, and you are privileged to be participants in it as subjects of the King.[18]

The disciples are instructed to enter the villages humbly (as lambs among wolves [Lk 10:3]) with no accoutrements of power (carry no purse, no bag, no sandals [v. 4]) and be present in the homes around the tables of the people they are sent to (v. 7), as guests devoid of power. And yet they bring the announcement that "the kingdom of God has come near to you" (v. 9). In their humility, and in their submission to what God is doing in this place, they clear space for the kingdom, for Jesus to become present. And by being humbly present, they can discern his presence and point to its breaking in.

So the posture problem is solved. We are always sent with something. We bring Christ's presence, the capacity to open space for his rule. And this is manifested in our eating, reconciling, being with the hurting, proclaiming the gospel, and the other disciplines we have covered in this book. But we do not control God's power in Christ. It is never our power. God is sovereign over all and working already in the places we are sent. So the posture we must assume is one of the incarnation, giving up all hubris, control, and arrogance. Instead, we come humbly and vulnerably to be present. Anything else and the power of God, his very kingdom, evacuates from our midst, and we become defensive, judgmental, controlling, and impotent for the kingdom.

This kind of *sentness* is essential to the identity of the church in mission. We are sent as emissaries of Christ with his presence and his authority. Yet, in those sent, a certain posture is necessary in order to be truly present to what God is doing in his reign. We must inhabit the incarnational posture of humility and vulnerability and submit to Jesus as Lord in each context in order to open space for his presence. Apart from being sent with his accompanying presence, there is no mission. We bring nothing. On the other hand, apart from being humbly present and tending to Christ and his work (not ours), we will never discern what God is doing, and our own power will supplant and deny God's power in Christ. All of this is what it means for the church to extend the presence of Christ in the world.

God Comes to Be Present in a Place

This is the way God has chosen to change the world. God will not force himself on the world. Instead he looks patiently for an entry point to become present. God will not come into the world, intervene violently, and destroy all sin. He rejected this option since the Noahic flood ("Never again" [Gen 9:11]). Instead, he chooses to enter the world at a place, in Abraham, Israel, Jesus, and then in the church, slowly working to manifest his restorative presence in the world through a people. As Catholic theologian Gerhard Lohfink says, "God desires to liberate and change the entire world but for that purpose he needs a beginning in the midst of the world, a visible place" from which he starts.[19]

So God finds someone or a people and sends them to a place as an entry point. Jesus, the Son, of course, was that ultimate entry point (although the prior entry point was Abraham and his history with Israel). The Son, God and human, was sent to be *with* us. God then extends that single entry point in Christ through a people called the church. The disciples and his church are sent as an extension of the Son. Today, the Son sits at the right hand of the Father, looking over the whole world to extend that entry point into every nook and cranny of the world. He is seeking a people who will be faithful to his presence in the world.

God needs just a few people who will call him Lord and be faithful to his presence in the places where they live. (Remember the conversation between God and Abraham about Sodom [Gen 18:16-33]?) In each of these places he will become present in a way that can be seen, in a way that can be accepted or rejected. This is the nature of faithful presence.

So God, who is already Lord of the world, comes to us in Christ by the Spirit to be present in our circumstances, our language, and our poverty. He comes in love and patience. He works in and through people who will join him. And here, in this place called the church, before the watching world, his authority and power become real. He reigns not as a despot but as the Lamb who was slain. Slowly, through his presence, he is setting things right, bringing reconciliation, forgiveness, and healing in and through a people. Each time a relationship is reconciled, an injustice is overturned, his presence becomes visible, his kingdom breaks in anew. This new social reality called the kingdom is birthed before the watching world and will continue until its completion in his return. It is the church. It is his faithful presence.

Appendix 4

Where Is the Church?
A Closer Look at Matthew 25

Returning to the back porch in the Michigan City beach house (see chap. 2), we remember the disconnect those people felt between their lives together in worship, the Lord's Table and discipleship, and their life in their neighborhoods, homes, and work. "Yes, we're out there helping hurting people, but nothing seems to be happening! No more people are gathering for worship." There is tendency to separate the disciplines we do together as Christians, like, for instance, the Lord's Table on Sunday morning and the disciplines we live in the neighborhood, the various tables we share in our homes, and neighborhood gatherings. This book, *Faithful Presence*, has tried to describe how they are all linked. The tables in the world are the extensions of the table we gather around as Christians on Sunday morning. There is no *in here* and *out there* (church in here, world out there). There is only one way of life lived seamlessly *among* the neighborhood as the church.

The history of the interpretation of the parable of the final judgment in Matthew 25 illustrates this dynamic. Jesus describes how the Son of Man is sitting on the throne of his glory at the end of time, separating the sheep from the goats, the righteous from the unrighteous (vv. 31-33). The Son of Man ends up welcoming the righteous into the kingdom by recognizing those who gave him food when he was hungry, drink when he was thirsty, clothes when he was naked, and visited him when he was sick and in prison (vv. 34-36). The righteous respond by asking, "When was it that we saw you hungry and gave you food, or thirsty and gave you something to drink?" The Son of Man answers, "Truly, I say to you, as you did it to one of the least of these my brothers, you did it to me" (v. 40 ESV).

Historically, there have been two dominant interpretations of this text, one associated with *in here* and the other with *out there*. Both interpretations center around the words, "least of these my brothers."[1] One interpretation (often referred to as the "particularist" interpretation) understands the "least of these my brothers" to refer to Jesus' disciples. These interpreters point to the occasions where Jesus appears to use similar words to refer specifically to his disciples (Mt 10:40-42; Mt 28:10). In this interpretation, the declaration of righteousness is to be based on how the world receives the church in mission amid suffering. The kingdom (and indeed the presence of Christ) is located exclusively in the church. We could say this interpretation substantiates the *in here* idea of the church.[2]

The other (nonrestrictive) interpretation says that "the least of these my brothers" refers to all of those who are in need, wherever they may be found. Here it is noted that of the thirty-eight times *brothers* is used in Matthew, only on three occasions does he use *brothers* to refer to Jesus' disciples. These interpreters note that the few instances where *brothers* is used to refer to Jesus' disciples, it does not correlate well with the way Jesus uses the word in Matthew 25 (e.g., "the little ones" in Mt 10:42 is used very differently than "least of these" in Mt 25). Furthermore Jesus' purpose for the parable is to motivate faithful discipleship, not console existing Christians.[3] It therefore seems most likely that "the least of these my brothers" refers to the needy. Those who will be declared righteous, therefore, are those who spend time ministering among the poor. Based on this interpretation, Jürgen Moltmann argues that since the church is wherever Christ is, and Christ is to be found present with "the least of these," the church is to be found with the poor. This interpretation substantiates the *out there* idea of the church, that the church exists outside the group of already gathering believing Christians, where God is working for justice.[4]

But are these the only options? Over against these two options, I propose a third: that the kingdom/presence of Jesus becomes manifest in the dynamic between "the disciples" (the *you* in "as you did it") and "the least of these my brothers." In fact, by Jesus referring to the hurting as "brothers" he is emphasizing the relationship of kinship (or family) that takes place as Christians come alongside and are present *with* the poor (see chap. 6). The declaration of who is righteous will be based on who was there in the presence of Christ.

To expand on this last thought, notice that the Son of Man in Matthew 25:32 is reflecting backward, discerning who was in the kingdom in the past. He is judging who is in the kingdom now based on who was actually in the kingdom during their earthly lives. Thus, the sense of the text is this: "When you were doing this, you were already in the kingdom because I was present there; the kingdom was breaking in. As such, when you, the church, were *with* the poor as family, that was a sign you were already participating in the kingdom."

This interpretation of Matthew 25 expands the boundaries of God's work beyond the church. It moves the borders of the church beyond the particularist interpretation. Yet, because it is the church encountering people on the margins, it provides the means to discern the kingdom there in concrete circumstances (something lost in the nonrestrictivist position) via the church. The kingdom is discerned when the church, as Christians in submission to Jesus as Lord, extends into the neighborhood, submitting to Christ as King in acts of being present with the poor. Here space is opened up. More people submit to Christ as King. Forgiveness, reconciliation, the gospel, the renewal of all things is discerned as the Christians become present among the poor. Here, once again, Christ's real presence is made manifest. The kingdom takes shape.

The church therefore cannot be described as only *in here* (particularist interpretation), where his people gather to submit to Christ, or *out there*, where "the least of these" are (Moltmann's nonretrictivist interpretation). It is always birthed *among*, where the church becomes present *with* "the least of these." The church cannot be located exclusively *in here*, in the close circle, or *out there*, solely in the half circle. Either option fails to grasp the encounter of the disciples with Christ among the poor. Only in one continuous life lived in all three circles is *faithful presence* realized.

Appendix 5

A Simple History of the Disciplines
from New Testament Church to Christendom

Practice	New Testament Church	Medieval	Reformation	Modern
Baptism	initiatory rite	infant	infant/believer's	personal testimony
Proclaiming the Gospel	Luke 4; 10	homily	didactic sermon central	expository—taking notes
The Lord's Table	Luke 22:14-30; 24:13-35	mass (no cup)	subordinate to Word	plastic cups and crackers
Reconciliation	Matthew 18:15-20	confessional/penance	personal/no mediator	conflict mediation
Being with the "Least of These"	Matthew 25:31-46	unction, church systems	civic/ecclesial	justice ministry
Being with Children	Matthew 18:1-5	confirmation	catechesis	kids ministry
Fivefold Gifting	Ephesians 4:1-16	priesthood	priesthood of believers, hierarchy	gift inventory/volunteers, CEO pastor
Kingdom Prayer	Mark 9:14-29, Lord's Prayer	Sunday morning liturgy	Sunday morning liturgy, personal prayer	prayer meetings, personal petition

Notes

INTRODUCTION

[1]James Davison Hunter, *To Change the World* (Oxford: Oxford University Press, 2010).

[2]Hunter's description of "faithful presence" in *To Change the World* (pp. 225-86) resembles neo-Anabaptism as articulated by Stanley Hauerwas and John Howard Yoder even though he criticizes them extensively on pages 150-66. In my estimation, Hunter carries out the standard sectarian critique against Yoder and Hauerwas while failing to grasp just how much their theology of church and culture is a strategy for engaging, as opposed to retreating, from culture.

[3]Hunter, in his book, never really describes the church itself as a social-political reality of God's faithful presence. He seems to carry on a Niebuhrian tendency to ignore the church itself as a viable politic and cultural presence (this Niebuhrian position is described and critiqued by John Howard Yoder most famously in his essay, "How H. Richard Niebuhr Reasoned: A Critique of Christ and Culture" in Glen Stassen, D. M. Yeager, and John Howard Yoder, *Authentic Transformation* [Nashville: Abingdon Press, 1996]). For Hunter, the realm of politics is limited to conflictual nation-state processes. Like Niebuhr, for Hunter this kind of power seems to be a necessary fact of life. Hunter then chastises the neo-Anabaptists for their refusal to engage in it. As a result, he sees the neo-Anabaptist response to this power as a withdrawal from culture. In the process Hunter doesn't see how the church itself can be a political witness to an alternative kind of power. He does not see how the church itself can be a political reality and by so doing become the incubator for new ways to see and engage the world that the world has not yet encountered. There are numerous overtures by Hunter that this indeed is what he wants to see but he has already neutered the church's wherewithal to be such a body by refusing the church's political nature ala Richard Niebuhr (for evidence of this see 169ff., 177ff., 184ff.). The church therefore is reduced to being an instrumentality of faithful presence as opposed to its very social reality from which all other engagement can flow.

1 GOD'S FAITHFUL PRESENCE

[1]A. W. Tozer, *The Pursuit of God* (Camp Hill, PA: Christian Publications, 1999), 27.

[2]John Walton, *The Lost World of Genesis One* (Downers Grove, IL: IVP Academic, 2009), 83.

[3]G. K. Beale argues that the Genesis account of the Garden of Eden portrays Eden as the first sanctuary, a recapitulation of the first temple (Gregory K. Beale, *The Temple and the Church's Mission* [Downers Grove, IL: IVP Books, 2004], 66-80. See also Jon D. Levenson, *Sinai and Zion: An Entry into the Jewish Bible* [New York: HarperOne, 1987]).

[4]Beale, *Temple and the Church's Mission,* chaps. 1, 12.

[5]As reported in Wayne Gordon, *Real Hope in Chicago* (Grand Rapids: Zondervan, 1995). Other details come from conversations with Wayne, who serves on faculty with me at Northern Seminary, Lombard, Illinois.

[6]This narrative concerning the monarchy of Israel was outlined by John Howard Yoder. For a summary see John Nugent, *Politics of Yahweh* (Eugene, OR: Cascade Books, 2011), chap. 4.

[7]See John Howard Yoder, *Preface to Theology: Christology and Theological Method* (Grand Rapids: Brazos, 2002), 243-48; John Howard Yoder, "To Serve Our God and to Rule the World," in *The Royal Priesthood* (Grand Rapids: Eerdmans, 1994), 133-35; N. T. Wright, *Simply Good News* (San Francisco: HarperOne, 2014), 37-42; and N. T. Wright, *How God Became King* (San Francisco: HarperOne, 2012), chap. 7.

[8]I follow here to some extent Scot McKnight, *The Kingdom Conspiracy* (Grand Rapids: Brazos, 2015), 74-76.

[9]This page draws heavily on Gordon Fee, *Paul, the Spirit, and the People of God* (Grand Rapids: Baker Academic, 1996), 17-19; and Gordon Fee, *God's Empowering Presence* (Peabody, MA: Hendrickson, 1994), chap. 15.

2 TO CHANGE THE WORLD

[1]On "heaven and earth" referring to the whole cosmic domain of the rule of God see N. T. Wright, *Surprised By Hope* (San Francisco: HarperOne, 2008), 18-20.

[2]Werner Foerster, "εχουςια," *Theological Dictionary of the New Testament* (Grand Rapids: Eerdmans, 1965), 2:566-74.

[3]According to Joseph Martos, twelfth-century lists of sacraments ranged from twelve to thirty (Joseph Martos, *Doors to the Sacred* [Ligouri, MO: Ligouri/ Triumph, 2001], 50). Oliver O'Donovan argues for only four (Oliver O'Donovan, *Desire of the Nations* [Cambridge: Cambridge University Press, 1999], 169-90). John Howard Yoder isolates five in his *Body Politics* (Scottdale PA: Herald Press, 1992).

[4]Although we should take note that marriage itself is a practice that opens space for God's mission in the world, making spaces for his presence to be made known and invited into. On this see David Matzko McCarthy, *Sex and Love in the Home*

(Eugene OR: Wipf & Stock, 2011); and Renzo Bonetti, *Matrimonio. Sacramento per la Missione* (Rome: Città Nuova, 2013).

[5]J. Denny Weaver describes how the sacraments became individualized or desocialized alongside the medieval church's shift from Christus Victor to satisfaction theories of the atonement in the West. This was part of the church's accommodation to living comfortably in Christendom. See J. Denny Weaver, *Non-Violent Atonement* (Grand Rapids: Eerdmans, 2001), 87-89.

[6]John Howard Yoder is an important theologian in my work, and I quote him often. Nonetheless, I recognize that Yoder has been implicated in abusive sexual behavior in his past, which I am always cognizant of while referencing his work. For more on this issue, see "Anabaptist Mennonite Biblical Seminary Statement on Teaching and Scholarship related to John Howard Yoder," February 27, 2012; approved April 30, 2012, www.ambs.edu/about/documents/AMBS-statement-on-JHY.pdf; and Sara Wenger Shenk, "Unfinished Business with John Howard Yoder," *Christian Churches Together*, accessed April 26, 2016, http://christianchurchestogether.org/unfinished-business-with-john-howard-yoder.

[7]John Howard Yoder, *Body Politics: Five Practices of the Christian Community Before the Watching World* (Scottdale, PA: Herald Press, 2001), 71-73.

[8]I have failed over the years to come up with a good replacement for the word *submission*. And so I will continue to use it in this book and redefine it in terms of its mutuality and the center point for leadership.

3 THE DISCIPLINE OF THE LORD'S TABLE

[1]Cogan Schneier, "Restaurateurs Split on Phones at the Table," *USA Today*, September 1, 2014, www.usatoday.com/story/tech/personal/2014/09/01/restaurants-ban-cell-phones/13724919.

[2]Slavoj Žižek, *Year of Dreaming Dangerously* (New York: Verso, 2012), 63.

[3]We are somberly reminded of the differences between Christians each time we gather around the Lord's Table.

[4]In Stanley Hauerwas's words, "I have no doubt that Jesus is present by His Spirit at work in the world outside the church, yet the church, the gathering around the Eucharist, is the one place where we know He is present. And so it is here where we learn to recognize Jesus and his work from whence we can move in the world and see him clearly there as well." This is my best recollection of a quote I once heard Hauerwas make, but cannot recollect where.

[5]Geoffrey Wainwright expounds on this eschatological reality around the Eucharist in his *Eucharist and Eschatology* (New York: Oxford University Press, 1981), 39-40. See also Alexander Schmemann, *Introduction to Liturgical Theology* (London: Faith Press, 1966), 41-42.

[6]R. Alan Streett describes the communal meal of Rome as an overt exercise in power and discrimination that supported the Roman economic system. The Lord's Supper

was a "subversive meal" that reversed this Roman meal, proclaiming Christ as Lord over even Caesar, welcoming people from all classes to eat together and equalizing all relations. See R. Alan Streett, *Subversive Meals: An Analysis of the Lord's Supper Under Roman Domination During the First Century* (Eugene, OR: Pickwick, 2013).

[7]Although I developed the three circles concept out of my own church leadership, the idea of three circles or three different spaces for the meal is not without precedent. Andrew McGowan delineates carefully how there were different settings for eating around the table in the first centuries of the church. See Andrew B. Mc-Gowan, *Ancient Christian Worship* (Grand Rapids: Baker Academic, 2014), 50-51. Russell E. Riche sees three different meal settings in some streams of Methodism. See his "Family Meal, Holy Communion, and Love Feats: Three Ecumenical Metaphors," in *Ecumenical and Interreligious Perspectives* (Nashville: Quarterly Review of Books, 1992), 17-29.

[8]I learned this way of referring to the table from the Church of the Brethren.

[9]John Chrysostom, quoted in William C. Mills, "Our Common Calling to Holiness and Sanctity," in *Doing More with Life: Connecting Christian Higher Education to a Call to Service*, ed. Michael Robert Miller (Waco, TX: Baylor University Press, 2007), 97.

[10]It could be, that the meeting in the home as described in 1 Corinthians 14 represents such a dotted circle kind of space. Twice in this chapter Paul wants their activities to be sensitive to the outsiders (*idiōtēs*) in their midst (vv. 16, 23, 24) although the table is not specifically mentioned.

[11]Geoffrey Wainwright delineates how "take, bless, break and give" signal the Eucharist for the primitive church in the New Testament. See Geoffrey Wainwright, *Eucharist and Eschatology* (New York: Oxford University Press, 1981), 35-36.

[12]We realize of course, at the time of the actual feeding of the five thousand, the Lord's Table had not been inaugurated by Christ himself. Nonetheless, the Gospel writer (reflecting the early church consciousness), writing after the ascension, saw this feeding as a foreshadowing of the practice of the Eucharist in the presence of Christ.

[13]I termed these kind of questions: the "up, in and out" questions. I learned this way of talking from Mike Breen. See Mike Breen and Steve Cockram, *Building a Discipleship Culture* (Pawleys Island, SC: 3DM Publishing, 2011), chap. 7.

[14]McGowan sees the order of the various tables in reverse. For him, what I define as the half circle leads to the close circle. He states that one way to see the Last Supper is as "the climax of his practice as a frequent, significant and controversial eater" among the outcasts (McGowan, *Ancient Christian Worship*, 26). To me, this reveals how intertwined all three forms of the meal was to Jesus' life.

[15]"Jesus' pre-eminent place as an associate of tax collectors and sinners is arguably not as host, but as guest. Again and again, Jesus is depicted not as offering hospitality to these marginalized but as accepting their hospitality (Mark 1:31; 2:15-17;

14:1-9; Luke 7:33-34, 36-50; 10:3-9, 38-42; 14:1-24; 15:1-2; 19:1-10)" (Andrew Mc-Gowan, "The Meals of Jesus and the Meals of the Church: Eucharistic Origins and Admission to Communion," in *Studia Liturgica Diversa: Essays in Honor of Paul F. Bradshaw*, ed. Maxwell Johnson and L. Edward Phillips [Portland, OR: Pastoral Press, 2004]. 106). Special thanks to Northern Seminary doctoral student Jonathan Massimi who referred this article to me.

[16]McGowan states that the existence of these stories so prominently in the Gospels indicates their importance to "the communities we may identify with the Gospels and their likely antecedents" (ibid., 111). See also Craig Blomberg, *Contagious Holiness: Jesus' Meals with Sinners* (Downers Grove, IL: InterVarsity Press, 2005).

[17]John Howard Yoder, *Body Politics* (Scottdale, PA: Herald Press, 1992), 14-16.

[18]First Corinthians 11 is most likely a reference to eating the agape meal improperly as part of the Lord's Table. See Dom Gregory Dix, *The Shape of the Liturgy* (San Francisco: Harper & Row, 1945), chap. 4.

[19]The actual separation of the agape meal from the more formal Lord's Table time probably happened later in the late second and early third centuries. See Chris D. Balzer, "The Lord's Supper: Meal or Sacrament?" *Reformed Theological Review* 61, no. 3 (December 2002): 117-30; and Dix, *Shape of the Liturgy*, 96-102.

[20]Christine Pohl, *Making Room* (Grand Rapids: Eerdmans, 1999), 29-33, 41-43.

[21]Space does not allow a full exploration of this history. I recommend the work of Joseph Martos, *Doors to the Sacred* (Ligouri, MO: Ligouri/Triumph, 2001), 221-26, as a starting point.

[22]William Cavanaugh, *Torture and Eucharist* (Malden, MA: Blackwell, 1998), 222.

[23]Dix famously reports, "It was in the Latin middle ages that the Eucharist became for the first time something 'said' rather than something 'done'" (Dix, *Shape of the Liturgy*, 13).

[24]Henri de Lubac, *Corpus Mysticum: The Eucharist and the Church in the Middle Ages* (Notre Dame, IN: University of Notre Dame Press, 2006).

[25]Martos, *Doors to the Sacred*, 214-31.

[26]In the words of Alexander Schmemann, "the Eucharist is not only the 'most important' of all offices, it is the source and goal of the entire liturgical life of the Church" (Alexander Schmemann, *Introduction to Liturgical Theology* [London: Faith Press, 1966], 20).

4 The Discipline of Reconciliation

[1]This was reported in Arianna Huffington, "Ferguson: The Untold Story," *Huffington Post*, August 21, 2014, www.huffingtonpost.com/arianna-huffington/ferguson-the-untold-story_b_5697928.html.

[2]Willie James Jennings, "After Ferguson: America Must Abandon 'Sick Christianity' at Ease with Violence," *Religion Dispatches*, December 9, 2014,

http://religiondispatches.org/after-ferguson-america-must-abandon-the-sick-christianity-at-ease-with-violence.

[3]John Howard Yoder makes this point in *Body Politics* (Scottdale PA: Herald Press, 1992), chap. 2.

[4]Robert A. Guelich, in his commentary, shows how the subject of this beatitude is the eschatological peace of Isaiah 9:5-6 and Zechariah 9:9-10, where the Messiah, the Prince of Peace, is described as the bringer of peace on earth. It therefore refers to the dynamic of the in-breaking kingdom being fulfilled in their midst. See Robert Guelich, *The Sermon on the Mount* (Waco, TX: Word, 1982), 106-7.

[5]David Fitch and Geoffrey Holsclaw, *Prodigal Christianity* (San Francisco: Jossey-Bass, 2013), chap. 8.

[6]James Cone argues that a problem in the early civil rights movement was the inability of white Protestant leaders to be present with the black person's plight. He highlights the Social Gospel conferences held in Mohonk, New York, on "the status of the Negro" in American society, where no black persons were invited. According to Cone, in response to why no black persons were invited to these meetings, Lyman Abbott said, "A patient is not invited to the consultation of the doctors on his case" (James Cone, *The Cross and the Lynching Tree* [Maryknoll, NY: Orbis Books, 2011], 62; see also 55-58). In my opinion, Cone's account reveals the lack of presence in the callous Euro-American people's inability to be present with the African American struggle throughout the history of the United States.

[7]Martin Luther King Jr., "Letter from Birmingham Jail," published as "The Negro Is Your Brother," *Atlantic Monthly* 212, no. 2 (August 1963): 78-88.

[8]Historian Everett Ferguson outlines how by the third century reconciliation became a practice put solely into the hands of "the bishops" and a sort of "transactionalism" takes hold in the practice. See his "Early Church Penance," *Restoration Quarterly* 36 (1994): 94. J. van Rossum notes the creation of the special office, a "priest-penitentiary" (J. van Rossum, "Priesthood and Confession in St. Symeon the New Theologian," *St. Vladimir's Theological Quarterly* 20 [1976]: 227).

[9]In recent years, since the publishing of *Ordo Paenitentiae* in 1973 by Pope Paul VI, the Roman Catholic Church has sought to reinstitute both the communal nature of reconciliation and the reality of Christ's presence in the midst of reconciliation. Not coincidentally, that *Ordo* changed the name of the sacrament from penance to reconciliation.

5 THE DISCIPLINE OF PROCLAIMING THE GOSPEL

[1]Allan V. Horwitz and Jerome C. Wakefield, "An Epidemic of Depression," *Psychiatric Times*, November 1, 2008, www.psychiatrictimes.com/major-depressive-disorder/epidemic-depression.

[2]I follow here Scot McKnight, *King Jesus Gospel* (Grand Rapids: Zondervan, 2012), among others, including N. T. Wright.

[3]C. H. Dodd, *The Apostolic Preaching and Its Developments* (London: Hodder & Stoughton, 1936), lec. 1.

[4]Ibid., 38-43.

[5]Some discredit Dodd's sharp distinction between teaching and preaching, arguing there is more overlap between the two in the New Testament than Dodd allowed for. See Robert Worley, *Preaching and Teaching in the Earliest Church* (Philadelphia: Westminster Press, 1967); and Robert Mounce, *The Essential Nature of New Testament Preaching* (Grand Rapids: Eerdmans, 1960). Despite the overlap however, the two words (*kēryssein* and *didaskein*) do describe two different functions. My account of proclamation is also indebted to the work of Karl Barth, Walter Brueggemann, and Thomas Long.

[6]Herman Ridderbos famously describes this pattern in all of Paul's letters. See Herman Ridderbos, *Paul and Outline of His Theology*, trans. J. R. de Witt (Grand Rapids: Eerdmans, 1975), 253-58.

[7]Alexander Schmemann, *For the Life of the World* (Crestwood, NY: St. Vladimir's Seminary Press, 1963), 33.

[8]There is a reliance on the tradition of emissary here in this text (i.e., the Jewish Hebrew tradition of one's representative being invested with the real power and authority of the one who has sent them). I am arguing for an intensification of this tradition by Jesus to include his special presence. The sent one is imbued with the same power, authority, and presence of the one who has sent them. This idea of presence is exhibited in Matthew 10:40-42, the parallel to Luke 10:16, where Jesus, using the words, "whoever welcomes you welcomes me," draws on the idea of his presence being welcomed in the missionary act of proclaiming the gospel. The word *welcome* (*dechomai*) connotes more explicitly the idea of welcoming my presence.

[9]Dietrich Bonhoeffer, *The Bonhoeffer Reader*, ed. Clifford Greene and Michael De-Jonge (Minneapolis: Fortress Press, 2013), 277.

[10]Dodd, *Apostolic Preaching*, 3-4.

[11]Andrew McGowan makes the case that most preaching in the first one hundred years of the church was "to the choir," "to those already connected to the community," to the "already convinced" (Andrew B. McGowan, *Early Christian Worship* [Grand Rapids: Baker Academic, 2014], 72). Robert C. Worley argues as well that Dodd overstated this distinction, and teaching and preaching happened across different settings. See Robert C. Worley, *Preaching and Teaching in the Earliest Church* (Philadelphia: Westminster Press, 1967). Special thanks to Scot McKnight for pointing me to Worley on this question.

[12]See Gordon Fee, *The First Epistle to the Corinthians*, New International Commentary on the New Testament (Grand Rapids: Eerdmans, 1987), 720.

[13]The Second Vatican Council says the purpose of the homily is not to "advise people on how to live their lives but to invite people into the liturgy of the Eucharist (or

the world of the Eucharist)." See Geoffrey Dunn, "Aristotle and the Art of Preaching," *Worship* 72 (1998), 234.

[14]Even though the proclaimer always maintains a posture as one among, they preach the gospel *over* the church as an all-engrossing reality to be accepted or rejected.

[15]On the relegation of proclamation to the sidelines in later church developments see J. Kevin Coyle, "From Homily to Sermon to Homily: The Content of Christian Preaching in Historical Perspective," *Liturgical Ministry* 1 (1992): 2-9.

[16]I have already written extensively on the inadequacies of expository and topical preaching in today's modern church. See David Fitch, *The Great Giveaway: Reclaiming the Mission of the Church* (Grand Rapids: Baker, 2005), chap. 6.

6 The Discipline of Being with the "Least of These"

[1]For early Christians, encountering Christ through actively being with the poor "was not just a metaphor; the church proclaimed that one actually encountered the presence of God in the poor" (Gary Anderson, *Charity* [New Haven, CT: Yale University Press, 2013], 6-7).

[2]Leonard Sweet, *From Tablet to Table* (Colorado Springs: NavPress, 2014), 153-55

[3]"His garments, described in OT terms (Prov 31:22), insinuate he lived like a king" (Joseph Fitzmyer, *The Gospel According to Luke X-XXIV*, Anchor Bible 28a [New York: Doubleday, 1985], 1130).

[4]Klyne Snodgrass, *Stories with Intent* (Grand Rapids: Eerdmans, 2008), 557.

[5]Snodgrass argues the word *elachistōn* ("least of these") is used differently for disciples in Matthew 5:19, "with a negative connotation for disciples." Elsewhere, they are referred to as "little ones" (*mikroi*) in Matthew 10:42; 18:6, 10, 14, in a totally different sense from *elachiston* in Matthew 25:40 (ibid., 556).

[6]Robert Lupton, *Toxic Charity: How Churches and Charities Hurt Those They Help and How to Reverse It* (San Francisco: HarperOne, 2012). See also Steve Corbett and Brian Fikkert, *When Helping Hurts: How to Alleviate Poverty Without Hurting the Poor . . . and Yourself* (Chicago: Moody Publishers, 2014).

[7]Michael Gorman, *Becoming the Gospel* (Grand Rapids: Eerdmans, 2015), 31.

[8]I heard this story firsthand from the pastor at a "Cultivate Learning Party" put on by Pernell Goodyear in London, Ontario. I have since heard stories similar to this one several times as I've traveled North America.

[9]Boniface Ramsey, "Almsgiving in the Latin Church: The Late Fourth and Early Fifth Centuries," *Theological Studies* 43, no. 2 (1982).

[10]Emmanuel Clapsis, "Wealth and Poverty in Christian Tradition," *Greek Orthodox Theological Review* 54 (2009): 182-83.

[11]Anderson, *Charity*, 3.

[12]Samuel Wells, *God's Companions: Reimagining Christian Ethics* (Oxford: Blackwell, 2006), 7.

[13]More than simply a reference to a commitment to the relief efforts toward the

Jerusalem church, Bruce Longenecker contends that Galatians 2:9-10 was a "single application of the more general principle of caring for the poor" (Bruce Longenecker, *Remember the Poor* [Grand Rapids: Eerdmans, 2010], 187).

[14]The Greek word *anamnēsis* in Luke 22:19 and 1 Corinthians 11:24, where Jesus asks the church to "remember" him when they eat the Lord's Supper, is the cognate root to the verb "remember the poor" in Galatians 2:10. The *ana* in Jesus' usage is an intensifier. In Galatians 2:10 then there is the allusion to "make oneself present to" the poor in the same way as we are to make ourselves present to Christ in the Eucharist.

[15]Longenecker, *Remember the Poor*, 310.

[16]Rodney Stark describes the ways early Christians provided care to the victims of plagues, often at the expense of their own lives. Whereas pagan elites and their priests simply fled the affected cities, some even leaving family members behind, Christians stayed behind to provide food, water, and friendship to their neighbors. Stark sees this as one of the factors that led to the growth of Christianity in its first few centuries. See Rodney Stark, *The Rise of Christianity* (San Francisco: Harper, 1997), 82 -86. See also Peter Brown, *Through the Eye of a Needle: Wealth, the Fall of Rome and the Making of Christianity in the West, 350-550 AD* (Princeton, NJ: Princeton University Press, 2012), where he argues that the church's commitment to the poor, even up to the fifth century, was what won over Roman society.

[17]Julian the Apostate, quoted in Stephen Neil, *A History of Christian Missions*, 2nd ed. (New York: Penguin, 1991), 37.

[18]A. M. Henry, *Christ in His Sacraments* (Chicago: Fides, 1958), 279.

[19]In the words of Gary Anderson, "The charitable deed lost, in the sixteenth century, its central role making God present to the believer and became simply a sign of the underlying personal faith of the believer. Bereft of this sacramental sensibility the donor no longer had any reason to meet the beggar in person. The needs of the indigent could be more ably assisted by civic organizations" (Anderson, *Charity*, 8).

7 THE DISCIPLINE OF BEING WITH CHILDREN

[1]Tracy Cutchlow, "Would You Call 911 on Another Parent?" *Washington Post*, March 3, 2015, www.washingtonpost.com/news/parenting/wp/2015/03/03/would-you-call-911-on-another-parent.

[2]Eun Kyung Kim, "'Free-Range' Parents Being Investigated by Child Protective Services Again," *Today.com*, April 13, 2015, www.today.com/parents/children-maryland-free-range-parents-detained-again-child-protective-service-t14646?cid=sm_fbn.

[3]This did dip after the Great Recession of 2008 in the West.

[4]"Why Is Family Dinner So Important?" *The Six O'Clock Scramble*, accessed May 20, 2015, www.thescramble.com/family-dinner-challenge-statistics. I learned of this statistic through Leonard Sweet, *From Tablet to Table* (Colorado Springs:

NavPress, 2014), 9. On the extensive research on the benefits of frequent family dinners see Anne Fischel, "The Most Important Thing You Can Do with Your Kids? Eat Dinner with Them," *Washington Post,* January 12, 2015, www.washingtonpost .com/posteverything/wp/2015/01/12/the-most-important-thing-you-can-do-with -your-kids-eat-dinner-with-them.

[5]Joseph Martos, *Doors to the Sacred* (Ligouri, MO: Ligouri/Triumph, 2001), 159.

[6]In Jesus' day "to be a child was to be a nobody" (John Dominic Crossan, *The Historical Jesus: The Life of a Mediterranean Peasant* [San Francisco: HarperSanFrancisco, 1991], 269).

[7]This storytelling method first developed by Anglicans in London has spread around the world. See the Godly Play website at www.godlyplay.org

[8]On this see Judith M. Gundry-Volf, "The Least and the Greatest: Children in the New Testament," in *The Child in Christian Thought,* ed. Marcia J. Bunge (Grand Rapids: Eerdmans, 2001), 55-58.

[9]Andrew Lincoln, *Ephesians,* Word Biblical Commentary 42 (Dallas: Word, 1990), 401-2.

[10]Mark Yaconelli, *Contemplative Youth Ministry: Practicing the Presence of Jesus* (Grand Rapids: Zondervan, 2006). Gordon Neufeld and Gabor Mate, *Hold on to Your Kids: Why Parents Need to Matter More Than Peers* (New York: Ballantine, 2005).

[11]For research on teenagers deserting the faith see Kenda Creasy Dean, *Almost Christian: What the Faith of Our Teenagers Is Telling the American Church* (New York: Oxford University Press, 2010); and Kara Powell and Chap Clark, *Sticky Faith: Everyday Ideas to Build Lasting faith in Your Kids* (Grand Rapids: Zondervan, 2011), 193-12.

[12]See Alvin J. Schmidt, *How Christianity Changed the World* (Grand Rapids: Zondervan, 2004), 52-54, Rodney Stark *The Rise of Christianity* (San Francisco: Harper Collins, 1997), 124-125.

[13]As Joseph Martos describes it, "Late in the fourth century Christianity was made the official religion of the Roman Empire, and the sheer numbers of those who wanted to join the church made the bishops' presence at all baptisms impossible" (Martos, *Doors to the Sacred,* 191).

[14]This regimented confirmation was finally sanctioned in 1274 at the Second Council of Lyons (ibid., 195).

8 The Discipline of the Fivefold Gifting

[1]C. J. Mahaney, "Why I'm Taking a Leave of Absence," *Gospel Coalition,* July 7, 2011, https://blogs.thegospelcoalition.org/justintaylor/2011/07/07/c-j-mahaney-why -im-taking-a-leave-of-absence.

[2]Paul Tripp, quoted in Sarah Pulliam Bailey, "Pastor's Letter on Mark Driscoll: Step Down from All Aspects of Ministry and Leadership," *Washington Post,* August

28, 2014, www.washingtonpost.com/national/religion/pastors-letter-on-mark
-driscoll-step-down-from-all-aspects-of-ministry-and-leadership/2014/08/28/06
2cd186-2ee3-11e4-be9e-60cc44c01e7f_story.html.

[3]See Marcus Barth, *Ephesians 4–6*, Anchor Bible Commentary 34A (New York: Doubleday, 1972), 472-76.

[4]This requires an extensive treatment beyond the scope of this book. I follow those who observe that the word *apostle* is used in the New Testament to refer beyond the original Twelve or Paul. See Acts 14:4; Romans 16:7; 2 Corinthians 8:23; Philippians 2:25; 1 Thessalonians 1:1; 2:7.

[5]See Alan Hirsch and Tim Catchim, *The Permanent Revolution* (San Francisco: Jossey-Bass, 2012), chap. 2; and J. R. Woodward, *Creating a Missional Culture* (Downers Grove, IL: IVP Books, 2012), 113-70.

[6]John Howard Yoder argues that collaborative leadership under the rule and worship of one God was always God's intent for Israel. Yoder says the priestly role, the prophets, the "elders in the gates," the judges all operated collaboratively in decentralized ways. All this was overthrown by the monarchy of Israel. See John Howard Yoder, *The Fullness of Christ* (Elgin, IL: Brethren Press, 1987), 6-8. See also John Nugent, *The Politics of Jesus* (Eugene, OR: Cascade, 2011), chap. 4.

[7]Many of these tests are available. The one I have found most helpful is in an appendix of Mike Breen's *Building a Discipleship Culture*, 2nd ed. (Pawleys Island, SC: 3DM Publishing, 2014).

[8]This follows John Zizioulas's account of ordination in *Being as Communion* (Crestwood, NY: St Vladimir's Seminary Press, 1993), 215.

[9]I am working off the well-known extensive treatment of Paul's use of *plērōma* (fullness) in Ephesians and Colossians found in Marcus Barth, *Ephesians 1–3*, Anchor Bible Commentary 34 (New York: Doubleday, 1974), 200-210. Barth finds overlap in this usage with the usage found in Ephesians 4:13 in *Ephesians 4–6*, Anchor Bible Commentary 34A (New York: Doubleday, 1998), 490.

[10]Robert Banks, *Paul's Idea of Community* (Grand Rapids: Baker Academic, 1994), 101.

[11]See Joseph Martos, *Doors to the Sacred* (Ligouri, MO: Ligouri/Triumph, 2001), 404-24.

[12]Dom Gregory Dix, *The Shape of the* Liturgy (San Francisco: Harper & Row, 1945), 34-35.

9 THE DISCIPLINE OF KINGDOM PRAYER

[1]On this see Scot McKnight, *Sermon on the Mount*, Story of God Bible Commentary (Grand Rapids: Zondervan, 2013), 178-79.

[2]N. T. Wright has written extensively on how heaven is "the control room for earth" where God reigns. See N. T. Wright, *Surprised by Hope* (San Francisco: HarperOne, 2008), chap. 7. *Heaven*, according to Robert Guelich, in Matthew refers to "the

sphere from which God effects his rule" (Robert Guelich, *Sermon on the Mount* [Waco, TX: Word, 1982], 288 -89).

[3]Vincent Donovan, *Christianity Rediscovered* (Maryknoll, NY: Orbis Books, 2004), 100-1.

[4]Joachim Jeremias, *The Prayers of Jesus* (New York: SCM Press, 1967), 54-57. See also his *New Testament Theology* (New York: Charles Scribner's Sons, 1971), 61-68.

[5]Coakley, though, does emphasize the contemplative aspect of prayer in Romans 8. Her "incorporative" view of the Trinity is expounded in Sarah Coakley, "Why Three? Some Further Reflections on the Origins of the Doctrine of the Trinity," in *The Making and Remaking of Christian Doctrine*, eds. Sarah Coakley and David A. Pailin (Oxford: Clarendon Press, 1993).

[6]Michael C. Xiong, "The Presence of God," *Alliance Life*, July-August 2015, www. cmalliance.org/alife/the-presence-of-god.

[7]Karl Barth, *The Christian Life* (Edinburgh, T&T Clark, 1981), 171.

[8]See Eugene Boring, *Mark* (Louisville: Westminster John Knox, 2006), 316-25.

[9]Ibid., 319.

[10]See William L. Lane, *Commentary on the Gospel of Mark* (Grand Rapids: Eerdmans, 1974), 409-11.

[11]"Have faith in God" (Mk 11:22), although disputable, could be translated, "You have the faithfulness of God," which would emphasize even more dependence on God and his faithfulness to his kingdom promises as opposed to a dependence on the faith of the disciples themselves.

[12]I heard Charles tell this story at the Global Impact conference of the Metro District, Christian and Missionary Alliance, New Jersey, February 20-21, 2015, where he spoke. I tell this story as best I can recall it and do not hold Charles responsible for the accuracy of all the details.

[13]This is one of Barth's most often used quotes. Although there are many similar quotes in his treatment of the Lord's Prayer in his *The Christian Life* (never completed *Church Dogmatics* 4.4) it is believed Barth actually said this in a lecture. To my knowledge, it is not in actual print in this prescribed form.

[14]According to Alan Kreider, the early church communities "fenced" their prayer. They believed discerning peace among one another, and being in unity before the Lord, was central to effectual prayer. The close circle was the necessary beginning point from which prayer could flow out from the community into the neighborhoods. See Alan Kreider, *The Patient Ferment of the Early Church* (Grand Rapids: Baker Academic, 2016), 212.

[15]McKnight, *Sermon on the Mount*, 174.

[16]McKnight uses these words to describe the two parts of Lord's Prayer (ibid., 173).

[17]Ibid., 188-90. Andrew McGowan, *Ancient Christian Worship* (Grand Rapids: Baker Academic, 2014), 192-94.

[18]See, for example, *Didache* 8.3. Texts like Acts 3:1 suggest that the practice of the hours was part of the disciples' life from the very beginning.

[19]Tertullian, *On Prayer* 24, quoted in McGowan, *Ancient Christian Worship*, 191.

[20]Ibid., 190-91.

Epilogue: How God Changes the World

[1]To the best of my recall, this is a quote from Alan Hirsch. I have been unable to locate where he said this or that anyone else has said this, for that matter.

[2]Michael Gorman says, "The opening vision of the majestic Christ present among the seven urban churches foreshadows the presence of God and the lamb in the new city" (Michael Gorman, *Reading Revelation Responsibly* [Eugene, OR: Cascade Books, 2011], 160).

[3]Not coincidentally, Gorman suggests that the Maranatha Prayer, "Come, Lord Jesus," of Revelation 22:20 should be read as a short form of the Lord's Prayer (ibid., 173).

[4]Some commentators argue that the Maranatha Prayer is part of early church liturgical prayer invoking Jesus' presence at the Eucharist. See Gerhard Krodel, *Revelation* (Minneapolis: Augsburg Press, 1989), 378; and Wilfrid J. Harrington, *Revelation* (Collegeville, MN: Liturgical Press, 1993), 226. Others contend its primary focus is on the second coming. See, for instance, Grant Osborne, *Revelation* (Grand Rapids: Baker Academic, 2002), 797.

Appendix 2

[1]Luke Bretherton describes the New Testament pattern of the "journeying guest" as becoming host at the meals. He cites the example of Peter going to Cornelius's house as guest but then becomes host when asked to interpret the Word. Likewise Jesus went to the house on Emmaus Road as a guest but later becomes the host at the breaking of the bread. Bretherton draws on David Moessner, *Lord of the Banquet: The Literary and Theological Significance of the Lukan Travel Narrative* (Minneapolis: Fortress Press, 1989), 184. See Luke Bretherton, *Hospitality as Holiness* (Burlington, VT: Ashgate, 2006), 135.

Appendix 3

[1]Darrell Guder, ed., *Missional Church: A Vision for the Sending of the Church in North America* (Grand Rapids: Eerdmans, 1998).

[2]Michael Goheen charts the duo challenge of ecclesiocentrism and Christocentrism (correlative to these two themes) in the work of Lesslie Newbigin, in his dissertation titled, "As the Father Has Sent Me, I Am Sending You: J. E. Lesslie Newbigin's Missionary Ecclesiology" (PhD diss., Utrecht University, 2001), http://dspace.library.uu.nl/handle/1874/597.

[3]For an excellent history of the movement and its various trajectories see Craig Van

Gelder and Dwight Zscheile, *The Missional Church in Perspective: Mapping Trends and Shaping the Conversation* (Grand Rapids: Baker Academic, 2011).

[4]Jürgen Moltmann, The Church in the Power of the Spirit (Minneapolis: Fortress Press, 1993), 64.

[5]Alan Hirsch, "What Do I Mean by Incarnational," Facebook, May 9, 2011, www.facebook.com/notes/alan-hirsch/what-do-i-mean-by-incarnational/1015018 9514096009.

[6]Alan Hirsch, *The Forgotten Ways* (Grand Rapids: Brazos, 2006), 142-44.

[7]The event language is reminiscent of Barth's theology of the Word. For the early Barth, especially, each gathering of the people around the Word is an "event." But as Joseph Mangina reminds us, Barth's event talk "simply refers to the reality that God's action can never be reduced to terms of this world causality." It does not imply that the church does not shape a visible reality continuous in time. I wish to emphasize this sense of "in-breaking" in this book. See Joseph L. Mangina, *Karl Barth: Theologian of Christian Witness* (Philadelphia: Westminster John Know, 2004), 134.

[8]"Little Jesuses" is Alan Hirsch's term in his *Forgotten Ways*, 113-14.

[9]For more on this twofold movement see David Fitch and Geoffrey Holsclaw, "Mission amid Empire: Relating Trinity, Mission, and Political Formation," *Missiology* 41, no. 4 (October 2013): 389-401.

[10]Karl Barth referred to this as "the dual existence of Christ in the in-between time." In this in-between time, Barth said Christ has both his heavenly historical and his earthly historical existence. "It is He who is both there and here. It is He who is both the Head and the body," Karl Barth, *Church Dogmatics* 4.2 (London: T&T Clark, 2010), 652-53.

[11]The preposition *para* means "with," "beside," "in the presence of," depending on the declension of the noun. The word *klētos* derives from the Greek *kaleō*, which means "to call."

[12]George Ladd describes how the Paraclete comes in parallel fashion to Jesus "to take his place and continue his ministry" (George Eldon Ladd, *New Testament Theology* [Grand Rapids: Eerdmans, 1993], 329).

[13]In similar fashion, Luke Bretherton argues that "hospitality is the social practice that structures relations between Christians and non-Christians in such a way as it recapitulates the ascension and Pentecost moments of the Christ event" (Luke Bretherton, *Hospitality as Holiness* [Burlington VT: Ashgate, 2006], 143). In essence, when we gather for a meal in the world we are recognizing that Jesus is both ruling there ahead of time (ascension), and, as we gather to eat and submit to his rule, is present by his Spirit (Pentecost). Ascension (his rule) and Pentecost (his presence) are brought together in a lived moment in a concrete place.

[14]Witness, according to Karl Barth, is typified in the act of John the Baptist pointing. Barth famously hung a copy of the Grunewald's painting of the crucifixion (from

the Isenheim Altarpiece) above his desk. This painting featured John the Baptist pointing. Barth however uses the idea of witness to work against the idea that the church in any way can mediate the presence of Christ to the world. See Barth, *Church Dogmatics* 4.1, 317-18.

[15]The idea of Christ extending his presence through the church has often been called *Christus prolongatus*. The danger associated with *Christus prolongatus* is that the church takes control of or becomes equal to Christ's presence in the world. This is linked to the triumphalist mistake or the colonialist mistake. In what follows I wish to differentiate my view of the church in mission from this view. The church can never control but only submit to Christ's presence. It is always defined as a witness to Christ's presence, embodying it, but never equivalent to it.

[16]Karl Barth continually worried about the Roman Catholic notion that the church replaces Christ in the history of redemption. See Karl Barth, "Roman Catholicism: A Question to the Protestant Church," in *Theology and Church: Shorter Writings 1920-1928* (San Francisco: Harper & Row 1962), 307-33; and *Church Dogmatics* 4.3.2, p. 729. For another negative view of the Roman Catholic notion of *Christus prolongatus* see Moltmann, *Church in the Power of the Spirit*, 70-75.

[17]Barth talked about this dynamic using the classic patristic terms *anhypostasis* and *enhypostasis*. *Anhypostasis* emphasizes that the human nature of Jesus Christ has no independent existence apart from the preexistent Word in the incarnation. See for example Barth, Church Dogmatics 4.2, pp. 49-50. This use of *anhypostasis* safeguards the utter dependence of the creature on the Creator. Barth characterized the church-Jesus relation in the same terms. The relationship therefore between Christ and the church always carries an asymmetrical character. The church is always totally dependent on Christ for its existence, and yet Christ is never dependent on the church for his existence. On this see for example ibid., 59-60.

[18]This approximates what Barth is getting at when he says, "Between its invisible being and that of Jesus Christ, between its distinction from the world and his, its confrontation of world-occurrence and his, there is indeed correspondence but no parity, let alone identity" (Barth, Church Dogmatics 4.3.2, p. 729).

[19]Gerhard Lohfink, *Does God Need the Church?* (Collegeville, MN: Liturgical Press, 1999), 38.

APPENDIX 4

[1]The Greek word for "brothers," *adelphon,* is retained in the translation as "brothers" despite its gender exclusion because it is these actual words that hold the lexical key for many interpreters of this text.

[2]See Martin Tripole, "A Church for the Poor and the World: At Issue with Moltmann's Ecclesiology," *Theological Studies* 42 (December 1981): 645-59.

[3]Much of this depends on the work of Klyne Snodgrass, *Stories with Intent* (Grand

Rapids: Eerdmans, 2008), 552-63. Special thanks to Ty Grigg, a former student of Snodgrass, for alerting me to his work on this passage.

[4]Moltmann's interpretation is found in Jürgen Moltmann, *The Church in the Power of the Spirit* (Minneapolis: Fortress Press, 1993), 126-30.

IVP PRAXIS

EQUIPPING LEADERS FOR MINISTRY

God has called us to ministry. But it's not enough to have a vision for ministry if you don't have the practical skills for it. Nor is it enough to do the work of ministry if what you do is headed in the wrong direction. We need both vision *and* expertise for effective ministry. We need *praxis*.

Praxis puts theory into practice. It brings cutting-edge ministry expertise from visionary practitioners. You'll find sound biblical and theological foundations for ministry in the real world, with concrete examples for effective action and pastoral ministry. Praxis books are more than the "how to"—they're also the "why to." And because *being* is every bit as important as *doing*, Praxis attends to the inner life of the leader as well as the outer work of ministry. Feed your soul, and feed your ministry.

If you are called to ministry, you know you can't do it on your own. Let Praxis provide the companions you need to equip God's people for life in the kingdom.

www.ivpress.com/praxis

Missio Alliance

Missio Alliance has arisen in response to the shared voice of pastors and ministry leaders from across the landscape of North American Christianity for a new "space" of togetherness and reflection amid the issues and challenges facing the church in our day. We are united by a desire for a fresh expression of evangelical faith, one significantly informed by the global evangelical family. Lausanne's Cape Town Commitment, "A Confession of Faith and a Call to Action," provides an excellent guidepost for our ethos and aims.[1]

Through partnerships with schools, denominational bodies, ministry organizations, and networks of churches and leaders, Missio Alliance addresses the most vital theological and cultural issues facing the North American Church in God's mission today. We do this primarily by convening gatherings, curating resources, and catalyzing innovation in leadership formation.

Rooted in the core convictions of evangelical orthodoxy, the ministry of Missio Alliance is animated by a strong and distinctive theological identity that emphasizes

Comprehensive Mutuality: Advancing the partnered voice and leadership of women and men among the beautiful diversity of the body of Christ across the lines of race, culture and theological heritage.

Hopeful Witness: Advancing a way of being the people of God in the world that reflects an unwavering and joyful hope in the lordship of Christ in the church and over all things.

Church in Mission: Advancing a vision of the local church in which our identity and the power of our testimony is found and expressed through our active participation in God's mission in the world.

In partnership with InterVarsity Press, we are pleased to offer a line of resources authored by a diverse range of theological practitioners. The resources in this series are selected based on the important way in which they address and embody these values, and thus, the unique contribution they offer in equipping Christian leaders for fuller and more faithful participation in God's mission.

missioalliance.org | twitter.com/missioalliance | facebook.com/missioalliance

---

[1]www.lausanne.org/content/ctc/ctcommitment